SHELBY

The Man. The Cars. The Legend.

Wallace A. Wyss

Iconografix

Iconografix
PO Box 446
Hudson, Wisconsin 54016 USA

Iconografix books are offered at a discount when sold in quantity for promotional use. Businesses or organizations seeking details should write to the Marketing Department, Iconografix, at the above address.

Library of Congress Control Number: 2006939236

ISBN-13: 978-1-58388-182-8
ISBN-10: 1-58388-182-4

07 08 09 10 11 12 6 5 4 3 2

Printed in China

Cover and book design by Dan Perry

Cover Photo Credit: *Joe Farkas, Ford Motor Co., Dearborn, MI*

Contents

Whoa now... Another book about Carroll Shelby? Can anyone ever get their fill of stories about the garrulous, gregarious, Texas gunfighter who seems to have had more lives, loves, and close calls than any random group of six or eight "ordinary" mortals combined?

Herein are laid out the gaffes, mistakes, deceptions, the lies and the liars who put them out. Revel in the rumors, innuendos, the certifiable craziness, the full-blown hubris, and note that, there in the very middle of it for all of four decades now, is the failed chicken rancher, that effulgent tub-thumper Carroll Shelby, a little bent-over with age but still standing.

My own recollections of Carroll Shelby go just about hand-in-hand with my life long love of road racing. I talked my stepfather into taking my brother and me to Riverside Raceway for the first-ever race run there. We were over watching the events on turn 8 when Mister Shelby augered heavily into the turn 6 dirt bank, shattering a good deal of his face. We were half a mile away but I can still hear the T6 crowd yell out and then fall silent almost as one.

I was at Pomona shivering in the rain when Shelby backed a big old Ferrari into a big old tree located along the back straightaway.

A year or two later, I got a ride around Pomona in the first-ever "A.C." Cobra (with Mister Shelby at the keyboard). By then I'd become involved with the Cal Club and worked as one of the college kid set-up crew who put up the snow fence and wrestled the hay bales into place to convert the giant LA County Fairgrounds parking lot into a sports car race course. The noon ride around the course with Shelby was a huge perk for some of the course crew members. All I can really remember is looking over the low-slung door and seeing the track coming at us very sideways under the streaking vehicle. Impressed? Oh yeah! Rolling the clock forward more decades than I really want to think about, I spent a couple of days two years ago hanging out with Mister Shelby at Irwindale Speedway, watching the "new" Cobra (code name "Daisy") being put through its paces. He knows me a little now and takes great pleasure in chiding me that his heart is "younger" than mine (mine is OEM and 65 as of this past July...his is about 50 or so). I indicated to him that never, in my short racing career, did I drive with a nitro tablet under my tongue; but that I did race a go-kart wearing bib overalls and have (by actual count) been married more times than him.

From my new perspective as the co-proprietor of a bookstore that itself has something of a "legendary" status, I note that Carroll Shelby's influence pervades almost every aisle in the place. "Ol' Shel" is a force, a feeling, a movement, and a (far) larger than life person that just about everyone in my particular world has a great story about.

There's a whole bunch of those tales in this book... Have at 'em!

Doug Stokes
Autobooks-Aerobooks
Burbank, California
August 2006

Introduction

Long ago, goin' on maybe 40 years-plus now, I was minding my own business, walking along a street in Detroit in a business district called Cadillac Square, when I heard a deep-throated roar. I looked up just in time to see a bright red sports car which I recognized as a 427 Cobra—with white side pipes as thick as fire hoses. The tires were screeching and great balls of fire were popping out of the exhaust, which caused a nearby mounted policeman's horse to rear up on its hind legs. At the wheel was a young brunette manhandling the wood-rimmed steering wheel for all she was worth as she deftly pulled to the curb, and screeched to a stop. She pointed straight at me.

"You," she commanded, "Which way's Cobo Hall?"

"I'll show you if you give me a ride there."

She opened the passenger door and I climbed in. Before I could secure the 3-inch wide racing seat belt, she had had found the John C. Lodge Freeway and opened her up to 140 mph-plus. I had to shout against the wind. "It's the other way."

She took an exit, U-turned and eventually we found our way to the Cobo Hall Convention Center, where Carroll Shelby and his entourage, on a tour called The Cobra Caravan, were still setting up for their public appearance.

That was my introduction to Carroll Shelby.

I visited his plant later on, and ran into him here, there and everywhere during the next few decades, including the lobby of a hotel in Monte Carlo. In 1977, I wrote a book on him that sold 50,000 copies.

When the book finally went out of print I thought that would be the end of it, because after all, by then Cobras weren't being made anymore and Shelby, he was what, over fifty?

Well, here we are more than a quarter century later. I'm older. And Shelby? He's a whole lot older but, somewhere in Nevada, he's still making Shelby Cobras.

So the reason this book exists is to tell the newcomers just who this guy Shelby is and why he and his Cobra became American icons that just won't politely fade away into the history books no matter who says they should.

I've updated the chronicle of events a bit since that old book, because Shelby's done so much more since I wrote my first book. Recently, in reading Brock Yates' book *Outlaw Machine: Harley-Davidson and the Search for the American Soul,* it occured to me that Shelby, like the folks at Harley-Davidson, has always been in search of that one goal: building a car with soul.

I've written about lots of other cars but somehow that red Cobra, those roaring exhausts, that fast-shifting brunette, the policeman's rearing horse—that single moment in time just won't be banished from my memory. Of all the people on that street that day, she picked me to ask directions of.

That's why this book exists....

Wallace Wyss
Cobra Ranch, Mendocino, CA

Chapter 1- Hell on Wheels

It was World War II.

The bomber flew low, dangerously low, thought the co-pilot. But the pilot had something in mind. The pilot tripped open the bomb bay door, and stood up, lurching toward the rear, leaving it up to the co-pilot to take over the controls. The pilot dropped something out the bomb bay and the co-pilot saw what it was—an army boot. The pilot came back and sat down with a grin.

"Needed something to weigh down my love letters," the pilot explained.

Outside, the co-pilot could see, on the lawn of the farmhouse below, a lady in a flowered dress was waving the boot, smiling.

A few months later, it was night, and the bomber was the same, but there was a new crew. The same pilot was walking toward the back, a grim look on his face as he zipped up his sheepskin flying jacket.

He jerked a thumb toward the smoke pouring out from under the instrument panel. "We're headin' out." He opened the bomb bay door. He pointed toward the first man in line, with his chute rigged to a static line.

"You first, Eddie." The young airman gulped, then leaped into the darkness.

One by one they leaped into the void. The plane flew on as the night air filled their chutes. The last man to jump was the pilot, Carroll Hall Shelby. He grinned to his crewmen as his chute popped open. "Relax boys, we're only over Texas."

Carroll Shelby was born in 1923, in Leesburg, Texas, a town what folks down there in East Texas call a "wide spot in the road," with a population of 200. His first passion growing up was cars. Shelby had an early taste for speed. One of his earliest memories is riding on the running board of his dad's Whippet and urging him to go ever faster. He also recalls a Willys Overland he had modified. But, second after that came his passion for airplanes.

Shelby had been a relatively quiet boy as a youth, not in trouble with the law, other than managing to earn a speeding ticket the very first time his father loaned him the family car. He was clocked doing 85 mph, about half the speed he would drive at for most of his later race driving career.

Shelby came from a God-fearing family. His mother Eloise had named him after a fire-breathing minister, a Reverend Carroll, and there was no alcohol or smoking tolerated around the house.

Another early passion was golf (a hero popular at the time was Ben Hogan) and one Dallas reporter says that Shelby, who worked part time as a caddy at Dallas's Tenison Golf course, was a bit of a golf hustler while a teen, pretending he didn't know golf all that well in order to work his way into a game where he could relieve the rubes of their excess cash. A con man at an early age? Let's just say that in rebellion against his mother's rules about swearing, drinking and dancing (and no fishin' on Sunday), Shelby rebelled by hanging out with some of Dallas's more nefarious types.

Barry Horn, a Dallas Morning News reporter, elicited this info in a 2001 interview, where Shelby says his real education came while at Tenison Park in Dallas, where his 'teachers' were the likes of "Titantic" Thompson, a man linked to fixing the 1919 baseball World Series. Then there were the known associates "Chicken" Louie Frantello and Benny Binion, the latter of whom was to become one of the pioneering Las Vegas casino owners when Las Vegas got going. But his association with gamblers apparently didn't result in Shelby being a gambler in traditional ways—no, his gambles were always on business deals. He was always willing to take a flyer on this venture or that.

Flying attracted him like a moth to the flame. He had been bitten by the flying bug at an early age and spent a good deal of his high school years out at the local airport near Leesburg, Texas, trying to cadge rides. You have to remember that Lindburgh had flown the Atlantic a few years earlier and was every American boy's hero at the time. After high school, Shelby thought he'd see the world through the military.

He joined up with the Army-Air Force in 1941, before Pearl Harbor, and almost didn't get accepted because he was a scrawny runt at 5 feet, 2 inches weighing barely 100 pounds. He wanted to be a pilot but there was this requirement that you had to be a college graduate in order to fly, but Pearl Harbor (Dec 7, 1941) changed all that and, at some point during the war, the Military bent the rules and started a special school for pilots who didn't have degrees. Its graduates were derided by some as "flying Sergeants" but many distinguished themselves in combat. One of Shelby's instructors was Chuck Yeager, an honored name among WWII flying heroes. Shelby earned his 2nd Lieutenant's bars but his plans of seeing the world didn't work out. He spent the entire war in Texas at one base after another.

It was a fairly uneventful war for Lt. Shelby if you didn't count the plane crashes, all of which occurred while teaching young airmen to fly a variety of planes. He was also a test pilot, testing planes that had been repaired to see if the repairs had been done right.

In December of 1943, he hitched up with his high school sweetheart Jeanne.

Following the war, he went out and did whatever job he could to make a dime. His father-in-law was in oil. Now ordinarily one could say "so Bob's your uncle"—a father-in-law in a well-fixed position could be counted on to get his son-in-law a good job, one where he wouldn't have to get his hands dirty. Shelby's father-in-law got him a job in oil, all right, but it was at the grunt level—an oil well "roughneck," the nickname for oil workers who traveled from well to well, capping wells, drilling wells, being a general all around worker. Shelby stuck it out for a while but he wanted a job where he'd be the boss.

He left to start his own business, one where he would be in charge. In fact, he started one after another. One was owning a fleet of dump trucks, another was cement contracting, ideal for the building boom that started with the GIs coming home. But the latter seemed like it was vulnerable to a downturn in housing demand, so he decided that he would do what he already knew—raise livestock.

Every country family had raised chickens in the depression years and he knew how to do that. He began raising chickens. His wife, Jeanne, liked the idea—he would be around home and he wouldn't be around any dangerous machinery, like an oil well. And they had children to watch over—two boys and a girl. It went okay for a while until a disease struck, knocking off half of his flock of 35,000 birds in one fell swoop. Shelby, trying to think positive, thought, "Well, that's tough, but I still got half my flock left."

Then the second half died.

That was what launched Shelby into searching for a new career. One that looked like a lot of fun was being a racecar driver. Shelby had, like many another high schooler, dabbled in hot rodding, putting flathead V8s into Model A Fords that were stripped of fenders and running boards and made as light as possible. A friend had even invited him to a drag race down a quarter mile strip at Grand Prairie Naval Air Base, Texas, driving a car made of an MG chassis, a flathead V8 and a homebuilt body. Shelby beat all the other cars. But drag racing back then didn't pay any money. The most you could expect was a cheap trophy.

Before the drag racing, Shelby developed his own contest of speed. He had found a hill on which he could get his Willys hot rod airborne. According to Bill Neale, his childhood buddy, Shelby would take one run after another, seeing how far he could stay in the air. His record was 60 feet.

More exotic in its appeal to Shelby was sports car racing. The same friend, Ed Wilkins, later invited Shelby to a sports car race in Caddo Mills, Texas, and turned over the wheel of his MG-TC to Shelby, a spindley-wheeled little thing imported from England with a sewing machine-sized engine. Shelby entered the race. It was the first time Shelby had ever been in a sports car and his first time in a sports car race.

He won, but not because of his driving finesse. It was because Shelby didn't play by gentlemen's rules. He came to the sport with a different philosophy. The top sports car drivers in those days were gentlemen, especially those at the top of the heap, wealthy International sportsmen like "Gentlemen Jim" Kimberly or Briggs Swift Cunningham, who showed up at races in places like Palm Springs or Watkins Glen donned in tailored driving jumpsuits, with enclosed trailers to haul their cars in, and a retinue of mechanics in matching livery not to mention beautiful ladies to help celebrate their victories.

They didn't race for money but purely for the sport of it. Shelby, right from the beginning, cut the dandies off on the inside of the curves, determined to win, even if it meant shoving them off into the haybales. He didn't care if he bent metal, the point was to win, right? Shelby did so well in the MG for a rookie that some race organizers invited him to drive the same MG in a race in Norman, Oklahoma, where he would be up against some real sports cars—Jaguar XK-120s—then considered a modern sports car with their curvacious bodywork and inline twin-cam six.

In a way, they might have been toying with him, thinking there's no way this hayseed in an MG could beat the Jags. But Shelby smoked them too. A Legend had begun.

The next car he was loaned, at another venue, was a Jaguar XK-120. This was a big step up from the MG—a real man's car (Gable drove one, after all) Shelby won the race, and soon owners of fast cars from all over the Southwest were calling, asking if he would like to race their car. Shelby wanted to take them all up on their offers but the fact was that sports car racing still didn't pay any money. In America, sports car racing at the time was still an amateur sport and amateurs didn't get paid. You raced because you wanted to race. The pit crews, the flag marshals, everybody volunteered. The only person who made money was the organizer. Often the venue was city, country or state owned so the only way the organizers could get access was to make it a charity event. So then not even the organizers made money.

This was all before the purpose-built sports car race tracks were built in America. Sports car racing then was still a rich man's hobby. Shelby had a tough time squaring these offers with his wife. The only other thing he had going to put bread on the table was breeding dogs and pheasants. But even though drivers weren't supposed to be paid, there were *ways* as they say.

A case in point was Ken Miles, the British-born racer who had immigrated to California in 1950, obstensibly to be a roving service rep for a car distributor. But in reality he was a full time racer. Hey, as long as the rent got paid, one way or another you could find compensation.

Doug Stokes, an authority on racing history, says that one of the ways drivers got paid under the table was for the car's owner to sell the car to the driver before the race, say for one dollar, then to buy the car back for $100 or $500 if the car did well. Yet another way was for the racing to be "on the clock" as part of a regular job. One racer, Doug Hooper, a Corvette racer at the time for Mickey Thompson, told Stokes that on race weekend, he would clock in as an employee on Friday morning and clock out Monday night so he'd be paid by the hour the whole weekend while he was racing.

In the early '50s, sports car racing was just getting started in America. Some of the courses were laid out on village streets like Watkins Glen in New York. Others on narrow roads through forests like Pebble Beach or in open areas like Torrey Pines, at Camp Callen, an abandoned WWII Army training base in northern San Diego. Still others were laid out on old horse racing tracks. And then there were those events run on the tarmac of Air Force bases, like March AFB in Riverside, CA, General Curtis LeMay (the same man who had directed the Allied Forces bombing raids in Europe in WWII) being a sports car buff who graciously allowed races to be run there. LeMay himself participated in some of the races, puffing on a cigar and wearing an unfastened AAF pilot's helmet as he barreled along in a Cad-Allard.

Some of the racing organizations were still adhering to the British rule of no sponsor names on the cars, so where was a sponsor to get publicity? It wasn't only American road racers that didn't have signs on their cars, it was throughout Europe, though oddly racing in England and on the Continent was not amateur, the racers could accept prize money, something not allowed in the more puritanical U.S. And there was a loophole of sorts—there was no rule about sponsor's names being on the transporter truck that brought the racecar. So even though the racecars were plain solid colors, the trucks had flamboyant signs, but instead of plugging their family business these dandies often used European names for racing teams like "Equipe" or "Ecurie" or "Scuderia," as if to say we are oh-so-European.

According to author Michael Lynch, co-author of *American Sports Car Racing in the Fifties*, despite not being able to promote their businesses, sponsors still showed up in America to fund drivers like Shelby merely because being associated with the excitement of racing was fun. "They had big social schedules every race weekend," says Lynch. "Cocktails at 6, swim parties, live bands—the cars were only part of the whole social scene. The wealthy not only won status by buying the latest Ferrari or Maserati out of Italy but cultivated even more status by corralling a 'name driver' like Carroll Shelby or Stirling Moss to drive their car in the main event."

"Then they could stroll through the pits, a bottle blonde on each arm, looking like a monied sponsor, one who can afford not only the best car available but the best damn driver money could buy."

Imagine being able to name drop something like this at the cocktail bar: "I would have driven the Maser up this weekend but I'm afraid that I loaned it to Carroll so he could run it at Torrey Pines next weekend." That was like a golfer of today saying "I would have brought my new clubs but Tiger Woods called and I loaned them to him for the weekend."

Though six feet tall and ruggedly handsome, Shelby didn't quite fit the mold of gentleman sports car racer. In fact, he deliberately cultivated a sort of cornpone hayseed image because it made him different in a world where the elitists would be talking about their latest travels to the Cote d 'Azur (French Riviera) or Havana. It was during this time that Shelby developed a "trademark" look, resulting from the time he was late for a race and had to rush to the racetrack straight from his farm. He climbed into the racecar still wearing his striped farmer's overalls (Bernard Cahier, the French photojournalist, calls them "locomotive engineer" overalls.) When he won, he was pictured nationwide accepting the trophy and race queen's kiss while still wearing his farmer's overalls. He got more attention than the other race winners that day. He decided "Hey, if the press likes the angle of a fast driving farmer, then they got one."

Shelby had ambitions of building his own racecar very early on in his driving career. He told interviewer Richard Symons, who produced the DVD "Cobra Ferrari Wars," that the first car he tried to build was one with his old buddy, Ed Wilkins, which they were building in Shelby's garage. The car was a hodgepodge of used parts.

That car didn't reach completion after Shelby's wife took a dislike to the noise and delivered an ultimatum: "Either you go or the car goes." The car went.

Shelby was disappointed but, wanting to keep harmony at home, went out and searched for sponsors with professionally built racecars. Shelby had a talent for finding sponsors who could put him behind the wheel of the latest foreign car. His first ride in an Allard came from a man named Roy Cherryholmes. The Allard was a car built in England by Sidney Allard which had either a Chrysler or Cadillac V8 under the hood, both hulking cast iron V8s of great weight but which boasted bountiful horsepower. (Allard was also the man who brought American style drag racing to Europe by building England's first "slingshot" dragster).

In early '52 and early '53 Shelby drove five straight races in an Allard-Cadillac J2X. He ran at Turner Air Force Base in Georgia, and at Caddo Mills and

Eagle Mountain Base in Texas. Out of those, he finished first three times. Shelby appreciated the Allard's American V8. It might have been a British car but it was more American hot rod than anything British. After Argentina, though, he never raced an Allard again.

Though purists at first distained the idea of a European car propelled by a crude pushrod American-sourced V8, the Cad-Allard could reach 150 mph, matching the speed of many a purebred Ferrari or Maserati. The steering was a bit odd but you could manhandle it around a course if you had the muscle.

It might have very well been his time behind the wheel of that Allard that gave Shelby the idea that became his formula: British car, American V8. It was a formula that would make him his fortune....

Chapter 2- Shelby Goes International

Inglewood, California, circa 1955.

The short, dark-complexioned man pointed toward the Ferraris.

"Get packed, Shel. We're going to Europe to buy some more of these."

Shelby nodded.

This was something new in his experience—a guy who could buy more than one Ferrari at a time.

"How many of these you fixin' to buy?" Shelby drawled.

The man looked at him as if he had just said something stupid.

"As many we need," the man snapped.

Shelby nodded sagely.

This guy Tony would take some gettin' used to. If things went right, he could see himself, as Texans say, "in tall cotton." (Or cookin' on the front burner...)

Shelby was one of the first American sports car racers to start a protest movement against the rules that insisted that drivers weren't supposed to be paid. He called his organization "RFM," short for "Run For the Money," and for some reason they wore British "bowler" hats at various events to show where their sympathies lay, perhaps because in England race drivers were paid for driving the same cars in similar length events. It was a long, tough battle, and no doubt what forced American drivers with any real talent—like Dan Gurney, Phil Hill, Masten Gregory, and Shelby—to go to Europe in the mid-1950s to look for race driving jobs that paid. After all, the risk was the same, Shelby and the others figuring you might as well be paid for putting your life on the line. That was why Shelby sought International rides—he couldn't afford to drive for fun.

Shelby's first International ride came courtesy of a Texan, Roy Cherryhomes. In 1952 Shelby was racing Cadillac-engined Allards for Charlie Brown and Roy Cherryhomes and in January of 1954 Cherryhomes entered his Allard in the Buenos Aires 1000km.

The four car entry from America had come about because one of American sports car racing's wealthiest patrons, "Gentlemen Jim" Kimberly, the prematurely snow-haired heir to the Kimberly-Clark paper fortune, had given a trophy to the Argentine Sports Car club. The Club subsequently invited four American drivers down to Argentina to race.

The other Americans invited were Californian Phil Hill, New Yorker Boris Said, and Kansas City, Missouri driver Masten Gregory, who was sharing a C-type Jag with his brother-in-law Dale Duncan.

The race was a mess, poorly organized and the Argentine drivers ran far behind the hard charging Americans. Crowd control in the race, which was run through city streets, and was so bad that least one racer was killed along with several people in the crowd. Shelby drove hard and barely finished, in 10th. At some point his engine caught fire, and a quick thinking Shelby was able to persuade Duncan to urinate on it and put the fire out. It worked!

"Shelby's Allard was held together with bailing wire, scotch tape and sweat," one observer noted. But he still won.

According to an article by Jim Mourning in *Modern Men* magazine in '58, "Shelby nursed the ailing Allard for the last 60 miles, finishing tenth overall and claiming the Kimberly Cup for the U.S..." as the highest finishing amateur in a field of professionals. It was also a world championship event, which considerably elevated Shelby's image.

But more important to Shelby was that it was while in Argentina that he met John Wyer, a tall close-lipped reserved Briton who was in charge of the Aston Martin team. Wyer saw talent in the young Texan and invited him to England, with the promise he would have the opportunity to drive a factory-prepared car. Shelby couldn't believe his good fortune—his first International race and here he was, being invited to England by the head of a factory racing team.

There was just one hitch in his getalong, as they say in Texas. As they left Argentina, apparently the ship carrying Cherryhome's Allard did not have dock workers skilled at loading cars and a box fell on the Allard, smashing it, according to Shelby, "flatter than hell." Shelby claimed Cherryhomes didn't offer him any cars after that but the records show that Cherryhomes did entrust him with a mount again, once he cooled off.

But there was a catch to Wyer's offer—it did not include an airplane ticket. It might have been that Wyer assumed that, Shelby, being Texan, was rolling in money like other Texans in car racing. But if there was anything Shelby was good at, it was finding and then sweet talking wealthy patrons. In short order, once he was back on home ground in Texas, he found Guy Mabee, a Midland, Texas oil millionaire who had already built his own one-off American sports car, one which his son had made a speed record at Bonneville with. Mabee talked of building production versions of the car that would blow off the foreign tin. He hired Shelby to develop it.

Shelby humored him on the project car but now that he had driven professional race cars, he knew that building a car from scratch that would be able to take on the products from professional automakers wasn't as easy as it looked. He adroitly steered Mabee in a direction that would help him—he implied he could get Mabee a deal on a new Aston if he would merely hand him one round trip airplane ticket to the UK. Mabee bought the story and handed Shelby the ticket.

But there were a few other races before he could go.

Shelby also drove a Wyer-managed Aston Martin at the 12 hours of Sebring March 7th, 1954, but the duo retired early. His co-driver was Washington D.C. hairdresser Charles Calvin Wallace. Charlie was a fast driver, logging a lot of rides behind the wheel of millionaire Briggs Cunningham's D-type Jag. But he was quite elderly as race drivers go, having been born in 1914 which made him nine years older then Shelby. Not that Shelby would count a man's age against him because he himself never had even sat is a racecar until he was 29.

Mabee called him in March '54 with a ride in a C-type Jag. He ran at Bergstrom Air Force base, finishing third behind a Ferrari piloted by Carlos Braniff of Argentina. First was "Gentleman Jim" Kimberly in a 4.5-liter Ferrari, the first such Ferrari in America. Kimberly made quite an impression in his bright red tailored racing uniform, the color no doubt chosen to set off even more his suntan and snow white hair.

Once Shelby arrived in Europe in May, 1954, Wyer set up his new discovery to race some factory cars. Driving a 2.9 liter Aston Martin DB3S/2, Shelby finished second at Aintree, then DNF'd in the same type of car at Le Mans in a ride shared with Belgian Paul Frere when a stub axle broke after they had completed 77 laps. It was that year, with weather the foulest in years—that Shelby learned what horrific conditions you could go through in a single 24 hour race. But the biggest danger wasn't the rain. It was the lethal differential in speed potential of various cars all participating on the same race. Shelby would be in a car that could do 170 mph and find himself rocketing past cars that could barely work up a speed of 100 mph. When one of the little cars would inexplicably pull out in front of him as he approached, it would take every bit of his driving skill to avoid them. More than once, Shelby recalled in interviews in later years, he was forced to swerve onto the grass to avoid a slower competitor who pulled into his path.

Shelby finished fifth in the Supercortemaggiore Grand Prix, a 1000 Km event at Monza, co-driving with Graham Whitehead, and followed that with third in an Aston Martin 1-2-3 clean sweep at Silverstone.

But after all this Mabee decided not to purchase an Aston for Shelby to race Stateside.

Wyer wasn't perturbed at the cancellation for now that they were on a winning streak, there were other customers for the car. Wyer was impressed that Shelby showed the discipline necessary to make a car last and the courage to run hard in the rain. Americans were not thought of as good drivers in the rain, at that point at least not like Londoner Stirling Moss, who enjoyed a world-renowned reputation for relishing driving in the rain, only admitting years after retirement that he in fact loathed it. He did it just to psych out his opponents.

Shelby sounded like a good follower of orders. He told Diana Bartley of *Speed Age* "You got to be a team man to get anywhere. You have to be able to follow orders and take the right advice—besides going fast. You can only reach the top as a team man."

This attitude no doubt sprang from two sources—his war-time stint as a flying instructor when you did things by the book (pilots have a saying: "There are old pilots and there are bold pilots but there are no old bold pilots"). And then there was the influence of that stern taskmaster John Wyer, who taught him that you developed a strategy for each race and stuck to it come hell or high water.

Shelby returned from England with money bulging out of the pockets of his chicken-pluckin' overalls—his first real winnings as a race driver.

1955 was the first year Shelby drove for Allen Giuberson, who Shelby knew well from his days working as an oil well roughneck—a real Texas Oilman. Giuberson had already sponsored his friend and competitor Philip Toll Hill in a Ferrari in the Carrera Panamericana twice, so Shelby knew he had the money and the cars. The only trouble with self-made guys like Giuberson, from Shelby's point of view, is that they were a little harder to work for than guys born with silver-spoon-firmly-in-mouth like Briggs Swift Cunningham or "Gentlemen Jim" Kimberly. The self-made men would be flush with cash when they hit an oil strike, but if they hit a dry spell, they would pull back on racing expenditures. Actually, Shelby did co-drive with Kimberly on at least one occasion but Kimberly kind of liked attention focused on him and with Shelby in the same pit, that would be impossible.

The best description of how Kimberly turned out for a race is the way Mike Sheehan described him in *Sports Car Market*: "an over-the-top Beau Brummel fashion plate…[with a] red transporters, red Ferrari, red helmet, red driving suit with button-down collar, red driving gloves, red suited mechanics and the best looking car and companions (doubtless in red as well.)"

Giuberson slotted Shelby for a drive in the 1955 12 Hours of Sebring, in his 3-liter Ferrari 750 Monza. Shelby and Hill drove hard, won the race and dutifully rolled in Victory Circle where they had fragrant garlands of orange blossoms put around their necks. Just when they were going to be kissed by the race queen, they got the bad news that the race officials were still dithering on just who actually won the race. Their "1st place" trophy was then summarily snatched away and re-awarded to the occupants of the car that pulled in behind them, the Cunningham Team's D-Jag piloted by Mike Hawthorn/Phil Walters. Both had completed 182 laps, so how'd'ya figure? After that fiasco, Sebring changed the way they scored races, a tacit admission that maybe Shelby and Hill had won (and a good excuse to bring your own scorers to a race). Shelby was remarkably philosophical about it, saying something to the effect of: "Too bad, we had fun drivin' it."

Shelby had driven the race in a Ferrari powered by an engine with only four cylinders, which to the purists was like driving one third of a Ferrari, because the Modena automaker is most famous for making V-12s. But he thought it handled better than the 4.5 liter V-12 he had also raced for Giuberson.

In July 1955, Shelby made his West Coast debut, winning the Torrey Pines race on a course laid out through Camp Callen, an abandoned army camp on the windswept hills of Torrey Pines overlooking the prosperous seaside village of La Jolla, north of San Diego. He was again piloting Giuberson's 4.5 liter Ferrari 375MM, a car that had been raced by the legendary team of Farina/Ascari at the '53 Nurburgring race. Shelby took first place. Right behind him was Phil Hill in a Ferrari Monza 3-liter owned by Beverly Hills car dealer, Austrian immigrant Johnnie Von Neumann (Mrs. Phil Hill, after hearing his name at an event once was overheard saying "I knew him when he was just "Johnnie Neumann.")

Hill had already carved out a reputation for himself, starting out a few years earlier than Shelby. Hill had one big advantage over Shelby—money. Although he was an equal in driving talent to Shelby, Hill had inherited a modest fortune at age 22 that allowed him to promptly go out and buy some proper modern sports cars, including an Aston Martin and a Ferrari (but despite the money, he wasn't a trust fund baby in the same way as Lance Reventlow was later; Hill always worked for his money, dropping out of USC to go to work at a Jaguar dealership as a line mechanic).

Hill had started racing at age 21 with a supercharged MG-TC. Later he brought a "purebred" (now a million dollar classic) Alfa 2.9 to race and although he did fine in the car, it was obsolete by postwar standards. His first race was in the '48-'49 period, when he was still a college student. At that point Shelby was still on the outside of racing looking in, sitting up in the stands watching races instead of being down there on the track behind the wheel, where he thought he rightfully deserved to be.

Also In the year 1955, Shelby hit paydirt. Or as oil well drillers say, "a gusher."

And just in time. But then, as they say in Texas, Shelby "could always draw a pat hand from a stacked deck."

Sure he was grateful as hell for the rides he got, but all the schlepping around from one race track to another, never knowing if he had a "ride" until he got there, was annoying. What he needed, Shelby concluded, was a sponsor with deep pockets, one who would let him choose the cars they needed rather than handing him some turkey and expecting him to win on driving talent alone. He needed a sponsor who could fund a racing effort for an entire season, not just for a day.

That "dream sponsor" finally came along one day in the fall of 1955 in the person of Antonio Parravano.

At one of the races Shelby had been in earlier, Shelby had gone back to his hotel room between races to freshen up, when the phone rang. Shelby answered—the caller was a man named "Tony."

Shelby needed no introduction. There was only one "Tony" in the world of sports car racing whose name was on everyone's lips. Tony Parravano, as advertised by the rumors that preceded him, was a successful building contractor in Southern California. He was a man immensely proud of his Italian roots, having been born in Aprino, Italy, back in 1917. He was bound and determined to buy some Italian race cars that would show how great the Italians were. (Not that anyone needed convincing, as at major sports car races like Sebring, the top five finishers at the time were either Ferraris or Maseratis). As early as 1952, Parravano had bought a Ferrari—a 340 America bodied by Ghia—and took it back to his home town in Sicily to show it off, local boy makes good and all that.

Parravano had already been a race driver sponsor in '53 when Jack McAfee, a racer who had a shop in Hollywood, talked him into sponsoring him in Parravano's Ferrari in the '53 Mexican road race. He finished fifth. Parravano himself drove the car in some minor events, fancying himself to be a driver whose talents were on a par with those he hired (he mostly confined his driving to "testing" each car when he first purchased it). Shelby met up with him a couple years later, after Parravano had already made and lost a fortune in frozen food but was making up for it by making a new fortune in home building on Los Angeles's now burgeoning west side.

"I want you to drive for me," Parravano demanded in the phone call. "Let's get together."

They met and Shelby saw that indeed Parravano was the genuine certified article, i.e. someone who could put his money where his mouth was, and by July 1955 Shelby found himself up in Seattle, at a venue called Seafair, behind the wheel of Parravano's gleaming Ferrari 375 Plus. Shelby finished second and right behind him was Ken Miles, driving a 4.5-liter Ferrari for Guiberson. Shelby also beat Phil Hill in a 3-liter Ferrari, which brought him a lot of notice as Hill was then America's hottest sports car driver. Miles was later to loom large at Shelby- American as Shelby's chief development driver in both Cobras and Ford GTs.

Parravano was like a man on fire. He already had several Ferraris (Ed Niles, the Ferrari expert, says that, at one point the Parravano stable housed 13 Maseratis and 11 Ferraris) but he wanted the latest ones. When he first hired Shelby, he took him on a tour of his current collection but then waved at them dismissively and ordered Shelby to get packed so they could go to Italy to buy some more.

"How many?" said Shelby, somewhat amazed.

Parravano looked at him like he'd just said something stupid. "As many as we need," he growled.

Enzo Ferrari liked the fact that Parravano stepped off the plane with money in hand because he hoped to unload his dogs on Parravano while he built newer, more competitive cars. Some steeped in the history of Ferrari feel that Enzo went even further, cleaning out the parts room of parts he didn't want, while leaving Parravano with the impression that he was getting the best stuff.

Parravano wasn't quite Ferrari's ideal customer. Once he bought a Ferrari from him, he would immediately take it over to Sergio Scaglietti, a local coach-builder who did most of Ferrari's coachbuilding on racecars, and tell him precisely how he wanted the styling changed on his Ferraris so that a Parravano car would be different from all the others of the same model. He had even modi-fied his '53 Ferrari by installing American-made Halibrand wheels.

This habit of Parravanos irked Ferrari because then the customers would say, "Why can't I have one like Parravano has?" leaving Enzo wondering, "Who the hell is the boss here, anyway?"

One of the mysteries of Parravano's cars was his habit of having extra gas tanks installed. Did he plan to fool the race organizers? Or was he smuggling something in those extra tanks? The smuggling angle was the only explanation for having the cars practically taken apart at customs on at least one occasion. Racecars, in fact, were ideal for stashing various substances, as they went from country to country, often air-freighted and you could stuff contraband any-where, even in the engine cylinders or frame tubes (Ironically, one famous name from that era, Zora Arkus-Duntov, bragged for years how he escaped the Nazis, driving out of Paris during the war in a Ford with gold hidden in the frame).

While in Europe, Parravano entered Shelby in two events. In August '55 Shelby ran at Oulton Park in England with Parravano's 4.4 liter Ferrari 121 LM, a six cylinder. He retired the car after suffering leg cramps and pulled in, not finishing the race. He later blamed the car, telling a writer, "Aston Martin just pissed on us."

Next, Shelby was entered in a race in Ireland, at Dundrod. His co-driver was Masten Gregory, a friend from America. The big cheese at this event was again Stirling Moss, part of a three-car Mercedes works team led by Fangio and Von

Trips. All three would be driving Mercedes SLRs and the competition would consist of Shelby and Gregory in a tiny 1.5 liter Porsche, Mike Hawthorn in a D-Jag and a few other cars—but everybody knew the Mercedes team were the top dogs. The expected Jaguar/Mercedes contest started right from the drop of the flag after the Le Mans-style start (where drivers line up on one side of the track and run to their cars on the others side), but on only the second lap tragedy struck when Jim Mayers, in a Cooper Climax, lost control at Deer's Leap and hit a stone gatepost, scattering wreckage all over the road. He was killed instantly and a second driver in a Connaught hit the wreckage and later died of injuries in the hospital.

The race continued with Moss establishing a long lead over Hawthorn but more tragedy followed when Mainwearing overturned his Elva at Tornagrough and was caught under the wreckage when his car burst into flames. Now the death toll was three.

Moss won but the Irish government was so shocked over three deaths in one event that it spelled the end of the Tourist Trophy races at Dundrod Circuit. Shelby finished 9th overall, while the Mercedes Benz "steamrollers"—those immaculate 300SLRs—finished 1-2-3.

In Jim Mourning's 1958 article in *Modern Man* quotes Shelby's view of what happened. Shelby told Mourning he was only on his second lap when he was confronted by a solid wall of flame as he crested Deer's Leap. "Either you do it or you don't," Shelby told Mourning. "So I put my foot in it all the way." Shelby emerged on the other side of the accident with only a dent in his car caused by hitting an engine left in the road from the wreck that had just occurred. Shelby's only "wound" was singed eyebrows.

Gregory, Shelby's co-driver at Dundrod, was another American driver of great promise. In fact, Shelby often told interviewers that Gregory was the "most talented American driver." Gregory also got a jump on Shelby by being able to start his driving career in the same way as Phil Hill by simply buying the fastest cars with inherited money. At age 21 in 1953, the "Kansas City flash" bought a C-type Jag. He was a competitor to Shelby for years but they were pals, though they presented an "odd couple" appearance, Shelby being 6 feet tall and change while Gregory stood only 5 ft. 6 in. and wore what Shelby called "coke bottle" eyeglasses. Oddly, Masten had a deep bass voice that one writer observed, "seemed to emanate from somewhere around his shoes, the voice all out of character with his diminutive size."

The story is told that, despite his schoolboy looks, Gregory was totally fearless. He was famed, or rather infamous, for regularly bailing out of his racecar just before said car hit a solid object. In fact when ESQUIRE profiled him, the illustration was a cheeky full two-page spread showing a toy racecar tumbling over and over, row after row, across two solid pages. Gregory wasn't always lucky enough to escape injuries during those high-speed bailouts. Shelby has reported in interviews that he "had to nurse Gregory back to health a couple of times."

Gregory was also well known for an incident in Italy that occurred on the road when some menacing looking types were following him in a road car. At some point, he merely moved the wheel and nudged his pursuers off the road, as nonchalantly as if he were lighting a Lucky.

A story that illustrates Gregory's loyalty is told in a biography of Gregory appropriately entitled *Totally Fearless* in which Shelby accidentally ran into a racecar ahead of him during a race start. The driver of the car ahead, taller than Shelby, came out of his car ready to pummel Shelby but Gregory jumped in-between and said something to the effect of "If you want him you will have to come through me." Apparently Gregory's demeanor was convincing and the angry car owner skulked off, leaving Shelby totally amazed.

In October '55 Parravano entered Shelby into the famed Targa Florio of Italy, his mount a 3-liter 750 Monza Ferrari. His Italian co-driver was Gino Munaron, his presence supposedly dictated by Enzo Ferrari though the car was not entered as an official Ferrari Team entry. Munaron soon drove the car off a cliff (Shelby says into a graveyard) and in his 1954 biography, Shelby expressed bitterness about Munaron's performance, feeling the Italian driver hadn't done due diligence and taken a full week to learn the 44-mile course, which was run on 1,000 year old roads built by the Romans. Shelby had taken that week, but Munaron had made it a waste of time.

Shelby says they were running third at the time which made him even madder when he thought of how Munaron had botched their effort. Of course whether they could have won is doubtful because that year they were up against the Mercedes machine, with Stirling Moss and fellow Englishman Peter Collins steamrollering along in their 300SLR to first place followed by a second team Mercedes piloted by Fangio/Kling.

One of the problems with working for Parravano is that he expected nothing less than a first place finish regardless of the fact that some of the cars they were sold were turkeys. Case in point—the Ferrari 121LM. Most drivers felt it didn't handle and it had a six, when you think the only reason to have a Ferrari is to have their superb V-12. Shelby didn't mind it, though.

Shelby kept track of what happened to cars in case he ever had to drive them. There is one instance where he was supposed to drive a Ferrari the next day but he had heard the gearbox had a habit of exploding in that car. So he snuck out to the track the night before and paid a welder to weld some sort of shield on the car to protect himself.

Shelby also ran his first Formula One Grand Prix race in October, 1955, finishing sixth at the wheel of a works-sponsored Formula One Maserati 250F in the Syracuse GP in Sicily. He finished right behind his friend, Harry Schell. Although Shelby's Formula One career was extremely brief, he later told an interviewer that was his big mistake—at that point he should have gone all the way, bought a Maserati F1 car and raced the entire season in Europe. Grand Prix cars back then weren't nearly as expensive as they are now and though Shelby was lean on funds, he could have swung it, especially with his record for sweet talking sponsors. But at that point, his children were in grade school and his mother ailing and he just didn't want to stay away from his family for a whole season. No, Shelby figured, that he would have to play ball with Parravano because the plain fact that Parravano, of all potential sponsors, had the money to buy Ferraris and Ferraris were at that point the fastest cars.

But it was not easy. Today people would say Parravano had a "type A" personality. Or that he was a Grade A- A-hole, take your pick.

For one thing, he thought he was a master mechanic. Bill Pollack, a racer at the time wrote an article where he referred to Parravano as "the man with the golden screwdriver because no matter how well a car might be running, Tony could not resist an open hood. The sight of three or six Weber carburetors was like sugar to a diabetic. He would reach in and start adjusting a perfectly fine running machine to the dismay of his mechanics."

Shelby began to be on the lookout for a better sponsor. Nothin' personal, you understand. He was merely following Texas wisdom, to whit: "Always drink upstream from the herd."

In '56 Shelby enjoyed three more drives that season in Parravano's cars, all on the same balmy weekend in February in Palm Springs, a favorite wintertime resort of snowbirds 100 miles east of Los Angeles. Shelby retired the Ferrari 121LM in two races but took a first in the mighty 410S in another of the event's races. He tried a Maserati 150S as well but it failed. Oddly that was to be his last race for Parravano.

Then it was on to Sebring in March '56 where his ol' buddy John Wyer had a Aston Martin DB3S/7 waiting for him. His co-driver was British driver Roy Salvadori who was to loom larger in Shelby's life later on. The duo finished fourth overall.

Right after Sebring, Shelby found himself on the West Coast again, racing a Ferrari 750 Monza belonging to Richard Hall, of Midland Texas. Hall was an oil man originally from Abilene who had become Shelby's partner in a business called "Carroll Shelby Sports Cars" at 5611 Yales St, Dallas. Hall was the money end and Shelby the name that brought in the customers. Hall had a brother, Jim, still in college down at Cal Tech in Pasadena, who was later to not only sponsor Shelby in a race or two but to be a high-tech competitor, embarrassing the hell out of the Ford team's GT40s with his Chaparrals.

Shelby's victory at Pebble in April, 1956 was marred by the death of a popular driver in the same event—Ernie McAfee—who was killed when a brake locked up on his Ferrari, spinning him into a tree. McAfee was respected driver who ran a Ferrari agency on the Sunset Strip in Los Angeles. The upshot of the accident was that there was no Pebble Beach road race scheduled for the following year. In a way McAfee's death marked the end of innocence for American road race promoters. If they wanted to make American sports car racing safe, they would have to build purpose-built race tracks.

Chapter 3- A Gentleman Sponsor

Cumberland Raceway, May 1956. The occasion: a pre-race cocktail party.

Carroll Shelby is watching as the hors d'oeuvres are brought in. Not just one tray, not just two but an endless line of them—thanks to his newest patron, John Edgar.

Shelby could see Edgar now, a charmer working his way through the crowd, a cocktail in one hand and a cigarette in the other. The band was striking up a rhumba and Edgar did a little dance step still holding the drink and cigarette and the crowd laughed.

Shelby signaled the bartender for a re-fill. This Edgar, he liked women, he liked fast cars, he liked to spend money. Clearly his kind of guy.

In May 1956, Shelby drove for the first time for John Edgar at Cumberland raceway. His mount? A tiny little Alfa Veloce Spyder with an equally tiny 1.3 liter four. Actually the car he was supposed to drive hadn't arrived so Shelby cadged the Alfa so he could get some practice in on the track. He finished fifth.

Also in May, Shelby went to Ft. Sumner and drove a Ferrari 375 MM for Temple Buell. He took two firsts.

Then it was to Ft. Worth to drive a tiny OSCA M14, the car built by the Maserati brothers when they started a new company after the war (having sold the name Maserati). OSCA's were built by the Maserati brother's Officine Specializate Construczione Automobili, thus the name OSCA. He took second in the OSCA but nobody seems sure of who the sponsor was.

Then his car dealership partner, Richard Hall, trailered his Ferrari 750 Monza to the Eagle Mountain track near Ft. Worth, and Shelby was able to race in his native Texas, taking a first and second in two events.

The middle of the month found Shelby admiring the view from the top of Mt. Washington, the highest mountain in the Northeast, towering some 8,000 feet above New Hampshire. The venue was a hillclimb. The car was a Ferrari 375GP car which really stood out. Ferrari Grand Prix cars just weren't that common in America. Shelby took first and enjoyed the party afterwards. Edgar was a model sponsor. The kind racers dream of. Generous to a fault and sincerely concerned with his driver's physical and mental well-being. Above all he was forgiving. That was important for when you pranged the sponsor's car.

Edgar also swung Shelby a drive in a Ferrari 121LM at Elkhart Lake, Wisconsin, and Beverly, Massachusetts, though the official entrant was listed as Chinetti who was, after all, a car dealer. Though Edgar was paying the bills, Chinetti was hawking cars and would have no doubt sold the car out from under Shelby in a nanosecond if a buyer appeared waving cash in hand. The cars were loaners, until the Ferraris Edgar had ordered arrived. Entering them under Chinetti's name told the crowd they were for sale.

One story about Chinetti shows how he operated. He had sold a Ferrari to a New Yorker named Jan de Vroom (what a perfect name for a sports car driver!) but then Chinetti up and cancelled the sale so he could lease it to Temple Buell when Moss became available. The reason? Moss was more certain to deliver a victory. The car would then be worth more. End of story.

At last, Shelby had the best car available, the most money available, and the best mechanic .

Edgar, in turn had a driver determined to make up for lost time (having started in racing a decade older than his fellow racer). Another good thing about the deal with Edgar was that it was agreed that Shelby was free to drive for other teams if Edgar didn't have a car available for a particular race. For Edgar, Shelby first piloted Ferraris, then Maseratis, the latter his choice of an snarling 3-liter 300S six or a growling V8 450S. The combination of car, sponsor and sponsor support was a winning combination. Shelby won 19 races in '56 and earned his second SCCA championship.

John Edgar was a wealthy Hollywood man whose family back in Ohio made millions from the manufacturing of professional grade Hobart kitchen supplies such as a motorized meat slicer. Edgar could afford to buy the latest Ferraris from Italy. Edgar was similar to Parravano in being a fount of money but he had less of a bulldog personality than Parravano and, more importantly, kept his screwdriver away from the engine.

In fact, Shelby found Edgar to be a true gentleman, and admired the life style Edgar had; living, as he did in as grand a style as any American could aspire to. In fact at one point he lived in a place called the Garden of Eden on the Sunset Strip, and toodled about town in a Bugatti 57C drophead coupe. He was famous for throwing lavish parties at every race. Edgar even funded a special high-speed transporter to haul his racecars to the track in style. Shelby was right to feel, as they say in Texas, "as happy as a gopher in soft dirt."

The Alfa Shelby had first driven for Edgar was a fluke. Once he got a real car in his hands he began taking firsts again. After Mt. Washington, he took the Grand Prix Ferrari to Giant's Despair hillclimb and took first and then Edgar's Ferrari 500 Testa Rossa to a private racetrack on a Senator's farm in Pennsylvania where he took first again.

Then it was Seattle, and two races at Montgomery where he took firsts both times. It was only at Thompson where he slowed down, both races retiring the Ferrari 857S before race end.

Shelby took a short break from the Edgar Equipe to drive two races for Kimberly-Clark paper heir William Kimberly. Both races were run with Kimberly as co-driver. Shelby took first in the OSCA M14 but in the Ferrari 121LM for some reason the car wasn't ready to start. Shelby didn't drive any more for Kimberly and you can see why—both had type A personalities and Kimberly rather liked the attention on himself and with Shelby around that was impossible.

Then it was Palm Springs in November, a joy for Shelby to bask in the balmy weather of the desert when the East was knee deep in snow. Shelby took first in Edgar's Ferrari 410S.

The 410 Sport was one hell of a car. According to historian and auction official Rick Carey, "It dominated the 1956 SCCA races it entered, winning virtually everywhere it appeared. With conscientious maintenance by Joe Landaker, who had joined Edgar's equipe along with Shelby from Tony Parravano's squad, the 410 Sport was unbeatable except by misfortune. Misfortune's ugly head, it seemed, was rarely raised." Carey says that after Shelby drove the car Seattle's Seafair raceway, he delivered the famous line: "It's a hog, but it goes."

Writer Steve Dawson's quotes Shelby as saying: "The 4.9 was a big car. It was the biggest and best car Ferrari ever made in '56—the 4.9 was the car of the year. It didn't have any bad vices."

So much for 'it's a hog.'

Apparently it was dead reliable. Mechanic Joe Landaker was quoted as saying: "We ordered spares with it and they flew in with the car. We had everything—gears, pistons, fuel pumps and distributors, stuff we though we would need. Nothing much ever went wrong with the car."

And now that it was winter, the big event was the Nassau races. Shelby cleaned up there, taking three firsts in three different races. When the Ferrari got back to California though, it didn't work well and was retired at two races at the pedestrian Pomona track, as unglamorous a venue as you could imagine, especially when compared to the glamour of some of the other tracks.

When they took it down to New Smyrna Beach in Florida, the Ferrari perked up and gave Shelby and Edgar two more firsts.

Cuba was a true exotic locale and Edgar was game to enter so in February '57 Edgar's 410S was shipped there to run in a race on a course laid out on the waterfront. Shelby finished second, not bad when you consider the bloke taking first was none other than Juan Manuel Fangio, easily the most famous driver on earth. Fangio was in a Maserati 300S. Shelby was driving a car that had been built for Fangio with a weird gas pedal in the middle. He got used to it. Cuba at that time was one non-stop party, owing to the fact that dictator Fugenico Batista, in league with some Americano gangsters, had set it up to be his own private fiefdom with plenty of booze, gambling and woman-chasing available for Americano turistas!

In March '57 Shelby went to Mansfield, Louisiana, to a small track where he drove a Triumph TR-3, certainly a car beneath his talents. No finish is recorded but the same day he took first at the same track in a Ferrari 375MM. The owner was a man named A.D. Logan who had finished 7th in the same car the day before.

Later in March he was back in Edgar's 410S at Stockton in California but the car didn't finish.

Shelby's record with Maseratis must have impressed the Orsi family, who owned Maserati, and when the Sebring 12 Hour came around March 24, 1957 Shelby was behind the wheel of a Maserati works-owned 300S. But he failed to finish the race.

For Edgar he began another sweep of the racetracks in the Maser 300S, taking a first and second at Palm Springs, plus two third place finishes in Hawaii.

Then came two races which will amaze Corvette fans. Shelby was hired by a fellow Texan, Ebb Rose, to race two Corvettes. The first was at Hammond, Louisiana, the mount an SR2, a sort of ersatz factory race car/dream car designed by Harley Earl to tempt his son away from buying and racing a Ferrari (the trick worked). Actually it was heavier than a stock Corvette but Shelby managed to finish second in it. Then Rose put him in an ex-Sebring factory racing Corvette and he also finished second at Cumberland, this time in the production class. How did Rose get ahold of these special cars? Well, it went back to the failure of the million dollar Corvette SS at Sebring that year. The beautifully finished car only made it 23 laps before its suspension collapsed. GM was so embarrassed they withdrew from racing, citing an agreement they had signed to not encourage racing. So the racecars were sold out the back door and Rose got two of them. He was later to become a sponsor at Indy.

That was Shelby's last drive in a Corvette, until he hatched a plan to make a Corvette based project.

The '57 season from May to December is a blur of races for Edgar, all in the Maserati 300S or the 450S, with the result a couple of DNFs and DNS (did not start) but many firsts, and seconds.

The organizers of sports car racing had learned their lesson with the makeshift tracks earlier on and new racetracks were popping up all over. Shelby drove at the inaugural race at the new Laguna Seca track on the Monterey peninsula in Nov. '57, with Edgar's 300S taking a first place on Saturday and a fourth place on Sunday. Ironically, decades later, at various Monterey Historic races—such as the years Maserati and Aston marques were the honored marque—Shelby would pilot his old race cars, by then the subject of million dollar restorations, on parade laps.

There was one race in '57, though, that Shelby will never forget, and that was in September at Riverside. It was a brand new track and Shelby was practicing the day before the big race. He flung Edgar's "big Boomer" Maserati 450S around Turn 6, some wind blew sand across the track obscuring where the track was and the next thing you know, Shelby's got the Maser's nose stuffed into a dirt bank and blood is running down his face.

The car was still right side up but Shelby's face hit the windshield. When he got to the hospital, it was discovered that he had back injuries as well and three vertebrae in his spine had to be fused. But worse yet, from a promoter's point-of-view was his facial injuries. Fortunately a skilled plastic surgeon was at hand, and, working from a publicity photo, he managed to piece Shelby's face back together, using a mere 72 stitches. It healed well, and Shelby didn't have to go through the rest of his life with a beard, like some other racers whose surgeons were less skilled.

The real irony of that crash was that Nov. 16, 1957 found Shelby back at Riverside in the same damn car, now pristine, and he raced it both days of the weekend, finishing second the first day and first the second day.

Temple Buell interrupted Edgar's parade in December to wrest Shelby away to pilot a 450S to first in Miami on the first day of a two-day event but the second day the car was retired.

There was one incident in '57 that steeled Shelby's ambition for what he was going to do after he hung up his helmet. It was after he received "the call." No, not a religious "calling" but the one every sports car racer hoped to get in the Fifties, the summons from Il Commendatore, Enzo Ferrari.

Shelby, like all sports car racers at the time, yearned to drive for Ferrari on the factory team. But he had mixed feelings about the creator of the legendary Italian car firm, Enzo Ferrari. In an interview with Richard Symons in the DVD *Cobra-Ferrari Wars*, Shelby tells of his year in Italy, where he became a good friend of Enzo's son Dino, but never warmed up to his authoritarian father, Enzo. Alfredo, called "Dino" from "Alfredino," or "little Alfredo," only lived to 1956. He had been sick for some time but had accomplished something at his father's fatory, designing a V6 for F1 that was later refined by Vittorio Jano and put into production.

On the video, Shelby tells a story of how old man Enzo would deliberately pit one driver on his team against another, telling each driver the other drivers were saying bad things about them. Shelby thought Enzo might have done that in order to make each driver more competitive with others on the team, but he felt such pressure tactics unnecessary and potentially dangerous. In fact, in several interviews in the late '90s, Shelby came right out and said "Ferrari killed Musso," implying that his friend Luigi Musso died in a race trying to win the old man's favor by beating the other Ferrari team drivers. Musso was one of the last great Italian drivers of the era but whether you can say Ferrari killed him is hard to say. It might have been his own pride, trying to drive beyond his capabilities in a vain attempt to show the Old Man he had what it took.

There were only so many driving slots at Ferrari and drivers from all over the world were willing to risk their lives to win a slot on the factory team.

Obviously Ferrari had been following his career. No dummy, Ferrari knew if he hired Americans and Americans won, he would sell more cars in America. So Shelby traipsed off to Modena.

The conversation with Enzo went something like this:

Ferrari: "How many races did you win this year?"

Shelby: "I reckon 19."

Ferrari looked at the list.

"Who came in second?"

Another version of the famous meeting is that Ferrari didn't want to talk about money, feeling every driver should be honored to be asked to drive for Ferrari.

A third version is that money was talked about but it was peanuts. Chicken feed. An insult. Enzo knew what buttons to push to light off Shelby. Shelby knew some Italian but whether he told off Ferrari in English or Italian isn't recorded. The message got across, though, something like "I'll be back here and beat your ass someday."

And from then on, he doubled his efforts to make that prediction come about. Shelby told interviewers decades later that Enzo had approached him not just one but three different times but he "didn't want to get into the mess of (Enzo) playing game with the drivers and not paying anything." Later, in another interview, Shelby was kinder toward the old man. "You can't blame Ferrari for not paying, drivers were there because they wanted to drive Ferraris because they had a better chance of winning a race."

A real irony is that Shelby's racing buddy, Dan Gurney (yes the same Dan Gurney that later drove on the Shelby factory team) was suckered by Enzo in the same pitch a year later. After driving a Ferrari at Le Mans in 1958, Gurney was invited by the Old Man to take a test run in a works car and was on the works Formula One in 1959. He ran only four races and earned two podium finishes, but found the Old Man's dictums intolerable and eventually left the team. Ritchie Ginther, another Shelby pal, was signed on by Ferrari in 1960 and stayed one year. It appears that one year of the Old Man was about as much as anyone could take.

One of the last races Shelby ran in '57 was the Nassau Speed Weeks. The car was the same car he had crashed at Riverside but now it was in fine fettle and in three events he took two 2nd places and a 3rd for John Edgar.

For Carroll Shelby, the '58 season was a mixed bag. He knew it was closer to the end of his career than the beginning. The writing was on the wall. If you look at the variety of cars Shelby drove that year, it is astonishing, everything from a Porsche RSK to a pieced-together hot rod that would be banned from any concours anywhere.

The season started with the Miami race for Buell, driving a 450S. He took first one day but the next day retired the car before the end of the race.

Then Wyer called. Aston had a car going into Sebring, a DBR1, would he mind terribly? Not at all, said Shelby, but he and co-driver Roy Salvadori didn't make it to the finish after being disqualified for re-fueling too early.

Shelby was hoping that he could continue on with Edgar if he couldn't wangle a factory F1 drive in Europe.

In April '58 Edgar bankrolled another trip to Cuba, but this time there was no partying. For by now Castro's bearded rebels were almost ready to take over and as a demonstration of how strong they were, they lifted Juan Manuel Fangio out of his hotel lobby the day before the race. It was a protest, they said "against the Batista tyranny." Actually they treated Fangio pretty well and he sent them Christmas cards for years after his release. The race was run so poorly that they didn't even know how to drop the flag properly so all the racecars overheated. Gregory jumped into the lead and was followed by Moss, Shelby, Von Trips and Hill in that order. At the end of the first lap, though, it was Moss way out front, Gregory second and Shelby in third, held back by the great weight of the 450S into which he had installed an extra gas tank so he wouldn't have to pit as often. Then the Cuban drivers showed their lack of skill when one Cuban, Cifuentes, lost control of his Ferrari 500 Testa Rossa and put it into the crowd, killing at least six and injuring many more. The red flag came out. Gregory dutifully slowed but Moss stood on it, capturing the lead. The race ended and the drivers voted not to re-start but Moss was declared the winner. Gregory was miffed so Moss shared the winnings with him. Shelby was a definite third. But the final finishing order never was determined.

Shelby was called by Aston again, to drive at Spa in May '58. He took a third in a DBR2.

Then it was to England to Crystal Palace where he was scheduled to drive a Cooper in a race for the first time but something happened and the car did not start.

There's one other story from '58—one that explains why Shelby never raced at Indy.

The story is that Shelby went out there in May of '58 to see if he could qualify at the Brickyard. He didn't like ovals, but that's what Indy was.

The Indy people weren't that friendly. They called sports car drivers "teabaggers."

Shelby borrowed a car from another would be qualifier and went out on the course. He was halfway through his test when he was black-flagged. He pulled into the pits and found chief starter Harlan Fengler waiting for him, a scowl on his face.

"Whose car is that?" Fengler demanded.

"Jack Ensley's." Shelby replied.

"Each car can only be used by one rookie." Fengler said.

That put Shelby in a quandary. Ensley hadn't tried to qualify yet. If Shelby continued that would mean Ensley couldn't get out there in his own car.

"Hell, I got a car waiting for me in Europe," Shelby drawled and left in a huff.

It wasn't a bluff. He did have a car waiting for him, an Aston Martin in which he finished third at Spa, May 18th, while his friend Masten Gregory took first in a Lister-Jag.

Shelby never went back to Indy as a driver but did as a team owner. (More about that later.)

At the Nurburgring in Germany in June '58 it was an Aston DBR/1 with Salvadori as co-driver but they retired the car.

Then Grand Prix beckoned and he was able to enter both the French and British GPs in a 250F rented from Centro Sud, a firm racers called "rent-a-racer."

Temple Buell came up with a 250F for Portugal but when the car broke in practice, Shelby jumped over to sharing a rented 250F that Masten Gregory had rented from Scuderia Centro Sud, a ersatz race team run by Gugliemo Dei, who always ran rough cars but lived in hope that one of the leading cars would break and suddenly provide one of the drivers renting his cars an opportunity. You could knock his cars but the fact was that many a promising young driver like Masten Gregory got his start in F1 in a Centro Sud entry. But when an old driver like Shelby was forced to rent a well-worn rent-a-racer from a shop like Centro Sud, it indicated that he was no longer being considered for a spot on a top team driving fresh mounts. They shared a fourth overall.

Then it was back to Brands Hatch in England where this time the Cooper was ready and Shelby finished 16th in one race and 11th in another.

One race he liked to drive was the Tourist Trophy in England, where for '58 Aston put him in a DBR1 with Lewis-Evans and they took third overall.

Now it was getting to be fall and cold in Europe so Shelby was happy to go back to Riverside, California, for the second year of racing there. He took a Maserati 450S owned by Buell but the car didn't finish.

A little over two weeks later, he took the same car to Riverside and finished first. That car was special—it had a larger than usual 5.7 liter engine.

Edgar bought the car and took it down to Nassau in December but it didn't finish.

In October and Nov. '58 he ran two races in the big-engined Maserati 450S for Temple Buell, one at Riverside where he retired the car before the end and the other at Palm Springs where he took first.

The '58 driving year for Shelby ended as it usually did, with fun in the sun at Nassau in December. That year he drove the big-engined Maser 450S for Edgar but the car was retired before the end of the race.

The year 1958 was also the first year that Scarabs appeared on the race-tracks of America. These were aluminum bodied sports cars built in California for Lance Reventlow, heir to not just the Woolworth (five and dime) money but the EF Hutton fortune as well. The Scarabs were powered by Chevrolet Corvette engines. The size and scope of the Reventlow operation in Venice, California, no doubt drove Shelby nuts. Shelby had to endure watching blonde handsome Reventlow play the role of dilletante sports car builder and racer who seemed to spend more time squiring around movie starlets like Jill St. John (who he later married) then tending to the serious business of building and racing sports cars. Shelby, of course, believed, that if he had the money he would tend solely to business notwithstanding the fact that he was doing plenty of squiring around himself and in fact had his own movie star in tow not much later, Jan Harrison, who he married shortly before the end of his driving career.

Shelby told *Vanity Fair's* profiler Robert Levine "I'm a terrible husband. I'm always running around somewhere with some new deal that's likely to break me tomorrow." In the interview Shelby tried to recall for Levine all his wives or even the correct number. There was, for instance, a wife from New Zealand (which this author identifies as Sue Stafford), a match which Shelby dismisses as merely a "six week deal for her to get into the country." And of his movie star marriage, Shelby told the interviewer "I don't count that second one because it happened in Mexico." One thing's sure—Shelby's appeal to women was undeniable. Carol Conners, the pert songwriter who penned the hit song "Hey, Little Cobra" told Levine "You couldn't be female and not find him interesting."

In January 1959 Shelby found himself down in New Zealand, where Temple Buell had fielded a lightweight Maserati 250F for him, the so-called "piccolo" car that had been built for Fangio but then Fangio had retired. Shelby worked his way up to third but then found himself plagued by an agonising cramp in one leg, complicated by the fact his brakes were beginning to fade.

Finally he pitted on lap 41, hopping around to try to restore life to his leg and his co-driver Harry Schell leapt into the car in his place to resume the race. He worked his way up near the front but lost any chance to catch Moss because of the failure of the drum brakes. In fact the brakes had been welded to the drum castings by the heat, torn clean off the shoes, and Schell had a hell of a time stopping the car. He and Shelby were credited with a fourth place finish.

Shelby did salvage something from the event—he met a young girl, who it is said hornswoggled him into marriage but then one wonders, given Shelby's reputation, and the fact she was half his age, who was doing the hornswoggling?

In March he was back in California, driving a Maserati 450S for Edgar at the unlovely Pomona venue.

He didn't finish the race. The car broke. More significantly, that turned out to be the very last race he ran for his favorite patron of all time, John Edgar.

Something had happened between him and Edgar.

Maybe it was the cars. Edgar had been talked into building a Pontiac-engined Maserati but the domestic engine wasn't up to the task. Then Shelby had talked him into building a Maserati-powered Lister, also a disaster.

But it wasn't the uncompetiveness of the cars he had, it was, as Michael Lynch, the historian, says, "the man was just plain tired." After all, Lynch points out, Edgar had been racing for ten years and was just plain tired of the whole scene. Before auto racing he'd been a hydroplane racer, and though he won a lot of races, he also suffered a lot of crashes. Those injuries were coming back to haunt him. He had lost a kidney and wasn't helping his health by being a chain smoker and heavy drinker.

Add to that the fact that Shelby wasn't winning races as much anymore. At least not like back in '56 and '57 when the press had nicknamed him "The Texas Tornado."

Then too, Edgar had the gnawing feeling that the European factories had been suckering him. Parravano before him had the same suspicion and for that reason both had switched from Ferraris to Maseratis in the hopes of better treatment but Edgar still felt they were being sold the losers. In one case Edgar paid for a Maserati that had finished second at Sebring and the factory promised to freshen the engine before sending it to him. When he took delivery he had it torn down and found it was still worn out from the race. The factory hadn't touched it!

Shelby moved on. To be a winner, you had to drive what was competitive (but he still was a loyal friend and continued to visit Edgar for many years as Edgar's health declined).

Shelby and his partner, Dick Hall, also began to import Listers from England. Built by Brian Lister, the front-engined cars were stout and had good handling. And could use a variety of engines. In England they favored Jaguar sixes but in America it was Chevy V8s.

Oddly, Shelby didn't race them himself.

Meanwhile, Shelby's social life was in a state of extreme flux. There was a divorce or two, a marriage or two, but who was keeping track? One reason that there is so much memory fade in this regard is that some of the weddings were, as they say in Texas, "hitched but not churched." No church, no ceremony, hence no wedding photographers.

Shelby worked on being a lady's man. There is one amusing story from the time he shared an apartment in London with Masten Gregory. Gregory looked like comedian Wally Cox, glasses and all. Shelby, tall in the saddle, looked more like Dean Martin, the crooner. Shelby and Gregory had a deal worked out where if one of them found a woman willing to stay the night and got home first he would leave the porch light on, warning the other not to interrupt them. One night Gregory got home in a pouring rain and the porchlight was on. He sat on the porch shivering all night until the morning when Shelby opened the door and said "Masten, what the hell you doin' out here?"

Gregory pointed toward the light.

Shelby said "Oh, you should have knocked. I came home alone and forgot to turn that off."

Pete Petersen, the founder of the Petersen Publishing empire, recalls trying to make inroads on Shelby's harem in the '50s: "Shel and I would go out to he races in Palm Springs and Santa Barbara," recalls Petersen. "While he was out on the track driving, I'd be poolside back at the hotel trying to hit on some of the women waiting for Shel. I'd tell them 'Why do you want to wait for Shelby? He'll come back all greasy and dirty and here I am all clean.' They always wanted to wait for him though."

Fortunately for Shelby, Aston Martin came back into his life as a sponsor in '59, with three rides, one at Sebring in a DBR1 with Salvadori—they didn't finish.

Then one at Silverstone in the new Aston DBR4/250 Grand Prix car which predictably didn't make it to the end of the race. Then it was the Dutch GP where the same car also retired before finishing.

The word "new" as applied to the Aston Martin GP car is a bit misleading. The car had actually been developed back in '57 so it was already well obsolete before it ever turned a wheel in combat. And it was front-engined when most of the competitors were going mid-engined.

At Nurburgring he was put into a mid-engined Porsche RSK but retired.

Then came Le Mans.

Things perked up considerably for Shelby at Le Mans. There Shelby was paired with his old friend Salvadori in an Aston DBR1/300, part of a first class three-car sports car effort mounted by Aston. It was a good running car, now with a seven main bearing inline six. Its only bad point was a rather agricultural gearbox (maybe made by one of David Brown tractor engineers at his farm tractor company?).

John Wyer, nicknamed "Death Ray" because a hard stare that it was said could curdle milk, ran the race team in so organized a fashion that he assessed the lap times his drivers recorded in practice and then pre-assigned each of his three teams fixed speeds at which they were to run the entire 24 hours. Belgian driver Paul Frere and the French driver Louis Trintignant were delegated to run the slowest speed, waiting for the leaders to break.

Salvadori and Shelby were directed to run their laps 2 seconds faster, and to be on the lookout for opportunities to develop while Stirling Moss and Jack Fairman were to be the teams' "rabbit," i.e. running flat out from the onset in order to tempt the Ferraris to try to catch them and break in the process.

Shelby and Salvadori figured they would put all their effort into late braking and fast cornering in order to save the engine and gearbox as much as possible. They even kept practice to a minimum to save the car for the race. In fact they skipped one whole day of practice, playing gin rummy instead of fretting about the race.

The race ran like clockwork for Aston. Moss tempted the Ferraris into following him and broke them in the process; but he broke himself with an engine failure. That left the way open for Shelby/Salvadori. Salvadori—maybe wearing the wrong shoes—suffered burns on his feet as a result of a pre-race decision to move the exhausts under the floorpan. But he kept on driving.

At one point Salvadori pulled into the pits complaining of a rear end vibration. Reg Parnell got under the car and found large chunks of tread missing on one of the rear Avon tires. That was changed and they went out on the course again, three laps behind the lead Ferrari. Salvadori was worried they would never catch up but then around 11 a.m. the next morning, the Hill Ferrari came into the pits steaming and the Shelby/Salvadori Aston moved into the lead.

The strategy worked. They won! A second team Aston finished right behind them. Analysts figured out later the Ferraris were undergeared and their drivers had over-revved them on the straights—they didn't last.

Immediately, with the victory, Carroll Shelby became one of the world's most famous racecar drivers. He won the biggest purse he had won so far, which by today's standards wouldn't be much but it was the prestige that counted. He hoped it would open some doors.

But in the end, it was not as much as he had hoped. At least not in Grand Prix which was regarded as a different kind of challenge.

After Le Mans, Shelby was also a member of the winning Aston team in the Tourist Trophy at Goodwood, thereby greatly assisting Aston Martin in their winning of the World Sports Car Championship.

Unfortunately for Shelby, while Aston was that year on top of the world with their sports car, their Formula One Aston Martin lacked speed, and his best result in an abbreviated season was eighth in the Portuguese Grand Prix.

One would think winning Le Mans would have put Shelby in Fat City. But winning Le Mans back in those days didn't make you rich. A year after his Le Mans win, Shelby was still scrounging around in search of yet another wealthy patron who could put him behind the wheel of a competitive racecar.

Shelby was quoted in an interview as being thankful for what Wyer had taught him. "John Wyer was the hardest old son of a bitch in the world to drive for, but he was fair, honest and straightforward. He was cantankerous but you always knew where you stood. And in integrity, in my book anyway he stood head and shoulders above Enzo Ferrari. He had a great influence on my life. I learned from him that you got to fight for what you get. And once you make up you mind where you want to go, go there no matter what gets in your way."

Shelby had always chafed at the noncommercial rules of the Sports Car Club of America. Fortunately, the commercial age of American racing had begun, and while the SCCA was dithering on whether to allow prize money or for drivers to be sponsored, Shelby, after being named Sports Illustrated Driver of the Year, began to get calls from commercial sponsors who would pay if he appeared in their ads, for products like Brylcreem hair pomade and Jantzen clothing. Soon Shelby's grinning visage was seen everywhere.

Shelby made another attempt to establish a home life of sorts. His marriage to Jan Harrison had a promising start, but it ended quickly. Shelby was not really the marrying kind or to be more accurate, the stay-married kind. Like the stereotype of car racers in '50s movies like *Johnny Dark*, he drove hard and he played hard, devil take the hindmost.

The year 1960 was also the year that Shelby had his last adventure in Cuba. Only this time the Cuban GP was being run by the Fidelistas, all bearded and khaki-clad, and had been re-named the "Freedom Grand Prix."

Shelby had cajoled wheeler dealer car dealer (Cadillacs were his speciality) Lloyd "Lucky" Casner into funding two Maseratis—one for him, and one for Stirling Moss. Two of Casner's Maseratis and a Ferrari were shipped down to Havana, the Ferrari intended as the practice car. One of the Maseratis never arrived—lost in shipping. And Casner turned over the Ferrari practice car for the race to Allen Markelson, a back marker who name never made much of a name in racing. Shelby ended up standing around the pits while Moss won. Markelson blew up the Ferrari in a few laps.

Casner's wheelings and dealings were typical of the tomfoolery a free lance driver like Shelby had to put up with. One memorable occasion involving Casner that year was in April, when Shelby cajoled Casner into loaning him a Maserati which Shelby then prepared at his own expense. When Shelby won the Examiner GP with it at Riverside, who shows up at the winner's circle first but Casner, snatching the check. When Shelby got out of the racecar, the garlands and race queen were there but no moola. Shelby got his revenge by hiding the Maser, forcing Casner to pay up in order to get his car back.

But Shelby was grateful to Casner for one thing, and that was for bringing Goodyear tires into sponsoring sports car racing. Goodyear was to be Shelby's mainstay for working money during the birth of the Cobra and it was Shelby who brought them in on the Ford Le Mans program.

Shelby's final season as a driver was 1960, his mount for most of that year a 2.9 liter Maserati T61 "birdcage," called that because its space frame was made of tiny tubes that looked like a birdcage when you removed the aluminum body. He won at Riverside in the Maser but at Continental Divide Raceway in Castle Rock, Colorado, in June, piloting a Harry Heuer-owned Chevrolet-powered Scarab to victory.

Harry Heuer, like Augie Pabst, was another brewery heir who took to the Scarab and who helped to make the Scarabs reputation on American racetracks. There might have been an element of patriotism in both men's decisions—they could afford any car they wanted, but chose to run one that was built in America.

Shelby was an heir to nobody. His father, a rural mailman, probably didn't even leave Shelby his Whippet—the first family car Shelby mentions in interviews.

Shelby found his last sponsor in 1960—J. Frank Harrison out of Chattanooga. Harrison, like Edgar, wanted the latest cars, to hell with the cost. And he had money, owing to the fact that his family had started a lil' ol' soft drink firm called Coca-Cola. Harrison bought two Tipo 61 birdcage Maseratis from Lloyd "Lucky" Casner and sponsored Jim Jeffords and Shelby to drive them the whole 1960 season.

But evidentially Harrison's sponsorship money didn't stretch to enough races because that final season saw Shelby driving every car he could get his hands on, for half a dozen sponsors. Among the oddballs were a Formula Junior (Mitter) at Roosevelt Field, on Long Island. In that race, he was up against an amazing roster of drivers, amazing only in who they became later—Rodger Ward, Jim Hall, Roger Penske, Walt Hansgen and the very fast, very young Rodriguez brothers from Mexico to name but a few.

Another oddball car Shelby raced that year was a mid-engined Porsche RSK at a small event at Vacaville, in California, that car owned by Johnnie Von Neumann, who had years before sponsored Miles in the same kind of car.

Shelby never quite forgot about Parravano, and no one knows precisely why he had left Parravano's employ but you have to admit that, in retrospect, Shelby's timing was right, especially when you consider what happened to Parravano.

On April 8th, 1960, he up and disappeared.

One day he was there, the next he wasn't. He was never to be seen again. Parravano had been having trouble with the IRS, since he liked money and didn't much like paying taxes and it's true he had a date to meet IRS officials but the amount he owed wasn't that bad, so it's unlikely he split the country just to outrun the IRS. Of course they did make things inconvenient for him. At one point, in a desperation move, Parravano rolled a half dozen or so of his best Ferraris onto trucks and told the truck drivers to run full-tilt boogie for the Mexican border. He had a hideway for them in Ensenada, on the Baja peninsula. Some made it across. Some didn't. Those that didn't were nabbed by the IRS and sold for pennies on the dollar in a parking lot sale to settle his debts (today any one of those cars would be worth millions).

Some say his disappearance smacks of a mob hit; and there were rumors that he was a money lender at usurious rates, which might have cut in on the mob's action. Hey, he was Sicilian, which leads you down some dark roads of surmise. A body was even found, identified and then un-identified. This was before DNA analysis made it a lead pipe cinch. At any rate, he was history and Shelby had moved on.

There was a hidden agenda in Shelby choosing all those diverse rides. One was that he knew that he wasn't going to be a team racer anymore, that he couldn't count on ever receiving a sponsored ride from an automaker again, so he might as well try out every kind of car he could so when he built his own car, he would be able to draw upon his memories of how each competitive car felt at speed. Shelby told Rob Meich of the *Las Vegas Sun*: "I enjoyed driving race cars, but that wasn't where I was trying to go," Shelby said. "I wanted to build my own car. In Europe, I hung around Aston Martin, Maserati and Ferrari, learning how they worked."

An irony was that, in that final year as a driver, not only did he drive the money-no-object Scarab powered by an American V8, but also a car that represented a diametrically opposed philosophy—one of the racecars built in America by Latin immigrant Max Balchowsky; cars known as "Old Yellers." These were Buick-powered hot rods lovingly assembled of junk parts by Balchowsky, a master mechanic. But, despite their crude looks, they were reliable enough and had enough brute torque that a skilled driver could could use one to beat the purebreds and Shelby led at least one race in one, at Elkhart Lake in July, 1960. He raced them twice but failed to finish both times.

But as much as he enjoyed the fun of beating the "purebreds" with what was in effect a four-wheeled junkyard dog, Shelby knew he would get the wrong kind of image if he spent too much time in a Balchowsky-built hot rod. Still, one wonders if the dirt cheap performance on tap in "Old Yeller" didn't harden

Shelby's resolve to put together his own sports car powered by an American V8? It taught him that where a car's parts came from made no difference as long as you had a good power to weight ratio and enough torque.

Shelby's last race as a driver took place at Laguna Seca in Monterey on Oct. 23, 1960. He finished second in J. Frank Harrison's T61 Birdcage Maserati. He was second overall to Moss but in that same event he beat several highly regarded drivers of the day including Jack Brabham, Bruce McLaren, Roger Penkse, Jim Hall, Ken Miles and Augie Pabst, proving he still had what it took, right up to his very last day of racing. He reportedly pulled into the pits, removed his helmet, peeled off his driving gloves and announced, "I'm done."

Years later, he recalled that day to a reporter: "Before the start, I didn't even think about it being my last race. I was in third, and my car wasn't runnin' very well. I was on about my fifth nitroglycerin pill. I came behind Jim Hall, and I started getting angina pains again, so I popped another nitro, slowed up for a lap, and then said 'aw, piss on it—I'm gonna finish the race and hang it up.' I made that decision during the race…I never looked back, never gave it another thought. My new priorities were to build my own cars."

He wasn't being offered the good rides anymore—at age 37 he knew he was washed up. He knew that it could only go downhill from there. And, truth was, the end of his driving career had been inevitable for Shelby had been nursing a secret. As a child, he had rhumatic fever, and reported to one interviewer, Jim Mourning, that he spent eight years in bed with a leaky heart valve because of it. It had affected his heart and, as an adult, he was mis-diagnosed and didn't get the right treatment so his condition progressively worsened.

He got through his last couple of seasons using the same trick after another driver observed his difficulty and clued him in on how he could get through the race—by popping a nitroglyercine pill under his tongue before starting out. Somewhere around 1960 a doctor recognized the condition as angina pectoris and told him that his heart wouldn't take it much longer. As it was, the doctor only gave him a couple years to live.

Shelby had had one hell of career. He drove in approximately 150 races in 8 years. Of those, he won at least a third and raced some 45 different types of cars. Shelby remained philosophical about it. That was the breaks. The way the cards were dealt.

But, there was reason for optimism. As they say in Texas "The Lord never closes one door without opening another." He had enjoyed one hell of a run and emerged relatively unscathed. Not that he wasn't close to the edge a few times, but as they also say in Texas: "He's so lucky they tried to hang 'em but the rope broke."

Shelby didn't want to go back to Texas. For one thing, his marriage there was long finished. And, for what he wanted to do, he needed to be in Los Angeles, a town full of craftsmen and people who made racing their business, not just an entertaining hobby that was something they could chat about at the next cocktail party.

Shelby no doubt was ribbed by friends about staying in California, often called "la la land" because it was such a magnet for dreamers (most of whom wanted to crack into the movie business). Shelby had his own dream—to build his own car.

The first clue the world had of his plan consisted of just two short paragraphs run in a regional magazine called *MotorRacing* Sept. 2, 1960. The article said that Carroll Shelby had started a company called "CS Engineering" in Hollywood. He was noodling on installing a Pontiac V8 in an Austin-Healey sized car.

Hell, maybe even in an Austin-Healey.

Hey, it was a start....

Silverstone England, 1961.

A sports car was out on the track. Behind the wheel was a tall man with a rugged countenance. He was winding the car out to redline in each gear, shifting it rough, and sliding it about in the rain.

He was not driving for fun. He was driving the car to deliberately break it. Every few minutes he succeeded and would coast to the pits for a diagnosis. Was it the clutch? The engine mounts? The brakes? An engineer would make notes on a growing list of parts it would be necessary to re-do in order to make this car be able to take the torque of a mighty American V8.

The driver took his helmet off and stepped out of the car. He put on his cowboy hat and grinned. Hell, they'd done enough work for a morning. Now it was time for some bangers and mash.

It was not a new idea, this building of an American sports car.

A few years before, Swift meat packing heir Briggs Cunningham had built his Cunningham sports cars, spending millions having bodywork built in Italy and using heavy V8s supplied by Chrysler. He had hung it up, after making a couple of tries in his own cars at Le Mans, and a third time with Chevrolet Corvettes.

Cunningham never finished high, but the French appreciated his sportsmanship. One got the feeling that he was more concerned with whether his chablis was properly chilled than if his cars could beat the Ferraris. Cunningham hung it up after the IRS ruled his "business" a hobby.

After him had come another high-roller, Lance Reventlow, with his Corvette-powered California-built Scarab sports cars. Reventlow ran a first class operation—complete with a rolling machine shop and very large enclosed transporters. But even Reventlow was forced to fold his operation after five years when, again, the IRS ruled it a hobby, not a business.

Shelby surely didn't have the deep pockets of those millionaire sportsmen. In fact, compared to Reventlow, you could say Shelby didn't even have pockets.

He would have to do it on the cheap. He saw as a short cut buying an existing car and adapting it.

With that in mind, Shelby approached his friend Donald Healey, for whom he had driven some Austin-Healeys in a successful attempt on the Bonneville salt flats in setting some world speed record runs. Shelby's idea was to do what hot rodders were already doing, dropping a Chevy V8 into a Healey and make a car that would go someplace in a hurry instead of just putting along. But Sir Donald Healey thought Healeys were selling just fine with their four cylinder or six cylinder engines, thank you. He didn't need Shelby and possibly the idea of making an Anglo-American car might have horrified him.

Shelby had already given up an idea he had tried a few years earlier, when he had cadged three brand spanking new Corvette chassis out of his buddy, Ed Cole, chief engineer at Chevrolet.

Using funds from fellow Texan Jim Hall's brother, Dick, and Gary Laughlin, Shelby sent the three chassis to Italy to be rebodied in aluminum by Sergio Scaglietti, who ran Ferrari's racecar body shop near the Ferrari factory.

Shelby and Dick Hall had started a sports car dealership in Dallas (Carroll Shelby Sports Cars) back in '56, selling Morgans, Listers, MGs, Austin Healeys and even Rolls and Bentley, but for Shelby his participation was mostly in name only because at that time he was gallivanting around the world racing. Some might say the dealership was just a way for some sports car racers to buy the latest sports cars wholesale.

The Corvette plan would have helped Shelby achieve his dream but from first inception, things went awry. When the alloy-bodied Corvettes arrived back from Italy, they somehow didn't look near as good as Ferraris with similar coachwork, though they were done by Sergio Scaglietti. They also weren't as fast as Ferraris because they were dead stock chassis, not developed and fine-tuned.

Shelby was willing to go ahead and develop them but then another problem popped up. Cole's bosses at GM had discovered his unauthorized generosity in side-tracking some Corvette chassis off the assembly line in St. Louis to Shelby. Feeling pressure from the Corvette continent that Shelby's version might well make the stock Corvette look overweight and downright dowdy, Cole thought it wise not to ship Shelby any more chassis. Cole told Shelby "Forget I ever sent you those cars."

Then Shelby got lucky. He had cajoled John Christy, the editor of *Sports Car Graphic* into letting him write a column. He also got some free ad space in the magazine and ran an ad for what he called grandly "The Carroll Shelby School of High Performance Driving."

He had hired a young man in Riverside, one Peter Hall Brock, to be his driving instructor at the local track, and corraled a few well-used racecars, including an Austin Healey Sprite, to use as student cars. And he offered a brochure in his ad for a price, this in order to discourage just anybody from writing for a brochure for a souvenir. This fee covered his printing cost and mailing.

It became a habit then, whenever Shelby would visit the magazine, to pick up the money generated by the ad. If there were sufficient contributions, he would then take the editor of *Sports Car Graphic* to lunch at a local hotel renowned for its bargain-priced luncheon menu and generous-sized Martinis.

During one of these luncheons Shelby was informed by John Christy, the editor, that *Sports Car Graphic* had received a press release announcing that that A.C. Cars Ltd., a company in England making a sweet little sports car called the A.C.-Bristol, was dropping the model on account of Bristol Aeroplane, their engine supplier, having announced that they were ceasing production of the inline six they were building under license from BMW, who had designed the engine before the war. Bristol was making luxury cars and had discovered the virtues of the Chrysler V8, an engine which had oodles of torque and had been used in the Facel Vega luxury cars from France. With that discovery, Bristol didn't need the six anymore.

Shelby thought this interesting. He knew the A.C.-Bristol well as a handy little racer in the E-production racing class with a stout twin tube frame and lightweight aluminum body. In fact, when Shelby had raced at Le Mans there was usually at least one in the race so he had blown by them hundreds of times. They were damn pretty, too, copied off some old Ferrari, maybe a 166MM barchetta, the kind that had won the Mille Miglia in Italy back in '49. But even if he could obtain A.C.-Bristol chassis and bodywork, he'd still only have half of what he needed.

He subsequently found out that Ken Rudd, a British A.C. dealer, had come up with a temporary fix for A.C.—an inline Ford Zephyr six that he offered in the A.C. Ace in three stages of tune. But none of them were as zingy as the car had been with the Bristol six.

Rudd was not saving the car as far as Shelby was concerned. And Shelby hardly wanted to have to deal with some ancient Ford six cylinder.

What A.C. *really* needed, Shelby concluded, was a V8.

Then fortune smiled upon him again. In 1961, Shelby attended the annual 4th of July Pike's Peak hillclimb, where he met Dave Evans of Ford Motor Co., who told him Ford was coming out with a lightweight iron block truck engine. Not an aluminum block. This V8 was such that it wouldn't weigh much more than the cast iron block six or four that you found in many a foreign car. Shelby asked for some sample engines for "development" and Evans said he would "see what he could do."

As many engineers as Ford had back in Dearborn, they knew the California hot rodders were onto something when it came to getting more power out of a given engine. Look what they had done with the small block Chevy V8 engine when it came out in '55, modifying them to produce over twice the power Chevrolet originally announced. What did Ford have to lose by throwing a couple of engines his way? Automakers are loathe to reveal what it cost to make a given item but odds are that a cast iron lump of a V8 engine at that time cost Ford less than a dinner for two at one of the posh eateries favored by auto execs, like the Detroit Athletic Club.

They sent him a 221 cubic-inch V8 version. Shelby liked what he saw. Once he knew he would be getting engines, Shelby wrote Derek Hurlock, one of the owners of A.C. Cars Ltd., a letter and stretched it a bit by saying he had Ford's backing on developing a sports car and would A.C. mind providing one A.C.-Bristol sans engine so he could try it with the Ford V8?

If it worked out, Shelby implied, he would be putting in an order for more chassis and bodies.

A.C. was convinced. First of all, all the cars they were presently producing, except for the A.C. Bristol and A.C. Zephyr—were dogs, totally obsolete in styling and without a prayer of matching the performance of their contemporaries. Secondly, they knew they were missing the boat on not having a new engine yet they had failed to find a suitable one.

And this chap Shelby, well, he won Le Mans for a British automaker—what more recommendation did you need? Shelby was a known entity in England. And they were no doubt impressed that Shelby was working with the giant Ford Motor Co.

Although the myth has been built up that Shelby and hot rodder Dean Moon built the first Cobra in Sante Fe Springs, English historians like to point out that the first Cobra actually ran under its own power in England in late 1961, while fitted with the 221, though one could argue that, at that point in time, it was still just an A.C. with an American V8 in it. (The Cobra history is an odd one of parallel universes—the UK version, in which the Brits are the heroes who conjured it all up, and the American version in which Shelby did it all with the role of the Brits reduced to being hardly more than mere bystanders.)

The car was driven at Silverstone by Shelby and at the MIRA test track by A.C. chief Derek Hurlock, who was evidently pleased enough with the car to schedule it for production.

They removed the engine and shipped Shelby the car, figuring rightly that the engine would be a lot easier to get on Shelby's side of the pond.

Meanwhile Ford had upped the ante and the next engine that arrived in Sante Fe Springs was a 260 cubic inch version of the "Fairlane" V8 and immediately the idea of offering the 221 was forgotten. The American hot rodders had a saying: "There is no substitute for cubic inches" and Shelby subscribed to that belief wholeheartedly.

When the A.C. Ace arrived from England, Shelby transported it to the Santa Fe Springs, California, shop of Dean Moon, a hot rodder who had made a fortune selling spun aluminum hub caps (Moon discs). After a short time fabricating new engine brackets and working a bigger radiator into the engine bay, they lowered in the Experimental Ford V8 (still with the hand painted words "XP" for "Experimental" painted on the valve covers) into the car and mated it to the Borg Warner T-10 gearbox borrowed from a Corvette. They started it up and it gave a gruff throaty roar at first, then settled down to a rough idle.

Shelby got behind the wheel, aimed it toward the open garage door and growled: "Get that engine lift out of the way. Let's see if this sumbitch goes."

It did. Two long black streaks of rubber left on the shop floor were testiment to that.

One story is that he and Moon then went out among the oil derricks, laying out a road course as they went and doing a bit of body damage during the excursion. Another is that Moon and Shelby cruised the local drive-in restaurants, hangouts for hot rodders, looking for a Corvette to humble but not finding one.

Shelby came back and began directing some of Moon's helpers to attack the body with brillo pads, scrubbing off the last vestige of thin English paint until the aluminum underneath had a dull gleam. He then had his artist buddy Dean Jeffries paint the world "Shelby" in stylized script on the nose and tail. The car didn't have a name yet but at least people would know what the hell it was when they saw it rocketing past.

Shelby knew this was it, his new beginning.

Chapter 5- The Early Cars

Venice, California, Spring 1962.

The truck backed into the off-loading area. The young Shelby mechanic, who only a year before had been in high school, walked over and set down his toolbox. He heard the surf was runnin' high in Malibu and would like to hit the beach but he was planning on getting married soon and needed the job. Surfing would have to wait until the weekend.

He popped open the trunklid and located the nuts that secured the chrome stylized A.C. lettering that came on the car from England. He had the badge off in seconds and then reached into his toolbox, took out a small plastic wrapped parcel and unwrapped it. It was a new chrome badge that said "SHELBY" on top and "COBRA" in smaller letters on the bottom with a tiny A.C. logo in the center. He began to affix it in place on the trunk lid, using the same mounting holes.

Hey, credit where credit is due.

From the very first moment that A.C. Cobras began arriving in America, Shelby began trying to weed out the "A.C."-labeled part of the car even though by doing so he was foregoing the chance to inherit some respect because the A.C.-Bristol was already a known and well respected car. Years later he still regretted that he had promised A.C. that he would keep their name in the picture at all (now, 40-plus years later, Shelby Cobras are still stubbornly called "A.C. Cobras").

F. Wilson McComb in his book *A.C. (Shelby) Cobra* quotes Derek Hurlock. "We were all very fed up about it at the time but it was typical of Carroll Shelby. He was like that. It was one of his failings. So we said, well it's the nature of the guy and being British, we let him get away with it. If it would have been the other way around, a Texan would have given them a knuckle sandwich, but no doubt the British were maintaining a stiff, upper lip."

But in the beginning Shelby didn't have the nerve to flat leave their name out of it, though it is said that he continued to resent the clever ways A.C. managed to keep their name on the car such as casting their logo into the foot pedal faces.

The name "Cobra" if you want to believe the PR releases of the time, came from a dream Shelby had. Supposedly, he kept a writing pad by his bed so if he awoke during the night he could write down any inspirations. One night he woke up and wrote down the name "Cobra."

In the morning, he still liked the name. But there was a fly in the ointment. The name belonged to a car company that had gone bust—Crosley, who made the eminently forgettable Hotshot.

They had used the name "CoBRA" (with the exact weird capitalization shown) on their engine because they had a built-up block, copper brazed from formed pieces of flat sheet stock, and they wanted to highlight that fact. Since Crosley was out of business, he was able to secure rights to the Cobra name for a song.

Shelby, in a speech in 2005, claimed that he had a lawyer on retainer at the time and had called him and asked him to find out if the name "Cobra" was free. "Don't go home until you find out," he told the lawyer and the lawyer must have succeeded.

As soon as he had the name "Cobra" locked in, Shelby had his own metal badges made up to make it look more official, being careful to make them just big enough to cover the holes that were left when you pried off the A.C. stylized letter badge on the hood and trunk of each car arriving from England.

After having the first Cobra polished to a high sheen and having the words POWERED by FORD painted on the side door so large you could read it from space, Shelby took his little roadster to Riverside racetrack for a demonstration run. The idea of the sign was to say to Ford executives, yes, indeed, your contribution to this project will not be forgotten. By the time the car reached production Shelby managed to reduce the Ford labeling to a mere 1-inch by 1 1/2-inch rectangle, reading POWERED by FORD on the side of the car.

But next he had to convince the public this wasn't some one-off car and that he wasn't just another dreamer with his dreammobile like the movie stars who sometimes had some sort of weird one-off built, (like crooner Bobby Darin with his Dia Costa show car, a Barris-style lead sled) but rarely got beyond that one car.

Shelby could hardly wait to show the completed Cobra to John Christy, his buddy at *Sports Car Graphic*. A rendezvous was set up to meet the editor and his photographer in LA's huge Griffith Park so the car could be shot for the magazine and Christy could do a preliminary drive report (it appeared in SCG's May '62 issue).

There was only one obstacle left to conquer before the photo shoot; one that Shelby had been putting off because it was so formidable a task he'd rather plow a cornfield with a mule-drawn plow, and that was putting up the convertible top. It wasn't like the E-type Jag, where you could reach behind you at a traffic light and flip it up in one stroke.

No that would be too easy. It was the ancient type, where you took a bunch of tubes out of the trunk, erected the framework and only then pulled the top over it. When you actually see a real Cobra with this top erected, the first thought that comes to mind is that they've stolen the top from some poor tyke's preambulator!

Christy felt like he had died and gone to heaven when he saw that yellow Cobra purr up the entranceway into Griffith Park. Christy almost felt it was his baby too because he never tired of telling other members of the motoring press that it was he who first apprised Shelby of the fact that A.C. had run out of engines.

Christy was bowled over by the car, writing: "It's one of the most impressive production sports cars we've ever driven. Its acceleration...can only be described as explosive and at least equal to that of the better hot Corvettes and [Ferrari] Berlinettas we've driven."

Christy, in his August '62 test of the first Cobra, went to great pains to tell *Sports Car Graphic* readers how different the Cobra was from your usual engine conversion. "First and foremost the Cobra is not merely an Ace with a Ford stuffed under the hood. That sort of thing has been tried before and has almost always been unsuccessful. Vitually everything but the frame rails has been re-designed, beefed up or replaced. The suspension arms are considerably stronger and reinforced with plating, the springs are considerably stiffer and the track has been widened four inches. Wheels used are 72-spoke Dunlops in the 15-inch size, rather than the narrower 16-inch units used before. The differential has been replaced with a much larger Salisbury unit, as fitted to the XKE Jaguar, and takes the same range of gears."

Christy was even loaned the car for an extended test drive and, though things fell off along the way, Shelby didn't mind because he was getting free ink. Not only didn't Christy mention the myriad flaws but with each part that broke, Shelby's crew were finding out what parts to make stronger. Among the ideas thrown out very early on was the inboard disc brakes. A.C. hadn't wanted them and, once he got them, Shelby didn't want them either, realizing they would cause delays in the pits because they would be harder to reach.

A lady named Joan Sherman, who identifies herself in the group memoir *Remembering the Shelby Years* as Shelby's secretary/girlfriend during the early days of the Cobra, says about Christy's test: "That car was put together with spit, glue and rubber bands so that Christy could take it out and give it a test run. We all kept our fingers crossed that the car would run long enough for Christy to make it back to the shop."

The Shelby crew needn't have worried. Most car journalists of the time were on the side of the manufacturer, rarely finding much to complain about. Christy may have rationalized his failure to list the car's failings by saying, "Hey, this was, after all, still a prototype, not representative of production models to come."

But there were unimbedded journalists in those days, one of the favorites being "Uncle" Tom McCahill, who wrote for one of the mechanic nuts-and-bolts type magazines. He tested an early Cobra and intoned "it accelerates so fast it will rip Granpa's head clean off."

The guy had a way with words. Another thing that made "Uncle Tom" stand apart is that he would always take his Labrador retriever on a test. He reportedly used the dog to gauge the trunk capacity. If the dog didn't like the car, well...

Shelby called up his customizer buddy Dean Jeffries. Like Barris and Cushenberry, Jeffries was riding the custom car wave, chopping tops, doing metal-flake paint jobs, making custom cars that were appearing in those beach blanket bingo movies that featured more girls in bikinis than they did actual beach. Jeffries picked a shade of pearl yellow. The price to paint the Cobra might have been $200 or more likely Shelby traded him something—is it mere coincidence that a full house Cobra engine complete with a quartet of Webers popped up in Jeffries' famed Maserati-chassied Manta Ray custom?

Shelby took the bright yellow Cobra back to Dearborn. The Ford executives were, by now, more pumped up on performance than they had been when they gave him the engines. Shelby's presentation was so hyper that Lee Iacocca, the head of Ford Division and a super salesman himself, was actually scared of him. When Shelby left the room for a moment, Iacocca reportedly told the others something to the effect of: "Give him some money before he eats the curtains."

The Detroiters didn't know what to make of Shelby. He was dressed in a suit but the strong Southern accent was still there. He looked like the kind of raw-boned guy you might meet outside a southern juke joint on a rainy night—the kind of guy who kept a cigarette pack in a rolled up shirtsleeve of his t-shirt and whose idea of fun was to go out squirrel hunting. One thing was sure, he wasn't trying to hide the fact he was from Texas. It brought to mind the old saying, "Never ask a man if he's from Texas. If he is, he'll tell you on his own. If he ain't, there's no need to embarrass him."

Shelby returned to California with a check for $25,000, enough to reimburse him for some of his out of pocket expenses to date, which he claims were up to $40,000 by then. He recalls the moment he got that check. Here, he had been broke for years and suddenly he was in Fat City. It must have felt like a million dollars. A Texan would say he was "squattin' in tall cotton" (Shelby, who had once picked cotton for 25 cents an hour as a lad knew that phrase a little too well).

Not only did he have enough money from Ford to make a second Cobra but he was able to prep the first one enough so that it could make its first auto show appearance at the New York Auto Show in April 1962 where Ford parked it at a corner of their display.

Ford had no idea what would transpire by the inclusion of the Cobra in their display. They just thought that the Cobra would be a nice show attraction, something showgoers would find interesting and perhaps induce them to wander over to the Ford booth where the hottest thing going was the Falcon Sprint and the 500XL Galaxie.

And, if truth be told, the little Cobra had cost them peanuts so far compared to the big dollars it took to build a concept car (called "dream cars" in those days) like the Futura, which had been bodied in Italy by Ghia (and met an ignominious fate later on when Ford gave it to customizer George Barris who made the derelict show car into the first Batmobile).

The early Cobras did occasionally get criticized, usually by editors not used to sports cars. Allen Grant, who was a Shelby team racer, told Royal Krieger of the Shelby-American magazine "There was one reporter who said the Cobra '...wasn't sophisticated and that is was brutish and that it ain't worth the money.' Grant was peeved and about to give the editor a piece of his mind when Shelby took him into a corner and told him to settle down. 'Let me give you a little advice,' Shelby said. 'There is only one thing worse than bad publicity and that is no publicity. So be thankful for what you get.'"

Ford had no idea back then that, merely by showing Shelby's little roadster, they were starting a performance revolution in the American car industry and that the Cobra would be the car leading that revolution.

You might call it the "domestic performance revolution" because although there were hot foreign cars on the American market, you seldom saw a Ferrari or Maserati. American cars were thought inept and clumsy back then, hardly able to get out of their own way with the exception of the "Rocket" Olds and the Corvette. And, even though the Cobra was chassied and bodied in England, it said "Ford" on the side and that was enough to give American enthusiasts some hope that American automakers were at long last waking up and building domestic performance cars that could give some competition to the exotics from abroad.

As a result of the New York Auto Show exposure, Shelby was swamped with orders. Some say 500. But he wisely booked only those he could fill in the near future because he knew the first way to dig a hole for his brand new company would be to take too many orders and then not be able to fill them. Excessive greed coupled with an inability to deliver had done in many another fledgling automaker and he didn't want to end up in the same junkpile as Madman Muntz, "Dutch" Darrin, Preston Tucker, or even his pal Cunningham. He aimed to deliver.

After the show Shelby showed his full order book to Ford. These were hard headed executives from Detroit, most of whom had never been to a European race. Le Mans they knew from nothing.

But orders in hand, especially orders accompanied by checks—that they understood. They told Shelby, "Okay. Let's do it."

The miracle of it all was how Shelby managed to keep the whole thing going while waiting for the cash to flow from Ford. He knew it would be coming eventually, but the problem was to keep everyone on board until it arrived. Allen Grant, one of his team racers, said, "My guess is that he borrowed a lot of money because in later conversation he said he was out on a limb back then."

An agreement was quickly and unceremoniously hammered out. A.C. would build the body-chassis, and Ford would supply the engine/transmission, plus misc. engineering and, most important, be standing right behind him to make sure Shelby's checks didn't bounce. Ford wanted to help Shelby but, for liability reasons, sought to make it appear that Shelby-American was a stand-alone firm. That way, if they were disappointed at some further point in time, they could cut him loose.

Accounts differ on just how Ford officials perceived Shelby during those early days. Some historians say Ford executives thought Shelby was a rich oilman. Understandable because most of the Texans in racing, including John Mecom, Jr. and Jim Hall were, in fact, rich oil men. In the West Coast newspaper, *Motoracing* (1956 issues), Shelby is frequently referred to as "Oilman Carroll Shelby" though if the truth were known the closest he had come to oil was working as a roughneck in the oil fields of East Texas.

Another account says Shelby confessed to Ford's Don Frey "I'm just a poor farmer."

Ray Brock, longtime publisher of *Hot Rod* magazine, told this author that Shelby at first had some at Ford convinced he was a wealthy Texan, more along the lines of Jim Hall. "When I told the guys at Ford that Shelby didn't own much more than his ten gallon hat, they were surprised," says Brock. Shelby was, as they say in Texas, "All hat and no cattle."

Nevertheless the Ford executives admired Shelby's boundless energy. It was obvious from the get-go that they were dealing with a man on a mission. It was either give him what he wants or get the hell out of the way before you get run over.

But even though granting co-operation and writing checks, Ford officials remained wary of being hornswoggled. In the book *Remembering the Shelby Years* by Don Frey, the key Ford executive approving the decision, says "Whenever I walked out of his office after a meeting, I always felt my pockets to make sure everything was still there."

Jacque Passino, another Ford executive, in charge of managing the relationship with Shelby, was even more guarded. "That simple Texas farmer is so dumb I've got to take six lawyers to the coast with me every time I go out there to discuss contracts," he joked.

Before meeting Ford officials, Shelby had done his homework, a fact which no doubt impressed Ford. The lunch he had bought Lew Spencer, an A.C. dealer back in California, paid off when he was able to present to Ford executives an itemized wholesale cost list of all the parts that went into the A.C.-Bristol, right down to the rearview mirror. They were the real figures.

You have to admire Shelby's business acumen. Most middlemen, when presenting a cost estimate to one of the world's largest automakers, wouldn't have been able to resist the temptation to pad the figures a tad to make sure they made themselves a profit from the word "go" but Shelby knew that nobody in the world is more expert at estimating the costs of building a car than a Detroit automaker and figured that he could be washed out right at the beginning if Ford thought he was feeding them padded figures so he could make a profit on each nut and bolt.

Shelby knew, if he was straight-arrow with Ford, there would be a pie in the sky bye and bye. And sooner rather than later.

But just to make sure their money didn't get lost once the project was "green lighted," Ford decided to send an expert on small business out to California to act as their junkyard dog, with a short leash on Shelby to make sure that he was spending their dollars wisely. After all, the history of independent would-be sports car makers, from Briggs Cunningham to "Madman" Muntz to Lance Reventlow, was littered with the wreckage of companies that didn't make it.

Ford brass made this decision late in the evening. They called down to the area where the young lions were, looking for a guy who was rumored to be from California who knew the territory. Well, it happened to be 6:30 p.m. and the guy from California had already gone home. So a young man named Ray Geddes answered. He was still working past 6 p.m.

Good sign.

And it turned out this "young lion" named Ray Geddes not only had a law degree but an engineering degree and had in fact owned his own small business, a business which he had sold for a profit.

Who better to send out to the Coast to set up a small business than him?

When Geddes arrived out in California, he dutifully set up the Shelby-American operation to be a "stand alone" business so it meant less liability for Ford.

This the PR flacks loved because they could work the classic David-and-Goliath angle. If the public thought that Shelby-American was making it all on its own, that projected a far feistier image than if they knew the truth that Shelby was paying all the bills with Ford's money. (This is substantiated in by bills of lading from A.C. for chassis and body which say in effect "bill to Ford through Shelby.")

Once he got organized, Geddes helped Shelby set up a pitch meeting in Detroit to find prospects to handle the car among Ford's dealer body. That first dealer showing was an unmitigated disaster—the Cobra Shelby brought over-heated and wouldn't start, the radiator blew up and the clutch pedal wouldn't go down. He wasn't able to give dealers rides.

Shelby was mortified but Iacocca was sanguine, and figured these were just some developmental glitches that could be fixed in a few minutes in the shop. Shelby's helplessness fits former early employee Bruce Burness' recollection that "Shelby didn't know anything about cars. It took me until years later to realize that his genius was in putting it all together."

But dealers signed up anyway, maybe because that bright yellow sports car with chrome wire wheels parked on stage was one hell of a lot more exciting than anything Ford had shipped them out of Dearborn lately. They knew it would build showroom traffic. Even decades later, Shelby voiced comments that showed he remains eternally grateful for Iacocca's understanding.

And Iacocca had a reason for backing Shelby. Right from the beginning, Ford was looking beyond any money they could make on selling Cobra cars. They planned on capitalizing off the Cobra in every way possible. They were developing a raft of high performance parts, from intake manifolds to valve covers and saw a great future in selling parts that had a Cobra and/or Shelby connection. (If you could only afford a Falcon Sprint, you could still buy Cobra-labeled grooved aluminum valve covers.)

There was no Mustang yet when the Cobras went to Ford showrooms so Ford ran ads for "Cobra parts" that could be added to the Fairlane or Falcon, both of which were available with the same 289 engine and which gained infinite amounts of stature for the owner among his peers in the high school parking lot when he opened the hood and showed off his "Cobra parts."

Naturally when the Mustang came along a couple years later, there was a natural connection as the same engine parts fit the Mustang. A separate company was even set up by Shelby to sell engine and dress-up accessories and the Shelby Parts Catalogs which flowed out to enthusiasts all over America are now treasured collector's items.

It took A.C. Cars, Ltd., some time to tool up for the production so, in the meantime, he stroked the press by having his one and only Cobra (which had been shown in raw aluminum first, then polished alloy) painted several times in succession: first yellow, then blue. The ruse worked: the public that read the buff books was soon under the illusion that Cobras were just rollin' out of the plant when the first production versions weren't even on the water yet from England. Dean Jeffries told some reporters that he painted the car four or five times in one week!

In fact it took three months for the second and third Cobras to come to America.

There is the misconception in the press that Shelby presented the Cobra to Ford as an *affair compleat* and it was "good to go" from the moment Ford first laid eyes on it. *Au contraire.*

Fred Goodell, a Ford engineer at the time, remembered it a bit differently when he told an interviewer from *Shelby-American* magazine of a meeting he had in '62 with his boss. As Goodell arrived, so he tells it, his boss told him,

"There's some guy who used to be a race driver who has come up with this idea. The Cobra," his boss announced the name of the car as he took him over to it, "and it's the goddamnest handling thing you ever saw in your life."

As Goodell was examining the car, he was told, "Mr. Ford wants to get this car to the point where his wife can drive it."

Goodell took the car out and immediately spun it out. He told the interviewer that he was about to go back and tell his boss, "You can't get there from here," when he considered that was maybe not such a good idea. Instead he took the car back to his shop area and persisted. He dropped the roll center, widened the tread, dropped the springs, tried various damper solutions like four shocks in back, four shocks in front and finally, he had something Mrs. Ford could drive.

While Shelby was waiting for the first cars, he and his crew (which at first consisted of no one but his girlfriend/secretary Joanie and later Joanie and Pete Brock, who doubled as his driving instructor out at the driving school) and scrambled to source parts.

Soon after the first cars arrived from England they found the A.C. radiator inadequate and Ford didn't have one that would do the job so Shelby had to send employees down to Chevy dealers to buy the aluminum Harrison radiator that had made its first appearance in the 1961 Corvette. You can bet back in Detroit someone at Chevrolet parts was mystified by the sudden upswing in demand in California for Corvette radiators! In fact, Chevy tried to make them unavailable but couldn't shut the supply off entirely because Corvette owners still needed them. Later on, when Chevy shut down a special run of lightweight Corvettes that Zora Arkus Duntov had tried to build without permission from the top brass, Shelby's team race driver Davey MacDonald was able to latch onto a supply of 100 aluminum radiators that had been stockpiled for the Corvette racing effort. They sold them to MacDonald because he had achieved so much as a Corvette racer.

Ford eventually pressed Button A and made brass radiators for it. Meanwhile, they were dialing in the handling. Don Roberts, a successful Cobra racer, described its handling to Dan Bianchi of SAAC (Shelby-American Automobile Club.) "I don't think a Cobra is particularly suited to any circuit. It hates slow turns, camber changes, high speed transient responses, hilltop correction (such as at Road Atlanta). Didn't I just describe a race car?"

He did find something to like. "It does like acceleration and braking which it does very well. As far as the handling it's really up to the driver to throw the car around like a go-cart and hang on."

The Moss gearbox in the A.C. Bristol was agricultural at best and Shelby was able to glom onto another Corvette part—the aluminum cased 4-speed Borg-Warner T-10 that had first been offered in the '57 Corvette as an option.

In order to race a car in FIA competition (the Federation Internationale d'Automobile is a French-based organization that sanctions many types of races) you have to file papers describing the car and prove you made the required minimum number of cars for it to be considered production.

Back then the requirement was 100 cars. That's all Shelby planned to make. His goal, back then, wasn't to make money selling cars but to go racing. But he reckoned you had to sell some road cars in order to finance the racing, just like Ferrari.

Shelby homologated the Cobra with the FIA based on CSX2000 (some reports say the first car was serial numbered CSX 2001) which might account for some discrepancies between what the Europeans thought a Cobra would be and what they turned out to be. Shelby hadn't exactly lied—it was just that many of the racing bits weren't yet developed when he filed the homologation papers.

Two examples were the wheels and the Weber manifold. Shelby had lined up some Halibrand mags but just didn't have them in hand when it came time to file the homologation papers with the FIA, so pictures of the wheels were sent to Ford along with pictures of the Cobra and the wheels were airbrushed onto the picture of the car.

Shelby also knew they would need a Weber intake manifold so, using some real Weber carburetors, they attached them to a chunk of wood carved to approximate an intake manifold and spray painted the wood silver. Those pictures too, went to the FIA with the homologation application.

When the second and third cars arrived, Shelby was faced with a new problem: no space to build the car.

Moon was a nice guy but maybe, for all of Shelby's happy talk, he never really expected Shelby's operation to hit a gusher with the first hole drilled. What he had expected would remain a back door operation helping to pay his mortgage was suddenly mushrooming into a full fledged car company! Shelby understood Moon's problem and now, with Geddes in tow carrying the Ford checkbook, Shelby went shopping for a larger facility and landed one almost within sight of the Pacific in Venice. Turned out it was Lance Reventlow's old shop, Reventlow having given up on the Corvette-powered Scarab after the IRS had looked at his books and concluded that five years in business without making a dime of profit meant this was a rich man's hobby, not a business and thus he was no longer privy to tax write offs.

Former employee Bruce Burness recalls that Reventlow got a kick out of being Shelby's landlord because this gave him a way to needle Shelby, who was essentially carrying on with more serious intent at the point where he himself had left off. Every month, recalls Burness, Reventlow would roar up in his Scarab street car, a hot babe in the seat beside him, and bellow at the top of his lungs "B-I-L-L-I-E SOL, get your ass down here" (alluding to a famed Texas swindler, Billie Sol Estes, who was in the headlines at the time, convicted for selling empty fertilizer tanks as full ones).

Shelby, after running around looking for the checkbook, would run down check in hand and Reventlow would roar off, a smug smile on his face. It was obvious that he didn't think the "chicken poop kid" (one of many nicknames for Shelby) would succeed but was having a ball needling him in the meantime.

Not only did Shelby get a shop full of machine tools but he was able to hire Reventlow's ace fabricator, Phil Remington. "Rem" had been a hot rodder before the war, running on the dry lakes of Muroc. He had been a flight mechanic on a bomber in the Pacific, and then after the war helped a millionaire named Stirling Edwards build his dream car back when Shelby was still raising broilers in

Texas. There wasn't anything on a race car that Rem couldn't fabricate, except maybe the tires.

Another plus was getting Warren Olson, a very capable man who had organized Reventlow's racing operations.

The wet-behind-the-ears kid that Shelby had employed in his driving school, Pete Brock, came over to the new operation and immediately proved his worth by taking on any task at hand, from designing stationary to writing and laying out some ads for the car magazines. His ads were so succinct, and so right on, they were an inspiration to performance car advertisers for decades to come.

It was Brock who thought of tying in the new reconstituted Shelby-as-manufacturer with the old Shelby-as-chicken-farmer-turned-race-car-driver, featuring a drawing of the striped farmer's overalls in a Shelby ad. Joan Sherman even insisted on the staffers wearing the same type overalls at races, whereupon Olson and his wife Simone left, disgusted at the cornball promotion. The idea was soon abandoned.

Brock also designed the Carroll Shelby block letter logo, the round Cobra snake's head logo that went on the car, the racing stripes that ran nose to tail (though he admits those were a simple reversal of the Cunningham theme which was blue stripes on white cars). He also did the T-shirt designs, and eventually the brochure for the driving school. He was your one-stop all-around artist. Shelby had 10,000 Brock-designed Cobra T-shirts printed at 38 cents each and "made sure that they were handed out to attractive women."

Shelby was a master at making his workers feel needed. In the *Shelby-American* magazine Allen Grant was quoted, "It was always a treat when Shelby did come down. He had the knack or ability to make you feel you were the most important person around the place. He wanted to make you feel that the company could not get along without you."

It was all coming together. Chassis, bodywork and wheels from England, Goodyear tires from Akron and gearboxes from Borg-Warner.

There were, of course, some bumps in the road. The cars were shipped by sea and when Shelby first laid eyes on the first cars to arrive by sea, he found out just how paper-thin the aluminum bodies were (which he always joked "were knocked together by winos under bridges"). They arrived with footprints sunk into the eggshell-thin metal, the result of stevedores taking short cuts walking across the cars when they crossed the ship holds.

Ford hated the aluminum body from the start, even though it was hard to beat the racing advantage of a body that weighed only 50—yes, fifty—pounds! Ford took one of the first Cobras and had it rebodied in fiberglass, in essence creating their own potential rival for the Corvette Stingray coupe of 1963. Ford couldn't help adding a brushed metal roof, even though that was a GM thing at the time (standard on the Eldorado Brougham in '58) but apparently the costs estimates for producing the body in fiberglass were too high for what they viewed as a short run thing so only the one fiberglass car, called the Cougar II, was built.

Then there was the paint fiasco, with cars arriving at the dealers the wrong colors. The story is that Shelby traced the source of that problem to a color-blind painter!

Shelby recruited shop workers from the ranks of racing mechanics. Although one would think they would be thrilled to be working at a company making sports cars, in the beginning the mechanics weren't that impressed. Many of them had been culled from USAC ranks where they built racecar chassis from the best of materials and the idea of working on production-based cars was a step down for them. The general feeling voiced by many was they would work for Shelby only until a racing job came up, like on an Indy team. And as for taking on Ferrari, most of them couldn't care less. They had seen Ferraris and Maseratis fail at The Brickyard so they weren't too impressed by the foreign tin.

And each car had to be tested. Shelby admitted decades later that the Cobra wasn't really engineered like you do when you start with a clean sheet of paper. In an interview conducted at the Saratoga Auto Museum in 2005 Shelby said: "The chassis was a 30-year old design when we started. All it was was two old buggy springs tied down to a space frame. We kept adding wider wheels and tires whenever we added horsepower. Finally we got to where the four tires stayed on the ground."

While the Venice shop was humming, Shelby, wearing a suit, would spend time hobknobbing in Hollywood with *Hot Rod* and *Motor Trend* editors and sometimes John and Elaine Bond at *Road & Track*. It was a critical stage, as he had seen many a fledgling automaker have his dream die when there was a negative review in the motoring press. Shelby told an editor at Petersen Publishing in 1971 (Sports Cars of the World): "You know the cars weren't that good to begin with. But the writers understood and were fair and never bad-mouthed the car. And they could have, too, bad-mouthed the steering and the overheating, but they were patient and helped us to the point where we could look anybody in the eye."

One of the nice things about Reventlow's choice of a Venice location was that there was a large swamp between the sleepy seaside town and the large airport to the south. That swamp was owned by a cagey old pilot named Howard Hughes who, in a deal with the city of Los Angeles, sold them the swamp, which they filled in so they could build a harbor community called Marina Del Rey.

By the time Shelby's shop was filling up with Cobras, the City had installed curving roads in Marina del Rey but there weren't yet any buildings.

It made one hell of a test track for Shelby employees like Miles to wring out each new Cobra on.

Of course the cops gave chase, but, funny, they never seemed to catch them. That might have been due to the fact that the Shelby shop was a favorite hangout for off-duty cops!

In a miracle of far-sightedness, Shelby, the old cowpoke from East Texas, who at times had pawned everything but his saddle and sixgun in order to keep going, managed to hang onto that first Cobra through thick and thin.

He told *Motor Trend*'s Matt Stone 40 years after that first Cobra was built that he had turned down $5 million for it. "It'll never be sold if I have anything to say about it," he told Stone. "I want that car to remain in my family forever. Every time I look at that old car, I think, 'Shelby, you lucky son-of-a-bitch.'"

Chapter 6- Hey Little Cobra

Riverside, California, October 1962.

Riverside in October can be, well, just like summer. It was a hot day in 1962 when the truck towing the trailer pulled into the pits and the spectators gathered around to watch the unloading of the Corvettes.

The Corvettes everyone knew about— the magazines had been full of pictures of the new aerodynamic Stingray coupes, their styling based on a one-off racecar created for GM VP Bill Mitchell on his own nickel.

As they were unloaded, everyone could see these coupes were pretty damn special—fuel injected, heavy duty springs, heavy-duty drum brakes. Not anywhere near what the Grand Sport was, that being a special lightweight Corvette, but they were reported to still be pretty hot for a streetable car.

Then the crowd walked over to the Cobra. It was a smaller car, hardly as impressive. Word was that this was one of Shelby's deals. Damned it wasn't but a lil' old Ace-Zephyr with a Ford small block jammed into it. Hell, he might as well be racing a Healey with a small block Chevy.

They weren't far wrong.

Shelby had entered it in a class called the "Experimental Production" class, which up until then no one had ever heard of. But, hell, everyone was there to see the Cobra race the Corvette, so the rules were bent and a new class created just for this one race.

A few hours later, the race began and Billy Krause, Shelby's first driver, shot out into the lead in the Cobra. Eventually he was a mile and a half ahead of the Corvettes, which were straining to keep up. But then he broke a rear hub carrier, and the suspension collapsed.

The Corvettes zoomed by.

In the pits, Carroll Shelby was sanguine about it. Hey, this is what racing was all about. Whatever broke they would make better.

While some of the spectators went home thinking: "The Corvettes got nuthin' to worry about," the wiser ones withheld comment. They had seen the early laps when the Cobra flat walked away from the Corvettes.

Sure, Doug Hooper, a Corvette pilot, took home the trophy, but it ain't over 'til it's over. In the long run, the Corvettes would be toast.

Carroll Shelby was of two minds when he built the Cobras. First, as a racer, he wanted to go racing. But in order to get Ford as a race team sponsor, he also had to build some street models to fulfill Ford's objective of putting Cobras in Ford showrooms across America to serve as "traffic builders."

But he knew the dealers wouldn't want the cars unless his cars won some racing laurels right quick. That explained the entry of the CSX2002 at Riverside. It was almost a dead stock car, except that the windshield was taken off and a small racing windscreen put in its place. The rear had a quick-fill fuel cap. The tires were Goodyear racing tires, and exhausts were straight through (no mufflers). It said "XP" on the doors meaning "experimental."

Right after the first race, Shelby sent A.C. instructions to change the motor, transmission and suspension mounts for heavier-duty units, and requested a change in fender contours to accomodate wider tires. He could see by the Riverside results that it was going to be an evolutionary process, with each change dictated by what broke in the last race. The day after the race Shelby's ace mechanic Phil Remington was already machining stronger hub carrier's of forged steel to replace the hub that had let them down.

The next event was the Nassau Speed Week, which was much less a series of races than it was one big week-long party in the Caribbean. Shelby accompanied Krause down there by plane, while two Cobras were shipped in by sea. The first most daunting thing was that Ferrari was there with some GTOs. What made it worse for Shelby at Nassau was that a team from Holman and Moody (H&M) showed up. H&M was a stock car racing outfit out of Charlotte, North Carolina. They had their hands into Ford's pocketbook for a long time. And here they were with a Cobra with Scarab ace Augie Pabst as driver. Shelby worried that their Cobra would do better than his entry, but it didn't.

If it had, the entire history of the Cobra might have been a whole lot different. Ironically the Shelby-American car ran strong but due to a mistake in refueling the car, a mistake made by Shelby himself, Krause ran out of gas!

Again, the Corvettes looked good and the Cobras looked bad. But by this time word was spreading: "If Shelby can ever get the bugs worked out, the Corvettes are history."

Holman and Moody also brought a weird fastback coupe 1962 Falcon to Nassau which they called the "Falcon Challenger." It had a stock 164-horse 260 cubic-inch V8, a four-speed, 3.50:1 gears, a handling package, larger tires and four-wheel Airheart disc brakes. Three were made. The one they brought to Nassau was faster than all get out, and was a genuine road racer, having been run in the 12 Hours of Sebring by Marvin Panch and Jocko Maggiacomo, but the Shelby-American team couldn't fathom the reason for its existence. What was Holman and Moody's angle with bringing this car? Fortunately the Falcon pooped out or else, later on, Holman and Moody might have been able to siphon off the Shelby Mustang production contract when that car came along. For the next few years, H&M would be lurking in the background acting as Shelby's nemesis, portrayed by Shelby as arch-villains waiting for him to slip up so they could jump in and save the bacon for their clients at Ford (they finally got their chance in '66 in at Le Mans).

Chevy couldn't beat the Cobra on a racetrack so they tried to seduce Shelby's first driver, Billy Krause. In an interview on a Maserati website Krause says: "The car wasn't that good in the beginning. It needed a lot of development. In the meantime Mickey Thompson kept calling me from Detroit. He was doing a deal with Chevrolet with this Corvette Stingray program. He said, 'We got those brand new, super light Corvettes coming. We are going to run Daytona. Sebring. Le Mans. We are going to do Indianapolis. Don't sign with Shelby.' Keep in mind at that time Shelby was totally underfinanced."

Krause felt that "...he did a bigger part in helping that Cobra program off the ground than Carroll would ever admit. I think that if I had not driven that car as hard as I did in the very beginning I am not sure Ford would have put up the money. But the main reason that I switched to Chevrolet was Mickey Thompson's Indy program which turned out to be a bad deal in the end. And of course Ralph Nader [After Nader's book against the Corvair, GM scrambled to redeem itself in the public eye, canceling tie-ins with racing]. This left me without a ride in the 1963 road races, including Sebring and Le Mans. Having left Shelby previously there were not many options left after GM pulled out."

Shelby was extraordinarily lucky at times, the approval of the 260 Cobras by the FIA as a "production sports car" a good case in point. At the time Shelby swung approval, only eight Cobras had been built out of the required 100, and later on he got the 289 Cobra homologated as a "production sports car" at a point when precisely zero had been built. The only explanation for this is that the FIA, knowing Ford money was behind Shelby, knew there was absolutely no doubt that he would have the money to build them, but with Ferrari and other small firms, you could rightfully suspect that they might try to get away with building only the number they needed, not the number actually required.

Some might view this finessing of the FIA as "smoke and mirrors" but one Shelby employee, Mark Popov-Dadiani quoted in *Remembering the Shelby Years* said "Everyone used to call Carroll 'Billie Sol' but that was the way he had to be in order to make it all happen and to keep all of us employed all those years."

At first Shelby had trouble recruiting drivers. The trouble was that he had been promising so many drivers that he would create a car for them to drive for so long that nobody believed him when he finally up and did it! Bob Bondurant is a case in point. In the book *Remembering the Shelby Years*, Bondurant recalls that Shelby told him numerous times he would have a car for him "in a few weeks." Bondurant, successful at driving Corvettes, just humored him saying: "Call me when you get it built and I will drive it." Finally one day after the Cobra was in production, Shelby called Bondurant out of the blue and said "I've got a car up in Seattle at a race that Miles was supposed to drive. He can't make it—can you fill in?" Bondurant, at that point dedicated to the Corvette and to his dealer sponsor, at first said "no" then figured, "Why the hell not drive the Cobra—because then I will know how to drive the Corvette against it." He agreed to take the ride, won the race and that was the beginning of his association with Shelby-American.

Back in the U.S., Shelby got his pitwork improved and, for a regional race in Riverside, fielded two 260 Cobras for Dave MacDonald and Ken Miles. Chevrolet again made available to West Coast racers some Z06 Corvettes, the semi-racing still streetable model that was supposed to blunt the charge of the Cobras. But the Cobras tromped them.

Miles added insult to injury when his Cobra proved to be so fast that he had time to stop in the pits for a drink of water on the way and still beat the Corvettes. He finished second behind MacDonald, and the best a Corvette could do was third.

Miles was a find. Shelby had raced against him for years, but didn't get to know him until he took on a little side deal known as the Tiger. Shelby had been contacted by Rootes, who had the slow selling Sunbeam Alpine. He took on the assignment of squeezing a small block Ford V8 into it, in effect "Cobraizing" it. After Miles had built a low cost first effort, the contract to do a second, more refined prototype came to Shelby.

Shelby liked the way Miles worked, and admired his driving (Miles being a champion earlier in his own homebuilt specials and in a mid-engined Porsche RSK spyder). Shelby hired Miles on at Shelby-American as a driver/development engineer. The cheeky Miles was opinionated, but was dedicated and proved to be invaluable to the Cobra's success.

According to Bill Pollack, who raced against Miles in the early 50s, "Miles wasn't the type to be a team player." This might have been because, ever since Miles had began racing in America, Miles had often been the only driver in the employ of a sponsor. One of the hardest things for a racer to adjust to, says Pollack, is when a team manager pre-assigns drivers to drive at a designated speed. "No driver likes being told that," says Pollack, "but if you are a driver for hire you do what you're told to do."

Already by that time 75 Cobras had been built. Shelby was on a roll.

For the racing mechanics, working at Shelby-American was grueling. In a speech at the Saratoga Auto Museum in 2005 Shelby commented, "Those guys would work 24 hours a day. Maybe they would sleep three hours and start working again. It wasn't work for them. They were doing it because they were doing what they wanted to do."

Shelby might have had a touch of the emplyer's rose-colored glasses syndrome. He tried to get away with not paying the mechanics who crewed for the race teams on weekends and eventually someone figured out how to file a complaint with the Labor Relations board. When the bill for back pay came to Shelby-American it was a whopper and suddenly there were a whole lot of mechanics who had more money in hand than they had ever had in their whole lives. Some quit, figuring they could find a better job.

Shelby also started a second racing front with the car the press called "the King Cobra." This too, was a car built in England, and again powered by a Shelby-installed 289. The tube frame, min-engine aluminum-body car was made by Cooper, who once had been strong in Formula One racing but whose designs were rapidly becoming obsolete. But Shelby persisted in ordering two of them for United States Road Racing Club (USRRC) racing and ran them for most of the '63 season with some success. There was a secret motive for doing this, but at the time he explained their presence by saying: "the guys in the shop want to go racing."

Before sending the new 289s though, Shelby wanted to test them under combat conditions so he entered two Cobras in a Cal Club race in the most unlikely place, the parking lot of Los Angeles Dodger Stadium, hardly a world class venue but a testbed nonetheless, and one only ten miles from his factory. And there were sizable cash prizes! MacDonald and Miles trounced the other cars but the race messed up the parking lot so bad the event was only run once more and never again.

Shav Glick, the famous *LA Times* sportswriter, in a nostalgia article published Dec. 15, 2003 recalled this event: "The course was too tight for the bigger, more powerful cars of the era, which were either forced to slow down or be battered by curbs, concrete pylons, light poles or other cars. Miles himself labeled it a 'Ken Miles Spyder Course.' In the hyped battle of production cars between the Ford Cobras and the new Chevrolet Stingray Corvettes, it was no contest as Carroll Shelby's Ford-powered A.C. Cobras left the Chevies of Bondurant, Dick Guldstrand and Paul Reinhart chasing shadows. With no straightaway, Miles' average winning speed was 65 mph. Cars were going faster than that right next door on the Pasadena Freeway."

In February 1963, the Cobras arrived at the Daytona Speedway in Florida for their first International Competition in a race called the Continental that was three hours long, not yet the 24-hour event it eventually became. Shelby sent three Cobras, one for MacDonald, one for Skip Hudson and the third for his longtime buddy and sometime rival, Dan Gurney, who had already raced at Le Mans and was to become a Shelby partner in building single seaters for Indy later on.

Gurney's job in the race though wasn't to win so much as it was to test an aluminum V8 for Ford instead of the usual cast iron one. While Shelby would have liked to go for a win with every Cobra, he was ever mindful that Ford was his client and the client wanted to see how the aluminum engine held up in racing conditions because they were thinking of using it at Indy. Unfortunately it fried.

Hudson crashed when a flywheel exploded and the Cobra effort then all rested on MacDonald's shoulders. When MacDonald came into the pits and shut his car off, a little later it wouldn't start. Shelby, realizing the starter solenoid was no good, took out a 50-cent piece and used it to bridge the gap and got the car started. MacDonald finished fourth overall behind two Ferraris and a Corvette. After this race, Chevrolet withdrew their support for Corvette racers, seeing that there was nothing they could do against the Cobras, which were 1,000 lbs. lighter than their plastic pachyderm.

The early days of the race teams sent out from Shelby-American were rife with rowdyness. Most of the mechanics were young, carefree and wanted to have a good time once the work was done (or before the transporters arrived carrying the race cars). There was frequent hazing, much post race consumption of alcoholic beverages and even the occasional swan dive from a balcony into the hotel swimming pool. Cherry bombs were the toy of the day, and they went off everywhere, sometimes set up to go off through elaborate booby traps that would go off when you opened a door. In one particularly memorable incident, someone knocked on Bob Bondurant's door. When he opened it, he was handed a newspaper and in that paper was a cherry bomb, which went off, showering him with shredded newspaper. On more than one occasion Shelby had to send an emissary, checkbook in hand, to deal with a motel manager to pay for the previous night's damage.

The surviving Shelby crew has remained tight-lipped about any "creativity" with the rules. Ed Leslie recalled that, soon after he was tied in with Shelby as a race driver, he was told to go and get a "safety kit." He wondered what it was, envisioning a first aid kit but then found out it was a roller cam kit. He also found out that the "Suspension Tuning Kit" on a Cobra consisted of an air gauge to check the tires.

By now the Cobras were running 289s, only 75 having been built with the 260. Shelby was on a roll as word spread about this fast American sports car.

The advent of the 289 model saw many incremental improvement—side vents put on the fenders, wider tires, wider fender flares, an alternator instead of a generator and a change in final drive to 3.77 from the original 3.54. The 289 models also had changes to the front wishbones, shorter pivot points, and changes to the uprights and spring connections. F. Wilson McComb, the British Cobra historian, attributes the source of all these changes to Alan Turner, A.C.'s Cobra engineer. McComb also calls the 289 models "Mk. II" though that phrase is seldom heard in the U.S.

A lot of the first 75 buyers of the 260 Cobras had complained about the vagueness of the worm and sector steering. By this time A.C. was installing sharper steering rack and pinion steering boxes, and the four cars Shelby-American sent to Sebring all had the new steering.

For each event, Shelby was fielding more Cobras. He figured, he already had the Corvettes on the run, so why not send them straight to oblivion? He entered three team Cobras in the 12 Hours of Sebring. The drivers selected were Davey MacDonald/Glen "Fireball" Roberts, Dan Gurney/Phil Hill, and Ken Miles/Lew Spencer.

Ironically Lew Spencer was his General Manager but a good enough driver that Shelby wanted him there, on the front lines so to speak, to see what the team needed. Shelby had recruited Spencer from his job where he was a car importer, in fact an importer of the A.C. "Ace" Bristol. Lew was also known as a winner behind the wheel of his Morgan, dubbed "Baby Doll."

For every race, a team has a strategy. Drivers are supposed to adhere to it, though there are those drivers who sometimes elect on their own to change the game plan. The Shelby-American plan for Sebring was to have MacDonald/Roberts run hard, tempting the opposition to catch up and break in the process. Running mid-way through the pack would be Gurney/Hill and taking up the slack at the rear would be Miles/Spencer.

The plan began to fall apart when the Miles/Spencer car first lost oil pressure, then Gurney hit a curb and the whole rack and pinion steering rack went. Then the MacDonald/Roberts car had problems and they went from 8th overall to nowhere.

The Gurney/Hill car had hit a marker cone which blocked off a brake cooling scoop and the brake on that side overheated. It still managed to finish 11th overall, but more important they still finished first in the GT class.

Shelby was not discouraged. He felt they were gaining on the Ferraris. The 1963 season was something to be proud of.

Shelby's long-range goal was to take a car to Le Mans and beat Ferrari, like he had told the old man he would do a few years earlier. But in 1963, he didn't really have a factory team yet so two private entries were readied—one by A.C. Cars Ltd. and the other by Shelby's first dealer, Ed Hugus. A.C. had two British drivers, Ninian Sanderson and Peter Bolton, while the American entry had former WWII paratrooper/car owner Hugus paired with British driver Peter Jopp. The great British driver, Stirling Moss, still recovering from a nasty accident that ended his driving career, was team manager.

Hugus had been selected because he had already run at Le Mans and, as he said, "the French like me." That could have had something to do with the fact he parachuted into France with the Normandy invasion to roust the Germans from the sacred soil of France. Plus he had already run hard there and proved himself a consummate professional. The third reason was most obvious—Hugus had the money to pay for his own entry. In fact, Hugus says he prepared both cars!

Both of the Cobras were 289 roadsters with solid Rudge wheels replacing the weak wire wheels. And they had aluminum fastback hardtops bolted in place (the shortened boot lids allowed the roofline to go further back than on the regular Cobra body). The hardtops were needed for aerodynamic reasons, the speeds approaching 170 mph, a tad windy for an open car and then too, it always rained at Le Mans and it was nice to have a roof over one's head.

Of course, Shelby being Shelby, there was a secret advantage to running the hardtops. The trick was in mounting the gas filler on the roof. The race scrutineers only checked the size of the gas tank but didn't measure the extra gallons of fuel that occupied the 4-inch wide filler tube. Of course, it might have made the drivers nervous to think there was a plastic filler tube full of gasoline right behind their heads but, hey, that wasn't enough to make any of them want to turn down a ride at Le Mans.

One of the two Cobras finished 7th overall, not a bad showing for a brand new marque. Though Ferraris had taken the first six places in the race, Shelby and Ford were pleased that Shelby's little Cobra proved it was a competitive car.

Back in the States the Cobra was getting new popularity from a song written by a pert little lady, Carol Conner, the song entitled "Hey, Little Cobra," sung by the Ripchords. The song was a pure bubble-gummer, mentioning a car just to hit on key words that teenagers like, not much different from "Little GTO," a song written a year or so later by Jim Wangers, a Detroit ad man, to promote Pontiac's muscle car, the GTO.

Shelby was also loaning cars to the movies, sneaking a Cobra into a scene here and there, and making side deals to promote such products as Pit Stop deodorant and his own Original Texas Chili. He also expanded his mail order speed equipment business and entered the wheel business, plus began buying and selling real estate property in Playa del Rey, a seaside community tucked in the sand dunes just up the road from his factory in Los Angeles and even managing to squire a few ladies around, among them a Miss Universe winner (1959) from Japan, who had innocently walked into his driver's school one day, not recognizing the gleam in the eye of the Big Bad Wolf.

By late 1963, Shelby was rolling ahead on all fronts. Back in Texas, they would say a man in his position was "on a gravy train with biscuit wheels."

Chapter 7- The Coupe

Shelby plant, Los Angeles International Airport, 1963.

The old man pulled up by the side of the hanger and walked in. The guys working on the racing coupe put down their tools. This was supposed to be a secured area. Who the hell was this old coot?

"It's O.K, boys," the man said. "Shel told me to come over and give my opinion."

The old man walked around, looked at the car's tubular body supports, tested the thickness of the aluminum bodywork with his two fingers, and then pondered the drawings on the wall, particularly the one that showed some newfangled wing on the back of the car.

He gave a nod. "Thanks, fellas," and walked off.

He reported straight to Shelby.

"Well, what did you think, Benny?" Shelby said, leaning back in his leather chair and planting his Gucci loafers on the desk.

Benny Howard lit up a cigarette and exhaled a cloud of smoke. He shook his head.

"Ain't gonna work, Carroll. It's a nice shape but you're still gonna need about 500 horses to get that sumbitch up to 180 mph."

The man delivering the opinion was Benny Howard, who had built and flown the Howard Specials before the war—a famous name in aeronautics. He was even a Vice President of Convair and founded Howard Aircraft in Chicago.

The year was 1963. Shelby knew what the Cobras were facing in U.S. racing. And he'd been to Europe when the Cobras raced at Le Mans.

One thing he realized right quick was that the Cobra roadsters—even with the fastback hardtops they had stuck on for Le Mans—were flat unable to catch the slippery Giotto Bizzarrini-designed Ferrari 250GTO coupes even though they had measurably larger engines than the Italian steeds (4.7 liters vs. 3 liters).

It didn't make it any easier that the Ferraris had 5-speed gearboxes and the Cobras four speeds.

In America, it had been a different story. The Cobras had effected a clean sweep of the racetracks, at least driving the much heavier Corvette competitors into temporary oblivion. And most of the Ferraris in the U.S. were being run by private teams, without direct factory support, so weren't as strong a threat as in Europe, their home territory.

But in Europe, where the tracks were different, and where a car could really get up to top speed, Shelby saw that the Cobra roadster was wanting in the aerodynamics department.

After all, its basic shape had come from a car introduced in 1953—the A.C. Ace. That car had in turn been copied off a series of specials, engineered by a man named John Tojeiro, which had used as their body style inspiration a 1949 Ferrari. Ferraris back then had been designed without any scientific aerodynamic testing. It was all what looked good to the eye.

So when his young—age 24—assistant, Pete Brock, walked into Shelby's office and said, "I can design a coupe body that will make the Cobra faster," Shelby was all ears.

Although he had hired Brock back in 1961 as his driving instructor for the Carroll Shelby School of High Performance Driving in Riverside, before he had started at Shelby, Brock had attended the Art Center College of Design, studying car design, and even worked briefly at General Motors as an intern. Brock had proved amazingly adept at conforming to every task Shelby threw at him, from writing ads to designing T-shirts.

Shelby also knew that Brock had already worked on a racecar secretly built for GM executive William L. Mitchell. That car became the Stingray racer, which Mitchell financed on his own nickel in SCCA racing, a car which won two National Championships. And which later inspired the '63 Corvette Stingray production cars. Shelby knew Brock could do it.

Shelby could see Brock's point that there was a way that he could slide a coupe version by the FIA, the International body that approved racecars for "homologation" as production cars. Shelby actually didn't want it to try to qualify it separately as an all new model, because in order for a given car to be considered production, the FIA rules at that point in time required a minimum of 100 cars to be built. He doubted there was a civilian market for 100 coupe versions of the Cobra and knew that he would be so busy with the racing program he didn't want to build coupes for the public.

But there was a loophole—maybe one big enough to drive a car through. If the body Brock designed went on a chassis that was essentially the same as the roadster, well, then it could be considered merely to be a variation on the already approved and homologated (as a production car) A.C. Cobra roadster.

Ferrari had already proved this by taking liberal advantage of this same rule when they had created the 250GTO ("O" for omologato meaning "homologated"). Ferrari had claimed it was only a slightly modified form of the short wheelbase 250GT but in reality it had a new suspension, new shocks, and a magnesium-cased transmission in addition to its slippery body shape (a shape that the FIA didn't see until it showed up at the track).

Ferrari had frankly bulldozed the FIA into permitting the GTO to run as a production car when in fact he built only around 39 cars, whereas Shelby knew that he would have had to build 100 coupes for the FIA to classify it as a brand new model. He didn't want to do that.

When Ferrari succeeded in opening a wedge in the rules to slip in the GTO, other manufacturers also began modifying their bodywork, including Jaguar who fielded a lightweight E-type with coachwork designed by aerodynamicist Malcolm Sayer and Aston Martin with their 212, 214 and 215 coupes.

Shelby figured if they can do it, so can we.

He gave permission to Brock to proceed and Brock began taping up his drawings on the wall for comment by the crew. He had to be hard shelled when he did that because the fact was that most Shelby employees, a good many of which came from the ranks of USAC oval car racing, were a skeptical lot. They had seen Brock run off on one tangent and another. They liked his enthusiasm but most doubted this wet-behind-the-ears youngster could design a car that that could beat a Ferrari.

The drawings showed a design which was similar to the GTO in front, having a long nose and faired in headlamps (under plexiglass). On the front hood, though, Brock designed in a "wastegate" which allowed air that had passed through the radiator some place to escape. And he had a fastback roof that continued in one unbroken line from the roof to the tail. Brock kept muttering about some obscure European named Dr. Wunibald Kamm, who had proposed before the war that cars should have long tapered teardrop shaped tails to best penetrate the air. Brock had discovered a book on Dr. Kamm's theories in the GM Library while working in Detroit and become a true disciple of the Doctor's theories. This solution was impractical for most cars, so handily Dr. Kamm had proposed a 'backup' theory which postulated: if you couldn't have the tapered tail, the next best thing was to abruptly chop off the tail of the car. That's what Brock wanted, the second design, the "Kamm effect" tail.

Brock's design owed a lot to the Maserati Type 151 coupe, of which there were at least four made. They too had faired-in headlamps and a fastback Kamm effect tail. When this interviewer asked Brock about how much inspiration for the Daytona coupe came from that car, Brock didn't register that he knew the car but there is a revealing picture of Brock racing a Cooper way back in '63, and the car he is following nose to tail around the track is a Kamm-backed fastback Maserati 151 coupe.

Brock was predicting to anyone that would listen that his design would allow the Cobra to increase its top speed to the 175-180 mph range, or about 15 to 20 mph faster than the open version. A plus would be that it would be much more stable at that speed as well.

The coupe project started in October 1963. Shelby assigned his best fabricator, Phil Remington, to the project as well as his best test engineer, Ken Miles. New Zealander John Ohlsen was assigned as well, along with Remington supervising

It's a wonder that it got done at all, what with there being a bit of bad blood between Miles and Remington that had occurred earlier with some racing roadsters when Remington was out of town and Miles re-set the suspensions of all the cars to suit him. When Remington returned, he ordered every car re-set to the settings they had on them before he left.

A 289 Cobra chassis, CSX 2014, a racecar that had been hit hard, was rolled in to serve as the mule chassis to mount plywood body formers on.

After the body panels had been added, and a substructure of tubes to hold the new body up, the panels were pounded out by a shop in Los Angeles. Cal Metal Shaping attached the body panels to the tubing of the frame and welded them together. The hood was a separate assembly, lifting in one piece with the fenders, unlike the roadster which had employed a traditional bonnett.

It was when the design was almost done that Shelby invited Benny Howard to take a look at the design and deliver his learned opinion. Howard knew a thing or two about aerodynamics.

Shelby sighed after Howard left. The bad news Howard had delivered put him in a quandary. He respected Brock. He respected Howard. The problem was that his engine builders had already tweaked the 289 Hi-Po engine to 390 hp and reported that was all there was in the 289, period. Shelby knew that he couldn't squeeze one more horsepower out of it—the small blocks were already blowing head gaskets left and right.

After Howard left, Shelby had walked back to Brock's office. He could see that Brock had already heard the news and was fretting.

"Keep going, Brock," Shelby said. "Howard oughta know—you can't tell a damn thing 'bout a car until you get the sumbitch on the track." Besides, Ford's Aeroneutronics Division, based in Newport Beach, had looked at it and made a few recommendations. They were into building missiles and knew a few things about airflow themselves, not to mention that their knowledge of aerodynamics was state of the art, not prewar like Howard's.

Looking back, Peter Brock says, "The 'Aero Guy' from Ford had no experience with race cars but being an 'expert' he offered a lot of advice on how to improve the coupes...primarily in the area of interior cooling and rear brake ducting. Nothing worked. Those 'solutions' were approved over my objections for political reason...and the drivers continued to bake."

Then there was another hitch. Brock's original design called for what he called a "ring airfoil" on the car, basically a horizontal wing encircling the rear of the fuselage but perched up from the body surface a few inches away, on little mounts so air could flow under it. Shelby was dubious about this device. He sent the coupe to Riverside for testing without having that part built. They could always, he told Brock, add it later if they saw that they really needed it. He probably made the decision to keep peace in the shop—the crew didn't revolt at the design of the car when it was done, but he knew if he added the weird wing, there would be more intransigence on the part of the crew. And that he didn't need.

The Shelby shop in Venice, near the Venice boardwalk, was a good 70 miles from Riverside, a track far inland. When the first coupe was trundled off by trailer to Riverside for that first test, all the employees in the shop continued to hammer on Cobra roadster production cars and King Cobra racecars, but almost to a man they were keeping an ear cocked for the first ring of the phone that might mean the guys testing at Riverside had some results.

When the call came in, the news was good. Miles had broken the track record by 3.5 seconds and been clocked at 180 mph down the main straight. Smiles broke out among the crew. Sonovabitch—the crewcut kid had been right! That was 20 mph faster than the roadsters and hell, Riverside didn't even have that long of a straight! God knows what could be done at a big track like Daytona!

Riverside was only the beginning. Then came the development. Miles wanted the suspension stiffer. That's when a triangulated subframe had to be added over the regular tube frame to stiffen up the chassis. Another addition was tiny vertical windwings standing just off the front A-pillars, these to divert the airflow to scoops on the sides of the rear 3/4 windows that fed cool air to the brakes.

One idea didn't work out so good: slots cut in the concave rear panel to cool off the brakes. Turned out exhaust gases entered and got to the interior. The slots were blocked off.

The coupe's racing debut was at the Daytona racetrack for the Daytona Continental in Florida February 16, 1964. It was being called the "Daytona" by the crew and someone had already painted that name on the front fenders.

It looked good. But Shelby's crew was a little worried. They arrived at the track to find no less than seven Ferrari 250GTOs waiting to pounce on their baby, though only one was a direct factory-supported "works" entry.

Shelby designated Bob Holbert and Davey McDonald as co-drivers.

Earlier Shelby had appointed Miles competition manager in an attempt to keep his most valuable test engineer from driving. Miles was cranky about that because he had been with the Daytona since the beginning and argued that the Daytona was even built around his dimensions.

Shelby wasn't worried that the drivers he assigned would need a "learning curve" because the coupe was a more rigid structure than the roadsters and was easier to handle.

During practice, Miles imposed an rpm limit of 6,300 on his drivers because he didn't want to blow the coupe's debut by having the drivers over-rev and blow the engine. Holbert promptly broke the GT lap record. The team looked at their stopwatches—Holbert was clocking laps three seconds faster than the Ferrari GTO's.

Miles figured, hey, if we are already ahead of them, let's lower the rpm even more, put less strain on the engine and see how we do then. He imposed a new rpm ceiling of 6,000 rpm and saw that Holbert was still outrunning the GTOs.

During the race itself, the coupe started out superbly, leading the race after the first couple of hours.

Trouble started after seven hours, when Holbert pulled in for an unscheduled pit stop, complaining of smoke in the cockpit. When the rear tires were pulled off for replacement, it was obvious fluid was leaking out of the differential. The correct fluid wasn't available in the pits so Shelby told the crew to fill the differential with the heaviest engine oil they could find—which turned out to be 30 weight—until they could find some differential grease. Holbert hit the track again.

The trouble was the engine oil was too thin to be used as differential oil. It was blowing out. Holbert was signaled to put into the pits again and this time the oil in the diff replenished with the right viscosity fluid. At the same time some wit thought "He's here—let's take advantage and top off the gas tank again." But the gas tank was still full because he hadn't been out on the track that long and the excess spilled out, down the body and hit a hot rear disc brake. The car erupted in flames with one mechanic, Ohlsen, still under the car. Ohlsen made it out with major burns. After they put the fire out, they got the bad news on the car: the wiring was burnt out and the differential damaged. The coupe was pulled from the race.

Later they determined that the differential's seals had deteriorated from overheating but it wasn't a design or engineering flaw. It was driver inexperience. Oh, the two drivers Shelby had picked were experienced drivers but they just hadn't been told that the coupe had a switch you had to trip in order to activate an electric pump. Without that pump to circulate the fluid through a cooler, the differential would overheat. The irony was that Miles knew about the pump and knew exactly when it was necessary to turn it on, but somehow that information didn't get to the new drivers.

Shelby still believed in the coupe. Its failure was just the result of a communication foul up. The coupe was reconditioned for the 12 Hours of Sebring coming in three weeks. McDonald and Holbert made no mistakes this time and won decisively.

But at the 1964 Sebring 12 Hour in March—run on a flat course laid out on an old airfield—it was discovered exactly how hot the coupe was inside. It was so hot, in fact, that it melted the driver's shoes! In desperation, scoops were added here and there to get more air in, but no matter what you did, the plain fact was that the coupe—with that fastback roof—was a lot hotter inside than a roadster.

The Cobras did well at Sebring, the coupe finishing fourth overall behind three Ferrari prototypes, and two other Cobra roadsters finishing 5th and 6th.

Ford, Shelby's patron, was impressed with how well the coupes had done and wrote him out a check that would cover the construction of several more. But where to build them? Building an all new body in England would be too expensive, Shelby thought, and not practical because the English could barely keep up with the production of roadster bodies he was ordering now and he knew they would raise what Texans call a "hissy fit" if he said "Oh, by the way, can you build some of this other body style?" It was no use asking A.C. He could go to the Italians but doubted they could make them that fast. But in the end, that's where he went, purely on the recommendation of his old friend, Alejandro de Tomaso. Shelby put in an order with Carrozzeria Gran Sport in Modena for two more, figuring an Italian carrozzeria could whack out coachwork faster than those toads in England. He then contacted A.C. Cars in England and told them to prepare two more chassis and send them straight on to Italy.

Originally, in order to make sure the Italians got it right, Shelby had planned to send the first coupe—the one bodied in California—over to Italy to serve as a model to check the new bodies against.

But the prototype was needed instead at Le Mans for testing, which meant the Italians were forced to improvise, using Brock's hand-drawn plans and photographs to shape the next two coupes.

The first European race for the coupe was at Spa, a Belgian track in the Ardennes Forest, in May. There they had it easy—they were only up against four Ferrari 250GTOs but some of these were a new breed of GTO with a body shape similar to the 250LM although they were front engined and the 250LM mid-engined. The Cobra team brought three roadsters and the one coupe, the latter for Phil Hill.

It was there, during practice, that Shelby discovered that Brock's insistence on the need for a rear spoiler was not to be ignored. Phil Hill, the team's main driver, came into the pits white-faced, reporting that he had felt the tail lifting off the ground at 180 mph plus.

Phil Remington, an ace craftsman, hammered a "lip" type rear deck spoiler together on the spot, something roughly similar in shape to the one Ferrari had found necessary to add to the 250GTOs soon after introduction. It was installed and tested, and Hill reported that the rear end of the Daytona coupe felt more rooted to the ground. He then went out and broke the track record and grabbed the pole position.

Hill was leading at the start but later on the car went out with some nasty problem regarding tainted fuel. There were rumors that the fuel had been sabotaged but that couldn't be proven. Was it Ferrari? You could never tell about Enzo. Shelby felt he was positively Machivelian, though Shelby's rivals would say that would be a case of the pot calling the kettle black!

But if there was any ever doubt in Shelby's mind about Brock's design, he was now fully convinced of its worth. The coupe had demonstrated at Spa that, under European racing conditions, it was every bit the mettle of the Ferraris. And it had soul; something you don't expect with a brand new car.

Meanwhile, back in Italy the coachbuilders were building the two new coupes but when the cars arrived back in California Shelby got a shock—they had gotten a measurement wrong and the result was that the two new cars had a different roofline than the prototype, maybe as much as 2 inches off! This was discovered but too late to change the cars so they were shipped to Le Mans for testing in April anyway.

When Shelby had the new cars tested by Chris Amon and Jochen Neerspasch, he got the bad news that the new coupes weren't as fast as the original had been. He was steamed. Had Enzo Ferrari, based in the same town as the coachbuilders, secretly instructed them to screw up his Cobras? But it turned out that a good driver could make up the difference, as Dan Gurney proved in the new coupe by not only finishing the race first in his class but recording the fastest GT lap at 3:58.7.

At the Le Mans tests in April 1964, the Cobra coupe was ignored, the press being much more fascinated by Ford's two mid-engined GT40s (so called because they were a mere 40 inches tall). The GT40s didn't do so well. Although they were clocking close to 200 mph down the Mulsanne straight, they both crashed at speed. Ford went home with their tail between their legs, mortified to find that their multi-million dollar Ford GTs were somehow unstable.

During the tests, in between runs with the Ford GT, Shelby invited Jo Schlesser, a journeyman French driver, to take a few laps in the Daytona coupe as well. Schlesser came back from his drive saying that he loved the coupe. He managed to get it up to a speed matching that of the Ford GTs, one of which he crashed later when GT testing was resumed. Shelby later hired him as a team driver in the Daytona coupe.

But the big surprise for Shelby at Le Mans practice was when a Cobra coupe designed by A.C. in England showed up, this one just as fast as the Brock version though it had a different body style. This was just one indication of how the relationship between the two firms was shaky—A.C. cheekily doing their own coupe without telling Shelby. And theirs would go 180 mph as well (as confirmed during an impromptu test by Jack Sears on the M1 motorway, a test that resulted in speed limits being imposed after there was a hue and cry in parliament about the danger of someone being able to drive that fast on a public road).

The Ferrari team, miffed at the success of the Cobra coupe, was watching the Shelby team closely for any infractions of the rules so they could bring them to the attention of track officials and get the car thrown out of the race. Sure enough, one of the Cobra coupes was disqualified for an illegal start after it had to be jump- started in the pits with a separate battery. The Ferrari team made sure the Le Mans officials knew that the Shelby team had broken the rules and the offending Cobra was black flagged off the course. It hurt because at the time it was leading the GT class and in the 10th hour of the race.

The coupe built entirely by A.C. had its own bad luck. It crashed and burned, and even hit a Ferrari in the process, which spun out and killed three youthful spectators who had been in an area they weren't supposed to be in.

The Gurney/Bondurant coupe finished fourth overall, behind three Ferrari prototypes. Bondurant told reporters he could have done better, but a leaking oil cooler had set his engine coolant to boiling and he had to run slow laps so he could hang in there.

The Ferrari/Cobra Daytona Coupe battle continued the rest of season with Ford ahead in points for the World's Manufacturer's Championship as they neared the end of the season.

In one race, the Tourist Trophy at Goodwood in August, when Gurney's Daytona finished in 3rd behind two Ferrari prototypes, the Ferrari team protested mightily and the cars were practically dissected by the officials, checking port sizes, gear ratios, everything for a deviation from the homologated version. However, the car checked out and Ferrari had to go away grumpy.

But you couldn't rule out the Ferrari team when it came to behind-the-scenes warfare. They were the masters. In Modena, old man Ferrari came up with a political move that would put Ferrari out ahead.

Shelby didn't find out until he began to make plans for the race scheduled for Monza, Italy.

Shelby now had two coupes ready for battle. Another was still in Modena being prepared for a 427. It was Shelby's secret weapon. Ferrari could field more than that of GT0s but knew they weren't as fast as the Cobra coupes. And those were small block coupes. If Shelby had a 7-liter coupe, well, that would be even more of a threat.

Enzo switched to Plan B, using his influence to have the one race of the series cancelled. Ferrari had more points than the Shelby team at that point. There wasn't another race on the schedule that would allow Shelby-American to catch up.

That's the PR version of why Shelby-American lost the Championship during the '64 season. Actually there *was* a Monza race in '64, but if you look at the entries you see they were all small displacement cars. So what Enzo had done was get the organizers to cancel the larger displacement cars by canceling the Group III FIA-sanctioned race that was the class the Cobras fell into. Supposedly this inbroglio started with the demand by the race organizers—carrying the water for ol' Enzo—that the FIA recognize Ferrari's mid-engined 250LM as a production car. The FIA was not about to be blackmailed into this so they said "no" whereupon the race organizers held a Monza race that did not count toward the World Championship and the Italian favorite, a 250LM piloted by Shelby's ol' driving partner, Roy Salvadori, won. Salvadori remembers "it was mostly Ferraris in the race."

Shelby learned a bitter lesson. It wasn't how good your cars were, or how good your drivers were. It was how much influence you could wield behind the scenes. Monza was in Italy and Enzo Ferrari was, in some eyes, as important as the King of Italy. No, more important than the King of Italy, who was just a figurehead. Rules were bent for the Ferrari team, then as now.

There were actually other events left on the 1964 racing schedule after Monza—two of the key ones being the Tour de France and Bridgehampton.

The Tour de France was an intriguing race in that you got to race on real race tracks, including a portion of the Le Mans track, but the downer was that racers had to drive hundreds of miles between the tracks in a sort of timed rally. This meant your support group had to guess where you were going to break down so they could be there with parts and service—not a good idea when the total amount of ground covered added up to thousands of miles. Ferrari had the advantage because there were several Ferrari dealers in France.

There was one memorable recollection of the Tour de France, though, from Bob Bondurant. At one point, near Reims, he and Jochen Neerspasch were driving like hell between the racetracks in a Daytona coupe when they ran into heavy traffic in one town. That didn't stop them—they drove on the wrong side of the road, and even on the sidewalk!

At one point they were running out of gas and pulled into a tiny gas station and jumped out, jamming both the guy's fuel hoses into the twin gas tanks of the Daytona. They couldn't speak French, and the gas station owner couldn't speak English. And they didn't have any money. So, tank full, they yanked out the hoses and took off, making the poor old man who ran the station think he'd just been robbed! When they reached the next checkpoint, Bondurant told someone from Shelby to go back and please pay the poor man.

The Bridgehampton Double 500 took place in Sept, '64, with Ken Miles finishing fourth overall but first in class in Grand Touring. Second in GT and sixth overall was Ronnie Bucknum in CSX2494. Bob Johnson was right behind him in a third Cobra roadster, finishing third in class. Ironically, the race was won overall by a "ghost" car, in that the Scarab company had ceased operations years earlier, but coming across the finish line first was Walt Hansgen in a Chevrolet-powered Scarab owned by J. Mecom Jr. A double irony is that mid-engined Scarab, the only one built, was the last project built by Phil Remington back when he worked for Scarab team.

But Ferrari's Monza trick foiled Shelby-American. They couldn't make up enough points in the last three events to beat Ferrari.

In '65 Ferrari didn't even enter any factory-sponsored cars in the GT class. He was still miffed about the FIA not approving his mid-engined 250LM as a production sports car despite his having failed to build the required minimum number. The FIA was in effect, punishing him for his trick with the GTO years before. This time if he couldn't field 100 250LM cars, they wouldn't homologate it. He decided to cede that area of the battlefield to Shelby while he went after the Ford GT40s running in the prototype class.

Cobra fans hoped to see the Daytona coupes get their revenge in '65, but Shelby, very busy making Shelby Mustangs, selling Cobras and preparing the Ford GT40 Mk1s and 7-liters for Le Mans, decided to farm out the Cobra Daytona racing effort to Alan Mann in England, whose shop had done such a bang-up job preparing the Falcon Sprints and the Tour de France Mustangs a few years earlier. It is presumed by most historians that the Cobra program was handed to Alan Mann because Shelby, with the Le Mans GT program, and Shelby Mustang and Cobra production was awee bit busy, but one historian, Marshall Gardner, has documentation (letters from Ford officials) that Ford was behind reassigning the Cobra racing program.

Shelby eventually sent over two drivers—Bob Bondurant and Alan Grant—to drive for Mann, but the American drivers were miffed when they got there because in race after race, Mann would tell them before the race what finishing order he expected, and more often than not, the American drivers were told to finish behind his British drivers.

Bob Bondurant, who already had decided that he was going to join Ferrari's team for '66, didn't like this and made it clear that, when he saw his opportunity, he was going to drive to win. Mann viewed this attitude as mutinous but that was nothing new as Americans have always been thought mutinous by the Brits, going back to the days of King George III, when they sent an army to quell the rowdy Colonists, only to have their royal tails soundly thrashed.

Ferrari running his teams through private dealers was a good move, for it was a private team run by his American distributor, Luigi Chinetti, that had their Ferrari 250LM finish first at Le Mans in '65, humbling the Ford GT team for the second year in a row.

At Le Mans in '65 no less than five Daytona coupes were entered along with the 4.7 liter and 7-liter Ford GT40s but when the smoke cleared 24 hours later only the Dick Thompson/Jack Sears Daytona was still running. They finished 8th overall.

You would think that, back in Dearborn, they would be pleased but the fact was that Ford was almost embarrassed by the Daytona's success in '65 because, at more than one event, their vaunted "high-tech" Ford GTs lost while the rude and crude Daytona coupes managed to finish.

Ford PR had projected an image of the Ford GTs as mid-engined supercars, state of the art, the ones that all the scientists and engineers at Ford in Dearborn had developed from scratch (a description Eric Broadley would no doubt take umbrage at, but in truth none of the Lola GT Mk. 6 was used, the GT40 being an all-new design). This, compared to the Daytona which, after all, from the Detroit engineers' point of view was nothing but a custom Cobra that had been pretty much by-guessed-and-by-goshed together by Brock, a 24 year old kid, for Chrissake, and a bunch of Shelby's hot rodders and oval racers with nary an engineering degree among them.

Ford couldn't have that situation continue. Sure, it was good enough for Cobras to win back in '63 when they didn't have the GT. But now that they had the GT, having the Cobras beat it wasn't good for the corporate image.

Following the '65 season, Ford support for the Daytona coupes totally evaporated. Henry Ford II making it crystal clear that he wanted Ford to win the Le Mans race outright and that he wouldn't be satisfied with the Daytonas winning the GT class instead. Henry Ford knew that the general public—the ones that only caught their racing news on the evening news—only remembered who won an event like Le Mans overall, not who won in each itty-bitty class.

The last gasp of the Daytona coupe was one the public never saw (in the sixties, anyway). Brock, who had been with Shelby three years, since before the first Ford GT was ever drawn on paper, had advocated going with the coupe the same way Shelby had gone with the roadster—upsizing to a 427 big block engine. He had talked Shelby into budgeting some money for an all new design, but Shelby, knowing Ford's interest in the Daytona was waning, farmed out the job of fabricating it to the lowest bidder—Radford—the company in England that did mods on road cars (such as three of the Beatle's Minis) and the upholstery for the Ford GTs. Brock was mortified.

What in God's name would an upholsterer know about making a racecar body? It turned out, not much. After a few months waiting impatiently for a report on progress, Brock talked Shelby into letting him fly to England to inspect their handiwork. When he got there, his worst fears were realized—it was far worse than he thought it would be—the car was not only off all his original dimensions but off by feet and not inches! He talked Shelby into shipping it home to the Shelby plant but when it arrived, instead of going into the shop it was parked around back with a "For Sale" sign on it. While it was on the water, word had come down from Dearborn. It was Ford GTs and not Daytona coupes that Henry Ford II wanted to see in the winner's circle. What was there about that that Shelby didn't understand?

The 427 coupe was sold unfinished. Unlike the 289 coupe it was unloved. The same crew who had called the 289 coupe the "Slug" before it had turned a wheel now called the 427 coupe the "Super Slug."

Years later a hobbyist bought it and it was completed but it was never to turn a wheel in combat for Shelby-American. Looking back, the Cobra coupes were truly the last hurrah of the original Shelby crew—the guys who had built the Shelby cars with all that they had learned on the dry lake beds of California, on the dirt ovals of a hundred fairground tracks and at Indy.

The second wave of employees, the brush-cut engineers wearing white shirts and ties who had come from Dearborn with the arrival of the Ford GTs succeeded too, but it wasn't the same at Shelby-American once they arrived. The original employees felt it. The fun was gone.

Ended too with the advent of the Dearborn brigade were some of Shelby's infamous back door projects, now that he had Ford Dearborn employees right there on site looking over his shoulder. One famous episode involved the Toyota 2000GT. At the time, Toyota wasn't a big automaker in America, with only a toe in the door selling cars like the Toyopet Tiara and Land Cruiser. They had bought this snazzy ready-made sports car from Yamaha, and figured who better to develop and race it than the famous Carroll Shelby? They sent some to Shelby to prepare. Well, the car was inspired by the E-type Jag, a fastback coupe with an inline six, but similar to the E-type Jag, you could rebuild the entire engine and when you were done end up with less power than you started with! Shelby's team campaigned the 2000GT racecars but they never had a prayer of catching the well-developed Porsches. At first this went un-noticed in Dearborn until one day a high-ranking Ford official turned a corner at Shelby's facility in California and saw all the work going on with cars that didn't look anything at all like Fords. The axe fell quickly.

And of course, among the secret projects there was the Shelby "moon rover." Or was it a flying saucer? Your author doubted any such thing ever existed until seeing a picture in a Japanese magazine of all the GT-350s lined up in the parking lot of the Shelby works and some *thing* floating overhead. Was it Martians spying on Shelby? Turns out, years later we find out, it was merely a military contractor in a neighboring hanger who was building a prototype for the Marines called the "Flying Platform." The gas turbine-powered job would get off the ground, but proved to be too unstable to develop further. But some Shelby employees are still convinced that this was another of Shel's secrets, no doubt fueled by the fact that astronauts were seen visiting Shelby-American (actually, one of them, Scott Carpenter, was there to buy a 427 Cobra).

Pete Brock wrote in *Vintage Motorsport*, "The Daytona Cobra Coupes were the last of the Specials, a watershed point in race car design. From 1965 onward, race car technology followed the lead set by the Broadley/Ford GT40, cars engineered on paper and built with the most technologically advanced materials available. Never again would there be a successful design distilled only form the cumulative experience of a team's race mechanics, who literally envisioned cars on the shop floor and built them as they proceeded. The Daytona coupes were the end of an era."

In the end, regarding the Daytona coupe, Shelby had the last laugh. He had pulled one over on not only Enzo but on the FIA as well. As John Christy noted: if anyone had ever really taken the body off a Daytona coupe and parked it next to a 289 roadster chassis, they would have seen that quite a few changes had been made in the coupe "in the matter of chassis and frame structure." Changes that would likely have disallowed its approval as being but a "mere body difference" over the roadster. It was as much different from the roadster as the Ferrari 250GTO was from the short wheelbase 250GT. But after all the victories had been won, and all the results recorded in all the record books, and all the trophies sent to Dearborn, it was too late for anyone to bring that up.

Enzo Ferrari never obtained a Cobra Daytona coupe to make that comparison. If he had, he would have found out just what it was like to be "snake-bit."

Chapter 8- The Big Block

Sometime in 1965. The Shelby Factory, Los Angeles International Airport.

The photographer rushed across the airport tarmac, slamming his car to a stop. He was sure he was at the right hanger, but there was no sign of activity.

Sweating heavily, he stopped his car and got out. He looked at his watch. He was on time.

Where the hell was Shelby?

But then he heard a muffled roar like you hear in the jungle when a lion coughs.

Couldn't be a 289, this sound was deeper. More basso profundo. A real engine.

The garage door began to roll up, revealing as it climbed a car in raw aluminum.

Shelby was behind the wheel. He goosed it and the car shot out. Shelby slammed on the brakes and the car stopped instantly. Leaving it running, Shelby stepped out and grinned them pearly whites.

"The 427?" the photographer asked.

"You got it," Shelby answered. He put his hand on the windshield and posed while the photographer got off a few shots. The photographer could feel the heat radiating up from the side pipes, which were as big and round as sewer drains.

"Well, what'd'ya think, Dave?" Shelby asked as he got behind the wheel again. "Is this SOB gonna kick some Corvette ass or what?"

As successful as it was, conquering the racetracks of America and Europe, the truth was that the 289 Cobra was a car with definite limitations.

But only in three areas: the engine, the chassis and the body shape. The engine you could do something about: drop in another one, one that would hang together. The chassis Shelby knew he could redesign, with the resources of Ford behind him. The body you could do something about but he'd done that with the small-block coupe.

Ken Miles, one of Shelby's ace fabricators, had taken the first step toward putting a big block into the Cobra back in December, '63 when, at Shelby's request, he shoehorned a 427 into a leaf sprung Cobra chassis. The result was squirrely because the leaf springs could not take the torque—they would wind up because of what Shelby called the "buggy springs" and then flex, throwing the car off line.

The first outing for the car—Miles believed racetrack testing was the way you discovered a car's flaws real fast—was at Sebring in 1964. The car's handling was so quirky that, during practice, Miles managed to find the only tree on the course and hit it. What a tree was doing on a race course would take a lot of explaining but suffice to say the car was squirrely beyond belief.

Miles suffered broken ribs as a result of the crash, but true to his legendary stoic qualities, he stayed up all night and hammered on the car and in the morning had a car his co-driver John Morton could enter. The engine blew, but as undeveloped as it was, it showed a big block had potential.

Later, a second version was built. This version had a 390 with 58-mm We-bers and a whole new body. The front hinged like an E-type coupe so the hood and fenders lifted as once piece. The doors were bottom-hinged. Miles took it to Nassau in December '64 but, after coping with mechanical problems galore the car finally blew its engine, putting it out of its misery.

The reason Shelby vitally needed a big block Cobra was simply to counter the competition. He knew that Chevrolet was coming out with a big block Corvette (the 396; later to become the 427) and he wanted an engine of equal or larger size to rain on their parade. The irony was that Chevrolet was officially not in racing, but for a company not in racing, there seemed to be an awful lot of money being spent on special duty parts that were strong enough to race with.

Shelby's old nemesis, Zora Arkus Duntov, who had earlier been slapped down by the GM Corporation, his employer, for making the lightweight Corvette Gran Sports, was at it again with the big block Corvette, cranking them out and sending the first ones off to private teams that could do something with them, like Penske.

Ford had its own big block, one mightier than the unestablished 396—the mighty 427. The 427 was a legendary engine in NASCAR circles where the side oiler version(with superior oiling than the normal version) could crank out 425 hp without half trying. More important it was dead reliable where the 289, for all the publicity Ford and Shelby cranked out to elevate it to legendary status, wasn't all that reliable, blowing head gaskets like crazy (because, say mechanics, Ford wouldn't let them use aftermarket head bolts that were stronger because Ford wanted to be able to say the engine was "all Ford").

Ford was upgrading to a big block on their Ford GT, which had finished few races with the 289. They absolutely hated to make the GT any heavier than it was, which the 427 most certainly did do, but they had to because they needed an engine with durability and the one quality the 427 had was that, in spades.

The 427 block was cast from high nickel content iron and used all of the features of the previous 390 hp and 406 High Performance V8s. It had a block cast with a thicker deck to cope with higher combustion pressures. It was a solid lifter engine. After casting, the block was stress relieved using a slow paced cooling process that reduced internal stresses. Completely cooled blocks were put through a special machining line. They located the block better in boring and machining which made it a more exacting product.

Some wonder if they were wise to use a cast iron crank. The main bearing journals were grooved for better lubrication. The con rods were the same type used in the High Performance 390. The 427 was one of the first to use forged pistons. At first they used flattop but later pop-up to increase compression. The cylinder heads and intake manifolds were flow tested together as they would be working together. In the first year, 1963, the engine had a high riser or low riser but by 1965 a medium riser was made available.

The most important part was the side oiler feature. The 427 block was rede-signed with a large oil passage along the left side of the block. Passages were drilled through the side of the block, through the left side oil passage to a vertical oil passage in order to feed oil under pressure ot the main bearing and cam bearings. The drilled holes in the side of the block were tapped and screw-in oil gallery plugs installed. Ford also switched to a forged steel crank in '65, with main bearing journals and rod journals cross-drilled to ensure 360 degrees of lubrication.

Shelby was convinced he needed to go the same route in the Cobra.

But he knew from Miles' experiments that, in order to build a bigger 427-powered Cobra, Ford would have to redesign the chassis of the Cobra. This they were willing to do because the 289 Cobra had done well without much help from them and still garnered them an outsize amount of publicity. But they made it clear to Shelby that the big block car would be a low budget, back-burner deal.

Ford assigned two of their engineers in Dearborn the job of redesigning the frame. They were Klaus Arning, a German-born engineer, and Bob Negstad, a performance engineer who had engineered the Mustang I experimental car.

Shelby, in a speech at the Saratoga Auto Museum in 2005 tells it slightly different—that he had met Arning at a social outing in Detroit and that Arning, proud of Ford's acquisition of a newfangled thing called a "computer," (this was the era, remember, when Detroit engineers still made most of their calculations using wooden devices called "slide rules") said "we can design a new frame for you."

Wherever the impetus came from, Shelby took Ford up on it.

F. Wilson McComb, the British author of a book called *A.C. (Shelby) Cobra*, says A.C.'s Alan Turner designed the frame, armed with early computer readouts of suspension settings sent from Detroit. (In the British versions it's always the Brits that are the heroes).

Suffice to say that the big block Cobra's suspension was the result of a collaboration between engineers in two countries, but Ford Dearborn definitely was involved with the first prototype. Pictures also show Shelby's key engineer, Phil Remington, over in England on some rainswept race course supervising the track test of the first 427 Cobra production car, while it was still in raw aluminum.

Arning speced the main tubes to be 4 inches in diameter rather than continue to use the small block's 3-inch diameter tubes. The tubes also were also speced to have a thicker wall thickness and were moved 2.5 inches further apart to accomodate the wider big block.

The new design called for modern coil springs to be used on all four corners instead of the obsolete leafs. The brakes were kept the same as on the 289s except for the Comp cars, which had larger 11.5-inch discs.

The knock-off wheels were kept, a European anachronism where you loosened or tightened the wheels by means of hammering on the ears on the center-locking nut with a large copper-headed mallet, which deformed with each blow. For the 427 Cobra they would be the Halibrand wheels used on the racing 289s.

Pete Brock also saw the opportunity to start a new career as a wheel designer and whipped out some wheels subsequently called "sunburst" but modern day Cobra owners don't much like them because they don't look like racing Halibrands, and were more brittle, a worrying thought when you are going over 150 mph.

Negstad would have liked to design some more modern bits as long as they were starting from the frame up but, incredibly, Shelby had budgeted so little money for the up-sized Cobra that in the book *Remembering the Shelby Years* Negstad recalled years later of when he was starting the project, going over to visit A.C. and being led to a warehouse where one of the Hurlocks (family that owned A.C.) opened a door, pointed to racks of old parts and said "That's what we've got to use." Negstad was shocked to find many of the bits were from already obsolete cars including

—steering column from a VW bus

—taillights from a Hillman

—spindles from Triumph Herald.

But he did change some things. The new suspension towers were made of steel tubing rather than the steel plate that had been used before. New wishbones were fabricated top and bottom all the way around.

Now that so much time has passed, no one can remember for sure if other engines were briefly considered before the 427. Ford first tested several 390 aluminum blocks, which wouldn't have weighed any more than the small block iron block 289 but the engines blew up. Then there was talk of a 351 and even of a 302.

But all other candidates were removed from the board once they took a serious look at the 427. This was an engine with an established record of victories in NASCAR.

Although the car was called the 427 Cobra, for an engine Shelby actually had a three-tiered offering. For the street originally it was the 425 hp 427 "side oiler," so called because it had a top end designed to get the oil circulated around the side of the engine to the mains. Then after the first 100 or so cars, they inexplicably switched to a Police Interceptor medium-riser 428 rated at 390 hp (and at 330 hp in the Mustang) while in the racing versions it was still the side oiler 427 rated at 485 hp with a prodigious 485 ft-lbs. of torque.

Neither Shelby or Ford ever officially announced that there was a 428 version nor was it mentioned in the ads. The engines looked alike once they were in the car (except for the intake manifold and carburetion) and Shelby spokesman Al Dowd once told your author: "If you looked like a weenie, we sold you the 428."

Shelby also made $200 more in profit if you left with a 428 under the hood rather than a 427 because the hotter performing engine cost them more.

Then the last 160 or so Cobras once again had the side-oiler 427 under the hood.

No one besides Dowd from Shelby-American has ever gone on record to explain why the "tame" 428s were installed in that middle period of the big block except to say there might have been a shortage of 427 side oiler engines, but you need not go much beyond the fact that the 427 side-oilers cost Shelby more. Today such a practice would be called "bait and switch," but those were fast and loose times with not much checking on what you got for what you paid.

There's also a long standing rumor that, since the U.S. was in the middle of a shooting war in Asia, there might some truth to the story that Navy SEALs needed some powerful engines for their fast STAB boats and selected the 427. Sounds good, in that such boats existed for infiltration/exfiltration, but it seems like the Viet Cong would have heard a 427 coming from one hell of a long way off!

The street cars usually had two Autolite carburetors. The high performance 427 side oiler in the Competition version had a single huge 750 cfm Holley carb atop an aluminum intake manifold. The full competition and S/C versions in addition had a metal bathtub-shaped airbox around the carb that sealed to the hood underside so that only cold air would be ingested from the hood scoop. The air scoop was actually dangerous to have if you didn't block it off properly with a wall of metal with circular perforations in it, because without that it could ingest a few gallons of water into your engine on a wet racetrack, a little detail that escaped many of those building Cobra replicas years later.

The gearbox was changed to a Ford "top loader" 4-speed formerly used in the Galaxie. Shelby had sold at least 15 small block Cobras with automatics so an experimental one was fitted to a 427 Cobra. Al Dowd, a Shelby executive, was driving it one day when it decided to downshift to low at 85 mph all by itself. The result was some hair-raising pirouettes on the 405 freeway. When Dowd got back to the shop, he told them where they could put their automatic and the subject was not revisited.

With the big engine, everything else on the drivetrain had to be beefed up to take the torque, including bigger half shafts, bigger hubs, more widely spaced bearings, tapered instead of roller.

Shelby didn't budget any money for a new body. So once they had the chassis, the crew building the car was forced to stretch the old one over the wider chassis to make do. Shelby's crew started out with the same center body section as the small block Cobra, but once they mounted the coil spring suspension, the larger brakes and huge new wheels and tires, then the old body wouldn't cover it so new metal was spliced in between the old body panels to be able to bring the fenders out to where they needed to be.

The same bonnet, trunk lid, doors and windscreen were used as on the small block Cobra. The result was a car that, while strongly related to the 289 Cobra, looked like a 289 on steroids. Much of the new shape came from the 289 Cobra FIA racecar, which had wider rear fenders (the Brits call them "wheel arches") yet it still had its own distinctive shape. Today, more than four decades later, the shape of the 427 Cobra remains one of the most muscular shapes ever seen on the road and has to be considered a "pure" design in that its shape was entirely dictated by its wider frame, and larger wheels and tires, a perfect illustration of the old Bauhaus design-school's maxim: "form follows function."

Just as they had done earlier with one of the small block frames, Ford glommed onto one of the first chassis of the big block car to see what they could do with a better body design. Since it was only going to be a styling exercise, they didn't care about the engine which is why it was fitted with a small block 289 instead of the thundering big block. The result was called the "XD Cobra" formally and the "Bordinat Cobra" informally, the second name because, within the company, it was thought that the only reason the car existed was that styling chief Eugene Bordinat wanted it built in order to show Bill Mitchell over at GM that he too had enough clout to have custom cars made for himself.

(Mitchell, of course, went over the top with his fleet of customs, even having a Ferrari V12 put into a Firebird!) The unusual feature of the XD Cobra, which looked something like a Corvette, was that the body was made of Royalex, a rubber-like material with "memory" to allow small dents to be popped out with the application of heat. It remained a one-off.

The first two big block Cobra racecars, ironically, still had the small block car's smaller grille cavity, which leads to endless confusion in picture identification of the first 427 Cobras racing. Suffice to say the first time a racing 427 overheated, out came the tin snips and a suitably larger grille mouth was created. Twin electric cooling fans also went on a lot of the cars used on the street, so that there would be some airflow while the car was stopped at a light.

The exhaust pipes on the road car were routed out under the rocker panels behind the door, but on Comp cars they were routed right through a hole cut in the body side below the "breathing gills." The four-into-one headers fed into a pipe of about 4 inches in diameter. This pipe ran along the rocker panels and was famous for painfully branding the ankles of passengers who weren't warned about this danger when entering/exiting The Beast.

The 427 immediately set news standards for its accelerative ability. It weighed but 2300 lbs., about 600 lbs. of which was represented by the engine.

The Competition version weighed even less because the high riser equipped engine was fitted with aluminum heads, and an aluminum intake manifold, and the car was sold sans bumpers.

To demonstrate its speed potential, one of the many Cobra PR men (Shelby would hire and fire them in droves) remembered the stunt a British automaker had done years earlier—seeing how long it would take to go from a standing start to 100 mph and back again. The Shelby PR releases claimed that Cobra team driver Ken Miles took a "street car" shod with Goodyear Blue Dot street tires and accelerated from 0 to 100 mph to 0 in 13.2 seconds. More impressive yet was the 0-60 mph time of only 4.2 seconds, a time that took a decade for any other road car to beat. Drag racing tests usually produced a trap speed of 110 mph with an ET just over 13 seconds.

How fast was it? Well, aerodynamics prevented it from ever catching the low slung GT40 coupe, which in Mk. II 427-powered form could reach 210 mph on Ford's test track. A good guess would be 175 mph for a stock 427 Cobra, but Dick Smith, who won several Championships in his race prepped S/C, was officially clocked at 198 mph at Daytona in 1966. That was scary because, as Smith admits "If you hit a bump at that speed, it might jump over a whole lane."

Truly in the white knuckle class was the amount of available torque on tap: over 425 ft-lbs. in the street model, something John Christy of Sports Car Graphic said, was "more what you expect in a dump truck."

Christy, testing one in *Sports Car Graphic*, pointed out that the torque was available from around 2800 rpm all the way to 6500 rpm. Even a judicious application of throttle could have your rear tires broiling at at any point, in any gear.

A ride could be truly terrifying for the uninitiated. In 1966, Ken Miles suckered an Australian reporter clad in a dress shirt, slacks and tie, into taking a ride around the Lakeside circuit "down under" in a Comp 427 equipped with a low cut racing windscreen for the driver only. The reporter enjoyed the ride but by the time they returned to the pits, the reporter noted his shirt had been ripped to shreds by them going 140 mph in the open car!

There was certainly no road car on the street at the time (other than the Ford GT40) that could touch it. No Ferrari. No Maserati. No Corvette. And the Dodge Patrol cars used by the California Highway Patrol topped out at a mere 140 mph, at which point your average 427 Cobra driver was still contemplating upshifting to fourth gear. Shelby originally planned to crank out several hundred 427 Cobras, hoping racers would buy them after they saw the factory team win.

The first few off the line were competition cars; some complete with dry sump oiling (recognized by the extra filler cap on the right front fender). Estimates vary on how many of these *Uber*-Cobras were made, estimates varying from, on the small side, three and on the large side twenty-two and maybe only the first one to three had the dry sump installed.

The trouble was, Shelby was so busy cranking out Shelby GT-350s on the one hand and remaining 289 Cobras and running Ford's Le Mans effort with the GTs that he flat didn't get enough 427 Cobras made by the time the FIA inspector arrived to count cars.

Big mistake. The magic number he had to have on hand was 100, lined up and ready for inspection.

This time Shelby's luck ran out, unlike when he had only a handful of the 260 Cobras and the 289 Cobras built but still won approval. This time the inspector was dutiful. When he couldn't count 100 big block Cobras all lined up (most experts agree there were 51 completed 427s at that point), he walked out, homologation denied.

Shelby was stuck. Sales plunged. Certainly, the lack of homologation put racers off because, if they were not able to run in A-Production, then they would have to run their 427 Cobra in the Prototype class where, as fast as it was, it would get its doors blown off by the much faster and more aerodynamic Ferraris. Secondly, the car might have also been thought of as too expensive by many racers.

For whatever reason, demand was slack and Shelby was left with a veritable sea of unpainted alloy stretching seemingly to the horizon. (These can be seen in the official 1965 aerial photo of the factory, where a magnifying glass reveals dozens of unsold unpainted 427 Cobras baking on the tarmac of LAX). One Cobra expert opined: "That dumb shit. He only had to make 49 more to make it legal."

Hey, easy to say with the hindsight gained by looking back over 40 years. The fact was, in judging Shelby's faux pax of 40-plus years ago, you have to reckon with the situation such as it was in the field of battle at the time.

Back in Dearborn, Ford was at that point tightly focused on a single objective—making the Ford GT a winner instead of a loser. They could care less about a class win with the Cobra. As far as they were concerned, the Cobra was already history.

Ford had already poured several million into the Ford GT and, goddamn it, that SOB better come across the finish line first at Le Mans in '65 or heads would roll at The Glass House (nickname for Ford World HQ in Dearborn).

Ford historian Tom Corcoran even claims that Shelby had to promise Ford that he wouldn't field any factory comp 427s in 1966. They didn't want any further embarrassment like Cobras beating Ford GTs.

Ford's attitude might have been akin to the situation of the U.S. Army-Air Force in 1945. If you walked in the Pentagon's door in 1945 and said you had found a way to make the prop fighter faster you would have been told "No thanks, we're going jet."

Ford's indifference to the 427 Cobra left Shelby in a quandary. Fortunately one of his dealer/salesmen came up with a face saving solution similar to what English automakers had been doing for generations—making a street replica of the racecar so that would-be racers could drive on the street a car that was essentially the same mechanically and cosmetically as the racecar.

For example when the British automaker Frazer-Nash made a racecar decades earlier, they made replicas for regular road drivers who wanted to "pose" as racers but didn't intend to race them. Turns out owning a "Le Mans replica" was a well established grand tradition in England. Jaguar did the same with the D-type. While the real D-type was a car worthy of winning Le Mans, which it did, the street version was that same car with the addition of some civilian items; i.e. a proper glass windshield, side curtains, a rudimentary folding roof and mufflers. It was called the XK-SS. With the S/C, Shelby was merely following a Grand Olde well-established British tradition.

Taking up on his saleman's suggestion, Shelby mounted just enough street equipment from the road car parts bins onto the already-built racecars so he could sell them as S/C models, "S/C" a phrase which can be interpreted to mean "street/competition," or "semi/competition."

The S/C was the one to have if you were a hot dog street racer because it was "barely" street legal (especially those side mount exhausts) but it was as fast as the racecar. And you could still take it to the track on weekends and race it. (Best to keep the rubber bushings though as the bronze ones used on the racecars could jar your fillings loose on the way to the track).

The S/C roadsters had a wee disadvantage—a bit less trunk room because they had humongous 42-gallon gas tanks compared to a mere 18-gallon version used in the road car. The S/C cars also were built without the glove box, ashtray, lighter and door parcel holders. They had a special instrument panel gauge layout.

Decades later, when Cobra clones started showing up all across America, the model that the customers clamored for most despite all its inconveniences, was the S/C because it was far more exciting than the road going 427 with its smooth hood and hidden exhaust pipes. The operating theory among Cobra buyers seemed to be: "If you're gonna be a bear, be a grizzly."

Automobile magazine put it best in 2004 when writing an article called "100 Coolest Cars:"

"There is nothing nice about a Cobra. It's stripped down to the essentials—a big engine, a small car, and four wide tires to keep the whole business on pavement. It's loud, smells like gasoline, and shakes, shudders, and bucks. It makes your arms tired and your feet hot. You nearly crash about once every 10 minutes. It's so damn wonderful that you can't believe it."

Except for a few races run by Miles and one with Phil Hill at the wheel, the Shelby-American team never ran the 427 big blocks as factory racecars. This was because Ford, with every eye focused on the Ford GT, had neglected to budget any funds for a team of factory 427 Comp cars. But the cars saw racing, Shelby selling them to several teams who ran them successfully.

One of the most successful 427 Cobra racing efforts was that run by the Essex Wire team who ran the U.S. Road Racing Championship (USRRC) with a Shelby Cobra 427 (CSX3009) and a Ford GT40. Essex made wire and one of their biggest customers was Ford. They thought running Fords would make Ford happy and it did. The white Cobra was nicknamed "Ollie the Dragon," because it had the un-nerving penchant of belching a two-foot length flame out the hood scoop when you started it cold. Team Leader Scott told a journalist that if you didn't keep throttling up, the big Weber downdraft carburetors would erupt in fire. Driving it was not easy. Dr. Dick Thompson told the same editor that the Cobra "was beautiful in the straightaway, but because it didn't have much in the way of brakes, it was always hairy in the turns."

As a pure application of "there is no substitute for cubic inches," the fact that the tires were too small to adequately put the power to the ground or that the car had the aerodynamics of a brick didn't hold it back. Ed Lowther, one of its drivers, once commented that the car was so good that "I can start the engine on this car, put it in gear and go to the men's room, and it will win the race by the time I get back!"

The Essex team Cobra 427 was eventually sold to Ed Lowther, who went on to win many races in it, though historians still argue if collectively it won more than, say, Sam Feinstein's big block, which was still racing long after Shelby had shut down Cobra production. In fact Feinstein's racing record in an "obsolete" big block Cobra proves that the big block Cobra had more "legs" than Shelby ever dreamed of. Sam bought Ollie from Lowther and raced it all the way from 1968 through 1976. The car has a record that includes finishes in the top ten in every USRRC race it entered. It clinched the 1966 SCCA A/P National Championship and came in second to Dick Smith's 427 Cobra in 1967, only seconds behind it at the finish. Sam finished third in CSX3009 in the SCCA A/P Northeast Division in 1968 and the next year, driving a backup 427 Cobra, finished second in the standings. In '70 and '71 he came back with Ollie, finishing second place in the SCCA A/P Northeast Division Championship in '70 and '71 and 3rd in '72. In '73, and now we're a long ways away from the shutdown of Cobra production, Feinstein was still soldering on, becoming the SCCA A-Production National Champion and A/P Northeast Divisional Champion and winning the ARRC at Road Atlanta. In 1974, Sam again took the NE Divisional Championship and finished 6th in the ARRC runoffs. On one track he defeated the British Leyland supported E-type Jag that had cost $100,000 to build. In 1975, some ten years after his Cobra was built, he dusted it off once more and took another A/P NE Divisional Championship. The car wanted to win. Proving that at one race, he qualified on the pole, was rammed in the back on the first lap, which lost him time trying to fix the rear axle...and still went out and finished fourth in the event.

So even though the small block Cobra was easier to race, the 427 Cobra was a car that fought being shunted off into the "obsolete" category for as long as it could. Then there were the forgotten years until vintage racing came along, giving it a new venue and now the big block Cobras once again have a chance to rule...

There were even a couple 427s built by Shelby-American especially for drag-racing, these known as "Dragonsnakes." One was campaigned across the U.S. by Shelby-American, another by a private team. Both, like their 289 predecessors, set many NHRA class records.

Shelby originally marketed the 427 Cobras for roughly $6,000 for the road car and $9,500 for the S/C. The full comp 427 was around $10,500.

Shelby only managed to unload 348 of the coil spring Cobras in the car's original era, the last one reportedly rolling out of the A.C. factory in 1967, that one bearing the serial number CSX3360. The original figures of how many they made of each model are still debated today. At the time figures first appeared in the various Shelby histories, they weren't that significant, but now that some big block Cobras are valued at $1 million each, the exact number made way back has become super critical to collectors.

Most experts agree that the majority of 427 Cobras—292 cars of that total—were street models. Most experts also agree that there were at least 19 full Comp cars, though some estimates go as high as 22. Most experts also agree that there were approximately 31 S/C Cars. In that total though are included the two prototypes, the one-off Daytona coupe, three that were only built as chassis, and the British/European market cars with coil sprung chassis but small block engine.

It's the oddballs that have popped up out of the woodwork that continue to confound any sincere attempt at a precise accounting. The still existent Super Coupe (427) accounts for only one big block chassis not built as a roadster, but then there's anywhere from one to three chassis that there's no record of Shelby-American having ever completed at the time. Not counting the 30-plus chassis that Shelby had serial numbers issued for but didn't build. Still, another oddball is the Ghia-bodied Cobra 427 roadster that Shelby had Ghia knock out in 1965 in the hopes of keeping the Cobra going—a design roundly rejected by Ford. That car's fate is unknown. It hasn't been seen in 40-plus years.

Plus Ford used up one coil spring chassis in the Bordinat Cobra show car, another big block not finished out as a roadster. And there's one 427 Comp roadster in England that frightens the women and children every time it goes out on the street, it cunningly clothed in the sheep's clothing of a 1953 Fiat 8V body (that one takes a lot of explaining involving a crash and a readily available Fiat body).

And so it goes, the mystery deepens.

Shelby might have inadvertently sewn the seeds for one source of confusion about how many 427 Cobras were made because, in a weak moment, Shelby allowed A.C. Cars Ltd. to continue the same arrangement with the big block Cobras that they had had previously enjoyed with the small block and set up a parallel production line for UK and European-market models.

The plan was that A.C. would use the improved big block coil spring chassis and 427 body style but their version—the Mk. III—would have only 289 engines and be fitted with wire wheels, so he wouldn't have to worry about them siphoning off his market. Not to mention A.C. feared no one in Europe could afford to drive it in 7-liter form. Call it "427 Cobra Light" if you will. The U.K. ones were right drive but A.C. also sold them in Germany and other European countries in LHD versions. The U.K. market versions had a serial number that began with the letters "COB" which logic leads one to conclude stood for "Cobra Of Britain." Continental models had a "COX" designation (for Cobra Export) and were left-hand drive. They weren't called Cobras and the serial number plate clearly identified them as being built by A.C. Cars Ltd, not by Shelby-American.

Shelby's generosity in allowing A.C. to produce parallel models for overseas sales came back to haunt Cobra collectors decades later.

The predictable happened: when Cobras began to soar in price Stateside, some speculators took COB—or COX—serial-numbered cars, doctored them to look like CSX Cobras (mostly involving changes in the cockpit "tub") and then boldly attached CSX i.d. number plates punched with the authentic serial numbers of real Cobras that had been thought to be totaled or burned out in accidents. The result caused consternation decades later when some of these cars reached the auction block, as owners in more than one country surfaced, claiming that they in fact owned a Cobra with the same chassis number! The reason for this is that the originals "thought" destroyed had in fact been rebuilt and were now competing with the "ghosts" that had appeared using their chassis number. The Cobra insiders called the newcomers "air cars" because, when you tried to trace their history back through the previous owners, at some point they seem to have materialized out of thin air.

Other flies in the ointment later appeared to confound any diligent documentarians—oddball facts like the time Bob Negstad, the Ford engineer who helped design the chassis, long after the last A.C. Cobra rolled out of Shelby-American, talked a Michigan company he was a consultant to into buying six to eight coil sprung Cobra chassis to use as the foundations for electric cars. And then there were at least four chassis ordered by movie production companies as the basis for movie stunt cars, such as in the film "Monte Carlo or Bust." How many of these chassis have since mysteriously metapmorphized into 427 Cobras? And, if so, what serial numbers do they use?

Over in England, A.C. dropped the A.C. 289 eventually, and commissioned a more svelte successor, something more along the lines of the Maserati Mistral spyder, this one built on a stretched 427 chassis, and bodied by Frua in Italy who also did the Maserati Mistral spyder. It was sold as the A.C. 428. Actually the very first one had a 427 and an alloy body but A.C. quickly discovered the 427 was far too much of a brute to drive on UK roads, so they sourced 428s, which were cheaper for them to buy as well, and mated them to automatics as well as ZF 5-speeds and sold just over 70 of them of them in both coupe and convertible form. Because the production versions had heavy steel bodies (though the prototype was aluminum), they weren't as swift as the 427 Cobra had been and topped out at near 145 mph. They lag far behind 427 Cobras in value. Americans view them only as potential fodder for the Cobra mill, figuring "Hey, what we have here are A.C. coil sprung chassis and A.C. registrations. If we can just shorten the wheelbase a tad...."

The value of the original 427 Cobras continues to climb to astronomical sums, especially when a car can be documented all the way back to the original owner. Those who watched eagle-eyed and bought them when they were forgotten entities made out like bandits; perhaps the most brilliant buys being those effected during the first Arab Oil Embargo of '73 when in California you were restricted to buying $3 worth of gas which is about how much fuel a 427 Cobra uses up on one good burnout. During that time 427 Cobra prices reached a low ebb of $7,500.

Decades later, after many a supercar has rolled across the stage at many a preview, the appearance of a 427 Cobra at any International Auto Show can threaten to upstage almost any new car. To stop that from happening, automakers usually insist replica cars or classic cars be displayed separately, preferably a few floors away from what they're trying to sell.

It was perhaps inevitable that Ford would drawn back to the idea of making their own big block Cobra again, drawn like a moth to the flame.

Shelby? Well, as you can see in a chapter ahead, he's making them too. But old timers like to tell the story of that period when big block Cobras were almost "throwaways." This was in the early '70s.

Shelby, as a member in good standing of a renegade group of aging playboys called *Los Visatores Conquistadores*, joined them in a one of their annual runs from Reno to Elko, Nevada.

Now Elko, if you have ever been there, is not one of your big Nevada metropolises. It probably has a total of five churches and five cathouses. And the barefoot boys were not going to the churches. Each member of the group selected his four wheel weapon of choice, and this, mind you, was when it was still considered more-or-less legal to drive an old tatty Ferrari 250P, GTO or LM on the street, sometimes still wearing its Le Mans inspection stickers. We're talking cars that could do 180-200 mph. Plus there was no speed limit to speak of in rural Nevada. (And now it can be revealed that the group had an "in" with the California Highway Patrol that caused the constabulary to "look the other way" as they were headed for the state line.)

Shelby naturally chose a 427 Cobra. Not an ordinary one. No, he was the boss, remember? Back when he had been making Cobras, he had a couple fitted with twin Paxton superchargers, one sold to comedian Bill Cosby and one for himself. (Cosby used it as a subject for a record album called *Bill Cosby at 200 mph*).

Well, turns out on the way to Elko, maybe the old Snakemeister put his foot into it a little too heavy and blew the engine. So he parked it by the side of the road and by the time he'd unhooked his long legs from under the wood-rimmed steering wheel, along came fellow Conquistadore Bob Estes in one of those new fangled Lamborghini Miuras, the one with the sidewinder V-12.

Shelby got into the Miura and off they went, leaving the still smoking 427 Cobra by the side of the road.

Abandon a 427 Cobra? A one-off with a zillion horsepower? (Actually it was a "two-off" rated at around 600 hp.) Well, to understand this, again you have to put this incident in its proper time context. At the time, Shelby was long since done with Cobras. It was the early '70s and nobody was collecting Cobras yet and vintage racing was primarily old prewar cars so nobody cared about Shelby's funky old sports car.

His thought at the time was probably: "Why worry? I can always build another."

Cap d'St. Antibes, France, 1960.

It was 1963. It was the crack of dawn on a peaceful Mediterranean sea. There was the shuffle of feet as the crewmen scrambled up on deck and assembled on the fantail of a large motor yacht.

They lined up, each inspecting the other's uniform before the Patron would emerge.

One man ran up the stars and stripes.

They were anchored off Cap d'St. Antibes, on the French Riviera. It was the start of another glorious summer day.

A few minutes later, the skipper came up on deck. Behind his back he was referred to as "The Deuce." He was clothed only in a white terrycloth bathrobe and velvet monogrammed slippers, and sipping a cup of coffee. He walked down the line as the crewmen stood at attention.

Once he passed, he spun around.

"At ease, gentlemen," he said, and then headed back down below deck.

The skipper was Henry Ford II, a former U.S. Naval officer, who liked to retain some Navy traditions even on his private yacht.

Henry Ford II was not a born racer like his grandfather, the first Henry. Ford Motor Company was a company that had an "institutional history" of racing—in 1901 Henry Ford raced an established auto builder/racer named Alexander Winton. Ford handily won that race and his victory helped to establish his name in the automobile industry. In later years, he stepped into sponsoring racing on occasion as a means of garnering favorable public opinion.

His grandson, Henry Ford II, might be termed a "neophyte" when it came to racing. HFII had no doubt been to races, like the Indy 500 where his father waved a ceremonial flag or two, and he himself was known to like fast cars (having been given a Ferrari in the early '50s by Enzo Ferrari, a car later used by Ford's Engineering group), but he was not what anyone would call a card-carrying "driving enthusiast" though he was enough of a fan for styling to have ordered hand-made cars from Europe such as the one Facel built for him in 1950.

All that changed in the early '60s when he bought a yacht and began spending part of each summer anchored off the Cote d'Azur, the playground for Europe's rich and famous.

Call it middle-age angst (he was, after all, approaching 50) but it was as if he had suddenly realized he was a billionaire and he could be free of the staid family life he had in Michigan and instead live life to its fullest in Europe. He had separated from his wife, Anne McDonnell and would eventually divorce her.

It was on the Continent that he renewed his acquaintance with Giovanni Agnelli, an heir to the Fiat fortune, and the "model" for all playboys everywhere who were dedicated to the pursuit of *La Dolce Vita*. The silver haired trim, tanned and fit Agnelli had been an officer during WWII (for both the Axis when Italy was fighting the U.S., and the Allies when Italy switched sides) and his jet set friends all had big yachts, Ferraris and beautiful women in copious quantities. They spent their days and nights each golden summer moving up and down the Riviera downing prodigious amounts of champagne, driving fast and dining on gourmet food in eateries perched high above the sea and the common folk.

Henry Ford II developed a taste for this life style. What was not to like?

In 1960, at a dinner organized by a relative, honoring Princess Grace of Monaco, Henry Ford II had been seated next to a blonde Italian divorcee, Maria Cristina Vettore Austin. They hit it off famously.

Later on, she reportedly attended the Le Mans race with HFII and asked him point-blank; "Why doesn't Ford build cars that can win a race like this?"

Henry Ford II was stuck for an answer.

The truth was that, despite Ford being one of the world's largest automakers, they were a firm renowned for producing prosaic bread-and-butter cars.

Ford didn't have a racing department and they didn't have full-time racing engineers.

Their biggest support in racing was for NASCAR stock car racers. They didn't produce a sports car (their one attempt, the Thunderbird, having bloated from a two seater after '57 into a four seater that was, surprisingly, still raced but no longer considered a sports car).

Agnelli had close ties with Ferrari and even sat on the Ferrari board of directors. And all the Europeans Ford met who were at all enthusiastic about sports cars had stylish fast and loud Ferraris, Maseratis or Aston Martins or something from the "second tier" of sports cars like an Alfa or Lancia or Jaguar. They wouldn't even think of owning an American car, which were characterized in European films as huge land barges barely able to get out of their own way on the twisty byways of the Continent.

Sports cars, by contrast, were a European tradition. After all, on the Continent, countries are close together and you could shoot across a whole country in a single day on roads with unlimited speeds in Germany and Italy. "Grand Touring" was a concept finely honed since the Twenties and there were many makers of Grand Touring or "GT" cars.

In America, only a handful of people owned European sports cars, and most of those buyers were on the West Coast or East Coast, not in Detroit.

John Wyer, later to manage Ford's first year racing effort, tells a somewhat different story of how Henry Ford II got interested in endurance racing, in his autobiography, *The Certain Sound*: "A party of Ford top execs, including Henry Ford himself, had visited the Sebring 12 Hours in the hopes of seeing a Cobra victory. Ferrari had run away with the race, finishing first, second and third and Mr. Ford was reported to have said, 'That's the way to go racing. Why don't we buy those red cars?'"

Exactly how much influence Maria Christina Vettore Austin had on Henry Ford II isn't documented. The official line is that Christina was an "acquaintance" until after his first marriage was dissolved. But unofficially she was part of that jet set scene and HFII was most anxious to measure up to the Europeans in her eyes.

Henry Ford II's new attitude toward racing happily coincided with the recommendations of a young hard-charging engineer back in Dearborn named Lido "Lee" Iacocca.

Originally put in engineering because he was an engineering grad, Iacocca showed a real penchant instead for sales and moved over there. He had shaped up sales in several Ford sales districts before being moved to the central office in Dearborn where by the early '60s he was put into the position of General Manager at Ford Division.

Iacocca was interested in Ford coming up with what he called "youth market" cars to accomodate the swelling army of "baby boomers" born after WWII. Ford's research showed that by the year 1965, several million of these "boomers" would reach car-buying age. He and a number of other young Ford executives began meeting informally on Saturday mornings at a hotel near Ford HQ, called the Fairlane Inn, where they would have breakfast and meanwhile draft recommendations for prototypes Ford ought to be making as well as plans for Ford's participation in racing.

The recommendations by the Fairlane group were brought back to the Ford World HQ building in Dearborn and seeded several exciting new directions. The bubble topped "dream cars" of the mid-Fifties, with their simulated "jet exhausts" were forgotten. Ford's move made Bill Mitchell over at GM look increasingly silly, as he persisted in creating bubble topped jet exhaust concepts for some time to come, still thinking Americans could be motivated by "space age" themes. Ford's new theme was Italian, complete with Italian names, such as the "Allegro," a fastback coupe. Another was a Thunderbird with a fastback called the "Italiane." Henry Ford II was thinking both high performance and thinking Italian. Henry was, in short, trying to build an Italian car his rich Italian friends would respect.

Why Italian? Because the Italians, as a group, were dominating International sports car racing. Where in the early '50s it had been British marques like Aston Martin and Jaguar that won the big races, by the mid-'50s, it was Ferrari and Maserati who were taking all the gold.

To identify with the Italians if even by only having an Italian name for a car was exciting for Ford designers.

The young turks in the Fairlane group also recommended Ford ditch their adherence to the ban that all the Detroit automakers had signed in '57 to not promote car racing. All the Detroit automakers had secretly been continuing to promote racing anyway and Ford decided it was hypocritical to keep pretending they were living up to the ban when they weren't. So the group brought their unofficial recommendations into the company and found they were accepted.

The result was a total U-turn for Ford, and the funding of what became known as the "Total Performance" campaign which eventually saw Ford supporting entries in NASCAR stock car racing, Indy racing, drag racing, rallying, sports car racing, and numerous smaller segments of motor racing.

One of the first fruits of the program in the sports car world was the participation of Falcon Sprints in the Monte Carlo rally. The irony was that the Sprints didn't actually win the event overall but American car enthusiasts were cheered merely by the fact that American cars were at last worthy of competing in a European event. They were proof that American cars were no longer too fat to get around on the twisty roads of Europe!

Soon after that the Shelby Cobras began winning in sports car racing, and Ford was on a roll. Since the Shelby Cobras used 260 engines first and later 289 engines which were offered in other Ford cars. It was a natural tie-in to offer "Cobra" parts over the parts counter for Ford passenger cars including the Falcon, Fairlane, and later the Mustang. It was a successful program, creating a new source of revenue from those who couldn't afford an actual Cobra or a Shelby Mustang. At least the wanna-be's could afford the parts that made those two cars so fast!

Ford Motor Company also had an Indianapolis entry, and was competing at the brickyard as early as 1963. But it was one thing to win "Indy." Doing that only got you lots of ink in America.

What Henry Ford II wanted to do was have a world class win by having Ford Motor Company win a major sports car event in Europe.

And in sports car racing, *the* major event was the 24 Hours of Le Mans.

The Le Mans race, an annual event run partly on the village streets of a French village called Le Mans, was a veritable institution in sports car racing. Jaguar had won it three times in the '50s but by the time Ford got interested, Ferrari had become a perennial winner.

In fact you could say "Le Mans" pretty much made the Ferrari marque's reputation because in the marque's very first year on the market—1949—a Ferrari piloted by Luigi Chinetti, Italian-born but living in America, won the race.

And they won it five more times by 1963.

At first, Henry Ford II looked at the situation the same way his grandfather had when the original Henry Ford had attempted to buy Italian luxury automaker Isotta-Franchini (a sale nixed by Benito Mussolini who did not want to see a great Italian marque be Americanized). You just take out your checkbook and buy 'em. The American philosophy was "everyone has their price."

Ah, but the question was: was Ferrari actually for sale? Well, yes, as a matter of fact, it was.

Enzo Ferrari, around 1961, was suffering from the effects of a "palace revolt" that occurred when a number of his key engineers, including the head engineer, Carlo Chiti, had walked out. The protest was against his dictatorial policies, and some say, against his wife Laura's constant meddling with the racing team.

The dissident group attempted to start their own sports car firm, ATS, but that firm only lasted a year or two, as a result of underfinancing, overambition and just plain bad luck.

Through an emissary in Germany, Enzo Ferrari had let Ford know he was interested in a partial buy-out. His goal was to jettison the passenger car division and keep the racing car division as his own. Ford had slightly different aims. They wanted to make a road car that would carry Ford-Ferrari badges and a race car that would carry Ferrari-Ford badges.

Enzo Ferrari's firm made less than 400 passenger cars a year at that point, something a single Ford factory could crank out in ten minutes. Financially, the volume would be small potatoes for Ford but it was the legendary name they wanted.

Despite the glamor of the name "Ferrari," Ford was not about to make an emotional buy. Bean counters to the core, Ford sent a team of accountants to take inventory of the entire Ferrari factory and, counting every last nut and bolt, they came up with an assessed value of $10 million. By Enzo's way of reckoning, what he had was worth more than $16 million.

But it wasn't money that resulted in the two weeks of discussion ending with the Ford team being sent packing. It was ego, pure and simple. Ford might have been happy calling any racecars they created "Ferrari-Fords" and the showroom cars "Ford-Ferraris" but Enzo didn't want his proud name shared.

Plus he was said to be annoyed that Ford didn't seem at all receptive to his suggestion that they cut loose Carroll Shelby as part of the deal. The brash Texan race driver had been a thorn in Ferrari side ever since years earlier, he had offered Shelby a factory ride for a paltry sum, and Shelby not only refused but told him off in no uncertain terms.

Enzo didn't want to have to deal with fighting Shelby within Ford ranks. When the Ford officials came home empty-handed, Henry Ford II's response was in effect: "Screw him—we'll build our own damn GT car."

It turns out Ford actually had a good head start sitting down in the basement of the World HQ building in Dearborn—a mid-engined car with an aluminum body that had been built as a show car.

Until then, most Detroit automakers' show cars (with a few exeptions) were clumsily built under their pristine bodywork, often barely able to be steered up onto the rotating platform at an auto show, but this one—the Mustang I—had been designed by a British-born engineer, Royston Lunn, who had built it on the order of a racecar—tube frame, alloy body, good weight distribution.

When they began planning an endurance racer, Ford engineers realized after they studied the winning Ferrari of the 1963 race—the 250P—that the only way to go would be mid-engined because a mid-engined car, with its engine between the front and rear axles, had a better "polar moment of inertia"—which meant, when you went to change lanes, it could move faster than a front-engined or rear-engined car. And they also determined they would need over 300 hp.

The Mustang I had only a four cylinder powerplant, but it was a start as far as a configuration for an endurance racer.

Ford stylists began designing clay models of a coupe which looked at first like a fastback version of the Mustang I. A coupe configuration was chosen rather than an open car because a coupe was more aerodynamically stable than an open car.

In a speech in 2005 at the Saratoga Auto Museum, Shelby summed up his early involvement: "We'd been doing pretty well with Cobras, but we knew we had to go to a midship-engined car to beat Ferrari. Don Frey, Ray Geddes and I went to Europe in '63 to see who we could have partner with us in building a car. We made a deal with Broadley, to have him come over and work for us. We hired John Wyer to build some cars."

Shelby had raced for Wyer, and knew that Wyer understood the game. In his autobiography, *The Certain Sound*, Wyer said, "Some people say that Aston only won because the Ferraris failed to finish. He debunks that, saying Le Mans is all about a battle of strategy and tactics."

Eric Broadley, founder of a firm called Lola, wasn't Ford's first choice. They knew the partner would have to be British because the English at that point were the most prolific racecar builders (and it was, after all, where Shelby had gone to source his Cobra sports car and a subsequent mid-engined club racer).

Among the other prime candidates was Colin Chapman, an engineer, and a somewhat dashing mustachioed ex-RAF-pilot who had been building his own sports cars since the '50s, each one more innovative than before. He was already Ford's partner in an Indy car, Ford having paid for Chapman to design a chassis to carry their 256 cubic-inch "Indy" engine.

Chapman may have concluded that, of all possible contenders, he had the inside track on receiving a contract from Ford should they seek to develop an endurance racing car.

But, if he thought that, he was dreaming because he had created enemies at Ford, those who had noted with displeasure that Chapman had garnered an outsize amount of publicity when the Lotus-Fords that Ford paid for first showed up at Indy. Ford had commissioned the cars but somehow, to Ford's annoyance, it was always the name "Lotus" which was mentioned first in the press reports, much to the chagrin of Ford. And, at times, it seemed as if Colin Chapman was getting more ink than his patrion, Henry Ford II!

Secondly, Chapman was producing a variety of cars, including GP cars, Ford's Indy cars and road cars so the question was: how much could he take on additionally?

Then Ford officials went to Le Mans and saw the Lola Mk. 6 in action. This was a low slung sports coupe designed by Eric Broadley, another creative English racecar builder, whose firm Lola only built racecars, not road cars as well like Lotus. Broadley had done a lot of clever things with the unitized steel-chassied car but the features that impressed Ford most was that it was:

—capable of nearly 200 mph
—mid-engined
—already Ford-powered.

Ironically the Lola Mk. 6 didn't finish. Driver David Hobbs missed a shift, jammed the gearbox and crashed. But the Ford contingent saw in this car the makings of a winner; a car with soul. They met with Broadley who, unlike Enzo Ferrari, was willing to deal. The truth was that Lola was on the ragged edge and Broadley needed the money. He was willing to join with Ford in a development deal for their car and signed on as a consultant for 18 months.

Shelby, in contrast to his usual up front style, remained a behind-the-scenes player in steering Ford to Broadley. Shelby had not only loaned Broadley the engine he had used in his car at Le Mans in '63, but loaned his ace fabricator Phil Remington to Broadley to help sort his car out before he shipped it to France.

This time Ford avoided the mistake they had let happen with Chapman and built a new facility in England called Ford Advanced Vehicles. The hope was that whatever emerged would not be called "Lola-Ford" by the press but simply a "Ford." John Wyer had left Aston Martin so he was considered the perfect man to run FAV.

Broadley was at loggerheads with the Ford engineers almost from the beginning. The car was built Ford's way, with Ford over-ruling Broadley at almost every critical juncture. Broadley had wanted an aluminum chassis; Ford went instead with a heavy steel unitized chassis. It would seem, in retrospect, they had too many people who thought they were in charge. Certainly Wyer was not happy with having to corral Broadley. Wyer wrote in his autobiography *The Certain Sound* that "Ford had sold the farm three times and we had more chiefs than Indians."

In his autobiography was a warning of the trouble that can ensue from such a situation: "any blurring of the lines in the chain of command on an organization chart will eventually lead to trouble." And it did.

The GT40 used a fiberglass body. As part of the deal, Ford took two of the remaining three Lola Mk.6s that had been built and began using them as mules, substituting parts they designed to test them out.

The engineering group at Ford had first thought of using the four cam Indy engine they scheduled for Indy in '65 but then decided it was too frenetic an engine to take a 24 hour race and dropped back to their second choice, a 256 cubic-inch (4.2 liter) alloy block pushrod V8 that could produce about 370 hp with four Weber carburetors.

The fly in the ointment was a 4-speed Italian gearbox made by Valerio Colotti. It had been used in Maseratis up to 5 liters before but was considered the weak link in the design.

Ford's styling department in Dearborn came up with a body shape they thought would work, but they were operating a bit in the dark since Ford Motor Company had never designed a car that went that fast, "fast" being over 200 mph. They made 3/8ths scale models and sent them for aerodynamic tests to the University of Maryland and various tweaks were made that they thought would give them something stable at speed.

But the proof is in the pudding, and you have to do on track testing to know what you have, not just extrapolate from scale models. In April 1964 Ford sent the first two prototypes to Le Mans for the annual test week where automakers are offered the chance to sort out the cars they plan to race in the 24-hour event in June.

Ford had two very experienced test drivers—one being former Le Mans winner Roy Salvadori (with Carroll Shelby in '59). The first problem they had was handling. In Wyer's autobiography he says the cars were acting so squirrely that it was found impossible to exceed 6000 rpm, equal to about 170 mph, whereas the cars were geared for over 200 mph at 7,000 rpm. In other words, they weren't proving to be any faster than the Cobra roadsters with hardtops or the Daytona Coupe. Then both GTs crashed, not from hitting anything but from simply becoming aerodynamically unstable and flying off the road at speed. Wyer feared the worst when Schlesser crashed and he saw wreckage strewn for 100 yards down the track. He says "I thought the driver had been killed but now there was Jo walking back to the pits."

Taking the cars back to England, Ford patched one together and began doing tests until they discovered the cause for the crashes—the rears of the cars were lifting at speed like an arrow without feathers. How could this happen when scale models had been tested in a wind tunnel at the University of Maryland? In his autobiography Wyer commented: "I was always distrustful of scale models." Then Ritchie Ginther, a California-based test driver, suggested "Why don't you add a rear spoiler?" Ginther had been on the Ferrari team in '61 when he had suggested they add those to the Ferrari 246 Dino and they had done so with good results. Once Ford designed a sharp-edged ducktail spoiler into the body shape at the back end, downforce that the spoiler generated kept the Ford GT stuck firmly to terra firma.

But the Ford GT obviously was not still ready to race. The cars were far from sorted out. Just one example cited by Wyer in his autobiography was the nylon fuel hoses. They melted from the heat loads. Wyer hadn't known they were using nylon until it was too late and they began to fail. But Le Mans beckoned and, taking the long view, Ford knew they needed more "real world" experience. So they went to the Nurburgring in Germany a few weeks later unprepared. This was their first real race with the car and they were going up against Ferrari who had been competing there for over a decade. But the test session was needed, even if it meant sending a first timer car up against the pros from Modena.

The Ford GT did well in practice, but during the race the suspension collapsed on the rough pre-war track.

After beefing up the car, a few weeks later, at Reims in France, Ford again entered the Ford GTs but this time it was the gearbox that failed. Some say the Indy engine itself was proving unreliable but that Ford blamed it on the gearbox so they wouldn't tip off Ferrari that their engine couldn't take it. In his autobiography, John Wyer says he knew that ZF in Germany had a prototype gearbox almost ready to go but he couldn't hurry them, the Germans being much too methodical to rush the program.

But an obvious sign that Ford had lost faith in the Indy engine was in the last two events of the season, when they switched to the same engine Shelby was using in the Cobra—the cast iron block 289, basically a hotted up version of what you could buy in the Falcon Sprint or Fairlane 500. John Wyer reported that it was only 41 pounds heavier than the alloy block engine it replaced.

The last race of the season was at Nassau, in the Bahamas. This event was run under rules that promoter Sherman "Red" Cruise made up as he went along so there were no points to be accumulated toward a championship. But the Ford GTs, as technologically advanced as they were, were humiliated there by some experimental tube-framed lightweight Corvette Grand Sports, part of a short-lived plan by Corvette engineer Zora Arkus-Duntov to make some cars that could beat the Cobras.

Despite the Nassau triumphs of the Grand Sports, the General Motors Corporation subsequently pulled the plug on Duntov's grandiose plan to mass produce the GS coupes and he had to find another way to promote Chevrolet racing since it was obvious that The Board was now intent on adhering to the 1957 ban on American automakers promoting racing.

According to Marshall Gardner, an FIA historian, Ford was seriously ticked—the John Wyer team had prepared the GT40s but won not a single race at this point. "Nassau was Wyer's Waterloo. It completely embarrassed the Ford senior management who all came to see the cars run, as well as holiday with their wives."

The European press had a field day over the repeated failure of the Ford GTs. It was as if the mighty Goliath had been felled by David and his slingshot.

Henry Ford had started the GT program on the idea of portraying Ford as a technology leader but so far they had been bested at every venue by a tiny Italian company, one they could buy and sell if only Ferrari would let them.

Chapter 10- Victory!

Shelby-American headquarters, Los Angeles, November 1964.

It was bright and sunny in California, one of those crystal clear days in winter when you can see forever. A great day for flying, thought Carroll Shelby. That's if he had the time, which he didn't.

Not anymore.

He made a lunch appointment at the Black Whale North of the Marina and then flicked through the piles of folders on his desk to see if there was anything he could handle quick before goin' over to the Whale.

He had a heap of work to do—there was ramping up small block Cobra production, scheduling more Cobra coupe production over in Italy, and of course the 427 Cobra he was developing. And then there was that dad-blamed Mustang Lee wanted him to make solely to embarass the hell out of Chevy's Corvette. Hell, the Mustang was already way beyond sales projections but there was no arguin' with Lee.

On his desk he saw a telegram from Miles, a preliminary report from Nassau. Miles still saw potential in the idea of making a big block Cobra in spite of the fact their prototype had blown its engine. But he half expected that—the "flip-top," the second generation big block prototype, had been cobbled together in what—a coupla weeks? For Ford's GT team, though, Nassau was a bruiser.

Bruce's GT only made it three laps into the preliminary Tourist Trophy race while Hill came in third in the preliminary race and lasted only to lap 17 lap of the next race. As drivers, they were both the best there was, so Shelby knew it had to be the cars where the problem was. For Penske, Hall and those guys (backed under the table by Chevy), it was like shootin' fish in a barrel.

The phone rang and his secretary poked her comely face in the door.

"Carroll?"

He looked up.

"Yes?"

"It's TWA. They got a coupla packages for you from Dearborn."

"Oh, yeah? Well, I'm fixin' to go out to lunch, I'll drop by on the way and pick 'em up."

She smiled.

"No, you're gonna have to send a truck. These are big packages...."

By November of '64, the Ford Corporation bit the bullet and finally called Carroll Shelby for help. Shelby was already on their payroll but somehow Ford had ignored the former Le Mans winner when it came to preparing the Ford GTs or running the team.

Why did they need him when they had John Wyer? First off, Wyer was not what you could call a "hail fellow well met." Shelby, by contrast, had an engaging personality and could "talk the birds out of the trees" as they say in Texas.

And Shelby was a good talent spotter. Plus he had won Le Mans in '59 for Aston, when the team manager was John Wyer. Wyer wasn't being fired, it was just that his responsibilities were being re-aligned. In his autobiography, Wyer comments dourly, "I was a commander who had failed to win battles and the reasons were unimportant."

Shelby was left a message to pick up two "packages" at Los Angeles International Airport. The "packages" were two Ford GTs, cars that a Texan would say "looked like they were rode hard and put away wet." They were covered with dirt and sea salt, obviously sent straight from Nassau. Shelby's brief: to sort the cars out. Shelby hired Ken Miles, an expatriate from England and Bob Bondurant, a promising Corvette racer he had been using in Cobras and Bruce McLaren, a racer from New Zealand who yearned to build his own sports cars. As they thrashed the GT40s at Riverside, one thing broke after another, and Shelby began throwing out whatever broke, including the Indy engine, the Italian gearbox and even the wire wheels.

He put in their place the Cobra engine, a 5-speed gearbox from Germany, the one made by ZF that Wyer had ordered the year before, and mag wheels from Halibrand, who had supplied Ford's racing Thunderbirds back when the T-bird was a racecar.

Shelby already knew a lot of what the car would need from the racing program in had run in the U.S. road racing club series with Cooper Monacos during the 1963 and 1964 seasons. He had ordered the English racers, which normally were powered by a hot four cylinder and stuffed 289 Cobra engines into them (the press insisted on calling the result "King Cobras") and found all sorts of problems with the 289 and the Colotti 4-speeds. Every flaw he found was summarized and the information sent directly to Ford so they could correct the problems in the Ford GTs.

Once Shelby got the Ford GT program, he had the Coopers, which were stone-age in comparison, rolled outside his factory with "for sale" signs on them, and got serious on behalf of his sponsor.

Shelby and Ford redesigned the Ford GT with a deeper grille cavity, a front spoiler, and much more prominent air vents in the hood to exhaust out hot air that had passed through the radiator.

An irony of Ford's endurance racing program was that the man Henry Ford II had put in charge was not a car guy when he was hired.

Henry Ford II realized that winning a race like Le Mans took a certain amount of strategizing. Leo Beebe, who had become a friend of Henry Ford II during WWII while they were both in the Navy, was a former high school coach teaching basketball, football, and track. When HFII left the Navy to take over Ford, he hired Beebe as a sort of personal troubleshooter. He knew Beebe had a special talent for motivating people just as he had motivated his athletes.

In 1964 Beebe was appointed Special Vehicles Manager at Ford. When he reported for duty, Iacocca handed him a tall order: win at Indy, win at Daytona in NASCAR and, oh, by the way, win at Le Mans as well.

Since he had never in his life been to a car race, Beebe faced a bit of a steep learning curve, but within a year he started delivering Ford victories.

The Europeans had looked down their noses at Shelby's Cobra engine. They ridiculed its low cost materials: its iron block instead of aluminum, its use of pushrods instead of overhead cams like European cars had and its low 6,500 redline where Ferraris screamed to as high as 10,000 rpm. They made fun of the lack of dry sump lubrication (Shelby had thrown it out). Ferrari thought they could beat the Ford GTs on fuel mileage alone, because the Ferraris had smaller engines that used less fuel.

Ferrari's biggest strength was that sports cars were the only cars they made where a company like Ford was used to making low cost cars for the masses like Fairlanes or Falcons and didn't know where you needed to spend the money to make a special part. Shelby had educated Ford fast on the Cobras but they still couldn't get them used to the idea of spending heavy bread on critical parts. It amazed Ford engineers to find out that one set of Ferrari pistons cost more than a whole Ford V8 for a Falcon. Ford was not used to making finely honed and expensive parts to such exacting tolerances. Asking Ford to produce a meticulously honed endurance racer was like going into a burger joint and ordering a gourmet meal that you would expect to be on a par with something you could order in a Michelin Guide 4-star restaurant.

For instance, Ford first used cast iron crankshafts, where Ferrari would whittle theirs out of solid billets of forged steel.

If we were talking rifles, it was Ford's lever-action Winchester cowboy rifle against a hand-made Weatherby. One was a tool, the other a work of art.

Ferrari was every sports car racer's dream company to work for. You knew they were going to stay in racing, where if you drove for Ford, you never knew when they might pull the plug at any time.

Now in charge of the whole GT racing program, Shelby again retained Ferrari's World Champion Phil Hill as his lead driver and signed on Ken Miles and Bruce McLaren, who had been in on the development program he had done on the GT40 after Ford's flopperoo the first season.

Ford had hoped to have American drivers, thinking perhaps it made the team more promotable, but the truth was that you could count the number of Americans on one hand that were used to running a venue like Le Mans at night in the rain at speeds near 200 mph. The only American names that came to mind were Le Mans veterans like Phil Hill, Ritchie Ginther, Walt Hansgen, Masten Gregory and Dan Gurney.

Shelby hired three of them but the "Kansas City Flash," Masten Gregory, Shelby's friend and rival from his early days of racing, escaped his dragnet. This was a serious mistake, as Ford would find out at Le Mans the following June. A biographer of Gregory says it was because Wyer thought Gregory had screwed up the Ford GT's gearbox while driving at Le Mans in '64 and was against hiring him, though even Wyer had to admit himself that it was a bad gearbox. Shelby didn't give a damn where someone was from—he hired the men he thought could do the job.

For '65 Ford's racing management also decided to go whole hog and use their "secret" weapon in the Ford GT—a 7-liter Ford engine. Actually that engine was hardly a secret. The 427 FE-series big block engine had been around for years in the hulking Galaxie, which was a NASCAR winner time and time again, but nobody at Ford had ever thought of it as a sports car engine. But, after seeing numerous small blocks blow up, Ford's racing czar, Leo Beebe, became exasperated and got around to asking: "What engine do we have around here that doesn't blow up?" and everybody pointed to the engine that had been winning in NASCAR for years—the awesome 7 liter 427 which could pump out 425 hp without half trying.

And do it all day long. True, it weighed 600 lbs., maybe twice what a Ferrari V-12 weighed, but the Ford GT chassis was strong enough to take it. Bob Negstad, Ford's racing engineer, especially liked it because it had 480 hp in racing trim and was still understressed at that rating. Negstad says "We drove the track manager at Ford's Romeo Proving Grounds crazy with the speeds we were running."

John Wyer, who had run the Ford GT Racing program in 1964, was dead set against the big block engine. When a Ford engineer pointed out it was a durable engine, Wyer countered with the droll comment "We race with cars, not engines," knowing that once the larger engine was adopted, everything in the drivetrain would have to be made heavier to cope with the added torque and weight.

Ford ordered some GTs with engine bays wide enough for the big block and also ordered their own transaxle designs, using gears from the front-engined Galaxie put into a transfer case.

Shelby's men knew the 427 intimately, as they were already using it in the 427 Cobra. They also knew the 289 was at the end of its rope—it had delivered a few Cobra Daytona coupes into the winner's circle (class wins; not overall wins) by sheer grit, but the 7-liter Ford GTs were running another 30 mph faster than the 170-mph Daytona coupes, so there was no use in trying to talk Ford into saving the small block version of the GT. Ford wasn't interested in any victories in this class or another. They wanted one result—first overall.

So Ford's effort in International endurance racing for '65 would be two pronged—first the small block 289 powered GT40s in the production GT class and then the 7-liter for the prototype class. For the 7-liter models Roy Lunn insisted on longer noses for better air penetration. The long nose cars still weren't stable so a "fix" was to attach fins to the tail, similar to those on a '59 Cadillac. These vertical stabilizers helped them track straight.

True, the 7-liters were clocked at an impressive 210 mph down the Mulsanne straight but at Le Mans, even with all the King's horses and all the King's men, Ford failed.

Not even the small block Ford GTs finished. Ford was almost embarrassed when the only Ford that finished at Le Mans in '65 was a Daytona coupe, which hobbled all the way to the end of the race, running on seven cylinders and with low oil pressure, but still, as you would expect of a car with the soul and spirit of a thoroughbred, finishing 8th overall.

The fact that the Daytona was still on the track at the end of the race was testimony that Shelby had the bugs worked out of the Cobra more than Ford had with the GT. Wyer subsequently commented in his autobiography Ford had spent 4 to 6 million and "were still not in sight of the target."

The diagnosis: the Kar Kraft-built 5-speed transaxles in the 7-liter GTs had failed. Worse yet, a Ferrari won. And the co-driver in the Ferrari? None other than Masten Gregory, an American from Kansas City—a guy Ford should have hired, if only to prevent him from driving for the enemy.

Enzo Ferrari had the last laugh on Ford that year, because in protest to the FIA (racing organization) refusal to homologate his 250LM as a production car the year before, he had pulled out his factory race team and let private entry Ferrari teams carry the ball so it was the private entry North American Racing Team that had won Le Mans for the Ferrari marque. That humiliated Ford more—it wasn't even a factory car that had beat them!

Shelby, in a 2005 panel discussion presented at a the Saratoga auto museum, laughed when he told the story: "Ferrari never gave Chinetti (owner of North American Racing Team) a good car. And driving it was Masten and Jochen Rindt, a Grand Prix driver who didn't have much interest in Le Mans cars. In fact, I heard Rindt disliked the car because it was running poorly and wanted to do a 'clutch job' on it (AKA a 'valve spring test,' where a racer over-revs the engine in neutral to blow it because he doesn't like the car) but somewhere around the fourth hour, Masten was runnin' in first and when he came into the pits he finds Rindt in his street clothes. Rindt thought they had a bum car and was fixin' to go home, so Gregory talks Rindt into putting on his driver's suit again and going out and Rindt figures 'well, I'll just drive the wheels off of it' so they both beat the hell out of it, runnin' it flat out for the next twelve hours. Masten was haunted by the idea it was going to blow up."

It didn't. The amazing thing was that the Gregory/Rindt Ferrari was actually running better at the end of the race than it was at the beginning. It was a car that, like a thoroughbred race horse, actually *liked* to go fast, in short, a car with abundant soul. It delivered them the victory.

Ah, the anguish in the Ford pits....

In his autobiography, John Wyer pointed out how much that loss hurt Ford's image: what had started as a PR excerise intended to improve the image of the company had so far done nothing but harm. First of all, Wyer pointed out, the giant comes and does it all wrong and that made the public root for the underdog. It was widely said in the European press that only Ford could have made Ferrari so popular.

There was a press conference following the race. Max Muhlemann, one of Shelby's legion of PR men, was quoted in the book *Remembering the Shelby Years* as being worried that Shelby would use the press conference to blast Ford for not preparing the cars right (Shelby was in effect handed the 7-liter cars already built and prepped by H&M and Kar Kraft, an in-house Ford shop in Dearborn, yet he had responsibility for running them). But instead Shelby just came out on the dais and dropped one line: "Next year, Ferrari's ass is mine."

Henry Ford II was not pleased.

Shelby told the publisher of the *Robb Report* in an interview in the year 2000 what happened when he went back to Dearborn in '65 after Le Mans. "Henry

Continued on page 113

American millionaire Briggs Cunningham tackled Le Mans several times, first using Cadillacs, but then trying his own designs. This is his 1953 Cunningham car, powered by a big Chrysler 5425cc 300-hp pushrod V8, with bodywork designed according to the theories of the famous aerodynamicist, Dr. Wunibald Kamm. With drivers Moran/Bennett, it finished in 10th in 1957.

Hizzoner himself, in Europe sometime back in the early '50s, still wearing his chicken-pluckin' overalls left over from his failed career as a poultry farmer. Shelby went to Europe in the company of fellow Americans Phil Hill, Dan Gurney, Masten Gregory and Ritchie Ginther, all in search of the elusive "factory ride." They all got the ride eventually, some with more than one factory team, but Shelby's driving career was cut short in 1960 when his heart ailment forced him to quit.

Portrait of a winning driver—Shelby with race queen. Shelby won so many races in '56 that his pearly whites were common in pictures shot in victory circles back then. He later married one of the race queens, though he likes to cross that one off his list of "official" marriages since both the marriage and divorce took place South of the Border! *From the Villem Oesthoek Collection*

Shelby drove a Maserati Tipo 61 "birdcage" his last year as a race driver. The car was called a "birdcage" because it was made of tubing so spindley that, without the aluminum body panels, it looked like a bird cage. It was powered by a powerful four-cylinder engine.

Where it all began for Shelby as an automaker—an A.C. Ace. The English car was sold since '53 with a variety of six cylinder engines, first with the ancient A.C. engine, then with the Bristol (derived from a BMW engine), and finally with a Ford Zephyr six. It was declining in popularity when Shelby came along, jammed in a hot-rodded Ford V8 and created the immortal Cobra.

The year is 1962. Still in Venice, running his company out of Lance Reventlow's old Scarab shop, Shel' rolls out three racing Cobras that went to Sebring in 1963. These were the first three rack-and-pinion steering cars.

1963 Le Mans. Ed Hugus, one time WWII paratrooper, runs around his Cobra as his car is refueled. Shelby snuck into Le Mans in '63 on cat's feet to test the weather before officially entering under the banner of the Shelby-American team. One of the two-car Cobra team, officially entered by the *London Times*, finished 9th overall—not bad for a brand new marque.

The essence of a small block Cobra, a 289, this one sporting the seldom-seen painted wire wheels. Originally, the chrome wire wheels were optional.

Ford hated the Cobra's eggshell-thin body so they took one of the first cars they got from Shelby and experimented with this svelte coupe body design wrought in fiberglass. But then they never went anywhere with it beyond the show circuit. It was called the "Cougar II," and still survives today in a Detroit historical museum.

The Cobra sports car sprang from the already existing A.C. Ace. The small blocks, like this 289, most resemble the later Ace models. When Shelby's Phil Remington first got to working on the Cobra, he had to modify the body in several places to accommodate wider wheels and tires and to stiffen the body (for instance, shortening the trunk lid depth).

A Daytona coupe. Shelby built but six, but they were enough to wrest the World Manufacturer's Championship in 1965 away from his archrival Ferrari. Ford withdrew support for Shelby's Daytona coupes for the '66 season, because as fast as they were, the Daytonas weren't fast enough to beat the Ferrari prototypes which is why Ford backed the Ford GTs instead.

One off-shoot Shelby did with Ford's approval in the sixties was the prototype Sunbeam Tiger. Shelby was a consultant when this car was developed out of the Sunbeam Alpine, basically a Cobra wannabe with a Cobra-type V8 engine. Shelby appeared in their ads, but he never considered it as a threat to his Cobras because it was heavy and shall we be generous and say "squirrelly" in handling.

British-born expatriate Ken Miles was arguably one of Shelby's greatest drivers. He frequently raced against Shelby in the early '50s when Shelby was still race driving, then later worked for him as a race and development driver. He was killed testing the experimental prototype Ford J-car, a predecessor to the Mk. IV, at Riverside in 1966.

Sebring '65. Shelby threw everything into this battle at Sebring in '65—look close and you see Daytona coupes, Ford GTs and Cobra roadsters. Ford was almost embarrassed to run their super high tech mid-engined GT40 alongside the Cobras (which descended from the 1953 A.C. Ace) but the GTs weren't reliable enough yet to go it alone.

Two Cobras—a 289 parked next to a 427. These are originals. Today, the small blocks would be worth over $400,000, even with no racing history. The big blocks run from $450,000 to $500,000 with no racing history. Add more for one with a documented racing record. The small blocks are easier to drive; not so wicked as the 427 which even Shelby says, "Will kill you in a second."

Phil Hill, a cultured USC student before he dropped out to become a mechanic at a Jag dealers and later a pro racer, was a World Driving Champion (for Ferrari) before he ever signed on as a driver for Shelby-American. He not only raced against Shelby in the '50s but even partnered with him as co-driver in a Ferrari at Sebring, a fiasco of a race where they fought their way to victory over 12 hours only to have their 1st place finish taken away by inept scorekeepers.

Ford's whoopy-do high tech car in the mid-'60s was the GT40-designed in Dearborn, built in England—but it laid a big egg in '64 racing, so sheepishly Ford went hat in hand to Shelby to make it right. Shown is the first GT40 Shelby developed, in practice at Le Mans in 1965. Shelby had changed the engine, gearbox, wheels and refined the body shape to make it a winner.

A big block 427 Cobra road car, as identified by the small gas cap and the presence of a glovebox door. The 427 Comp cars and 427 S/C cars had no glovebox, and a bigger Monza "Quick-fill" snap open gas cap nestled into a cavity in the right rear fender. The Comps and S/Cs also had side pipes sprouting right out of the body side and larger gas tanks.

You want to add fuel to the fire over whether the A.C. Cobras of 1962-'67 were British cars or American cars? Well, as documentary evidence on the British side, we introduce into evidence this shot from the A.C. Cars Ltd. assembly line in Thames-Ditton, England, of 427 chassis being hand rolled down what the Brits laughingly called an "assembly line." There was no "line speed" like in Ford's automated Dearborn factory, and it was frequently interrupted for the regulation "cuppa." The chassis, bodywork, seats. upholstery, windscreen, springs, brakes and suspension arms were all made in the Olde Sode for this most American of American cars.

Another stalwart from Shelby's early days of racing who later stood him in good stead when Ford handed him the Ford GT to develop was Ritchie Ginther, a Californian who had raced against Shelby earlier when Shelby was a race driver. Ginther had started his driving career earlier than Shelby and even won a coveted spot on the Ferrari factory team, a spot Shelby claims he was offered but refused.

The Cobra Daytona coupe, whipped up by a young protégé of Shelby's over the beefed-up chassis of a Cobra roadster, proved the equal of the Ferrari 250GTO fastback in speed. Here is a Daytona at Sebring in '65. It was powered by the same 4.7 liter 289 that powered the Cobra small block roadsters. Only six were made and today each is worth several million dollars.

Your stock fastback 1966 Mustang. With a 289 "Hi-Po" K-code engine, it was a pretty hot number all by itself but today it is worth about one-fifth of what a '66 Shelby Mustang is, though, in point of fact, they were both born in the same Ford factory once upon a time.

Ford also budgeted Shelby a pittance to build some for-racing-only Shelbys for SCCA racing in '65 and '66. This GT-350 was called the "R" model and had a heftier horsepower output, plexiglass side windows set into aluminum frames, a double-size gas tank (made out of two stock gas tanks welded together) and other features. This is a prototype while it was still being finalized. Wheels are American Torq-Thrust "D" that only the R-models came with.

Le Mans '66. Chris Amon waves as co-driver Bruce McLaren aims their winning GT40 Mk. II down the dirt return road. Ford spent over $12 million to reach this point, but the victory still pays dividends for Ford in the showroom four decades later.

Shelby's world-wise and cynical factory workers called the Daytona coupe the "slug" but they called this 7-liter version the "Super Slug," pictured here at the Monterey Historic. Shelby bankrolled it initially after Pete Brock pleaded for a follow-up to the small block coupe but then pulled the plug when Ford made it clear all they wanted to see in winner's circles was the higher-tech Ford GT. It was finished two decades later by enthusiasts.

Shelby's cosmetic changes to the Mustang 2-plus-2 fastbacks to make them Shelbys were small indeed in '65 and '66, mostly unseen at first glance. The items that visually separate this '66 Shelby from the Mustang fastback of the time in the '66 shown here are the rear 3/4 windows, the hood scoop and side scoops. Wheels are stock '65-style Cragers, leading one to assume this is an early '66, which were left-over '65s.

The Ford GT didn't achieve Henry Ford II's goal—winning the 24 Hours of Le Mans—until '66 when it trounced the competition. Here's the opening moment of the race in '66, as Ford GTs tear out from the grid. Enzo Ferrari only sent a handful of factory cars to contest the dozen or so GTs, which was a big mistake.

The car that Ken Miles was driving when he crashed was an all-new design called the "J-car." It had a tub made of honeycomb aluminum sheets, a roof periscope, automatic transmission, and a number of other experimental features that Miles was evaluating. *Steve Fields collection*

At the 1967 Le Mans, Dan Gurney, racing's eternal barefoot boy with cheek, gives everyone a *Moet de Chandon* champagne shower whether they wanted it or not, starting a tradition among race winners. Henry Ford II wanted to make certain Europeans got the message that Ford could win Le Mans anytime they wanted so he budgeted another effort in '67, this time with the Mk. IV, which evolved from the J-car. Gurney and Foyt shared the winning car.

England in the the Sixties. Almost as a sop, Shelby agreed to let A.C. Cars Ltd. produce their own Cobras for sale in Europe, so first A.C. made small block body-style cars with small block engines for U.K. and Continental markets but then as Shelby went big block, A.C. created these so-called "A.C. 289" models, using the 427 Cobra's coil spring chassis and wider fender body but the small 289 V8 (4.7 liter) engine. Decades later, enthusiasts are tracking these down and stuffing

big blocks into them, making them into ersatz big block 427 Cobras. In the background, behind A.C. director Derek Hurlock, is an Italian-bodied A.C. AC428 coupe, the firm's effort at finding success for the 427 Cobra chassis in a more luxuriously appointed form. Just 27 open AC428s and 51 coupes were made before A.C. dropped the model after their Italian body builder couldn't fill the orders they had fast enough to meet demand.

The '67 and '68 Shelby Mustangs got a bigger budget in styling so Shelby could differentiate them more radically from the Mustang from whence they sprang. This is a '68, the first year a convertible was officially offered. A roof rollover bar was standard.

Shelby with two '68 Shelby Mustangs. Note the name "Cobra." In one of his all-time worst business deals ever, Shelby immediately sold the name "Cobra" to Ford for the princely sum of one dollar and Ford began plastering it on everything, including the Shelby Mustang.

OK, so they aren't titled as "Shelbys" and they weren't raced by Shelby-American, but by a "new" builder called Shelby Racing Co. Underneath these Team Mustang cars from 1968 were basically the GT-350's chassis mods. Unfortunately, in '68 Ford insisted on supplying the "tunnel port" 302 engines which blew up by the dozens. It was to lead to a gradual distancing of Shelby and Ford as partners. Though not Shelbys per se, many of these Shelby Trans-Am cars have been rescued from the crusher and are racing again in vintage racing, once again trouncing the

Camaros and Chrysler cars they beat the first time around.

While running a so-called "skunk works" for Chrysler, Shelby developed dozens of projects that never made it to Shelby-branded production cars, such as the heads for this 16-valve engine. A 16-valve four did make it into the TC by Maserati made by Chrysler but it used a head design from Maserati.

In the early '80s, Chrysler hired on Shelby to work with their front wheel drive cars. Some were built by Shelby and badged as Shelbys, others built by Dodge and carried Shelby decals. Chrysler totally fouled up any potential for collector value by over-using the name "Shelby" but still, all one has to say is that today's hot front wheel drive Chrysler cars owe their popularity to early efforts by Shelby to create a market by weaning Americans away from thinking V8-powered rear drive ground-pounders were the only way to find driving fun.

Almost four decades since he penned the original, Superformance of South Africa, a replica Cobra manufacturer, tied in with Shelby's '60s protégé, Pete Brock, to do a reprise of his Daytona coupe. It was premiered as the "Brock coupe." At first Shelby tried to block importation of his former protégé's creation to the U.S. But then, realizing it would take too long for him to tool up his own Daytonas, he inked a deal with Superformance to sell their car as a "Shelby coupe."

Shelby's one big venture at a modern design done on his own nickel was the Series 1, an Oldsmobile-powered car introduced in 1999. It was initially a flop with only around 250 of the planned run of 500 completed. Shelby still claims it was an advanced car, and as this book went to press, a new group of believers was mounting an effort to revive a mildly-restyled version to sell at a much higher price.

The Kirkham brothers, anticipating that the real history of the Cobra was made mostly by the small blocks, managed to come up with an aluminum body that would fit their big block 427 Cobra-style replica chassis. So now replica buyers can have the best of both worlds—the more subtle small block styling but the big block car's improved coil sprung chassis.

Hard life at the races. Tom McIntyre is doing a non-restoration job on his 427 Cobra; letting the chips fall where they may from racetrack use. When Shelby was racing the Cobras, stone damage on the soft aluminum was so bad the factory team cars were repainted between races.

Shelby's war with the Clonesters took a worrisome turn when the A.C. Mk. IV made its debut in America. An aluminum-bodied clone made by A.C. in England with an off-the-shelf Mustang 302, it had potential, being better built than all the replicas of the time. Unfortunately for its U.S. importers, it didn't have a big block and was rather timid in performance, so it died off, leaving the fiberglass-bodied cloned 427-powered Cobra replicas sporting ground-pounding big blocks a clear field.

Exotic cars with fancy Italian names come into popularity and fade away every decade or so, but there is something eternally endearing about the Cobra. This is a small block 289 spotted at a Palm Springs vintage race. Transverse stripes across the hood are in imitation of identifiers used by race teams to tell each of their team's cars apart from one another since the factory cars usually had identical paint jobs.

The press release for the Shelby CSX read: "While the CSX's extremely tractable 175 horsepower intercooled turbo engine will challenge any of today's 'muscle cars' in straight line acceleration, the Shelby really comes into its own on twisting backroads, where its sports car handling straightens out the turns. From its sleek front airdam and lower side 'skirts' to its wraparound rear spoiler, Shelby's CSX coupe is designed to cut through the air while hugging the road." Chrysler's ad agency copywriters really stretched to make Shelby's front-drive cars sound like the cat's pajamas but

Shelby never had a sufficient budget while at Chrysler to change the body like he had enjoyed at Ford in the late Sixties.

Laguna Seca racetrack, Monterey Historics, the tenth Cobra built. A 289 Cobra gets ready for a run. Note this one has two inset side pipes along the rocker panels—a side exhaust treatment usually only seen on Shelby's Daytona coupes. Owner Lynn Pack chose to emulate the style of some factory racers.

The Indy Pace Car for 1996 was the Viper GTS coupe, pretty much a "steal" from the Daytona Cobra shape even down to the 1965 Shelby team's dark blue-with-white-stripes paint scheme. The driver that year was Robert Lutz of Chrysler, the jet set executive credited with conceiving the idea of Chrysler building a Cobra-like car in the first place.

When Ford made a one-off concept car based on the styling of the '60s Ford GT40 race car in 2002, it was so much of a hit that they decided to put it into production. Signing Shelby on as consultant in 2003, the Ford GTs were coming down the assembly line by 2005, selling for an average of $200,000, $60,000 over the initial window sticker price.

Here, at Fontana in 2005, is a 2005 Ford GT next to the Shelby GT-5000 Concept. Improvements over regular include revised shocks, springs rates and upgraded stabilizer bars.

The Olds-powered Series I roadster was a totally modern car and almost put Shelby under. He regrouped and escaped being dragged down with it but by 2006 was already cooperating with a new firm intent on reviving what he considers one of his greatest cars.

A '07 Hertz Shelby GT-H. In a replay of the year 1966, Ford convinced Hertz to stock some Shelby Mustangs for rental to customers. The engine isn't the same as the regular '07 Shelby GT500 Mustang, though, instead it's a 325 hp version of the 4.6 V8 coupled to a five-speed automatic. Rest assured it has a throaty sound and the distinction of being made at the Shelby factory in Las Vegas. Since initially the only way consumers could buy them was to buy them from Hertz when they were retired (50 in August 2007), Ford announced the "Shelby GT," a model with all the same specs as the Hertz Shelby but without the Hertz color scheme, to be available to the public.

Ford called Don Frey, Leo Beebe and me in and said 'boys, here's your name tag.' It said 'Ford Wins Le Mans in '66.' After we got over having a heart attack, we walked back down the hall. It was Don Frey who pointed out that Mr. Ford didn't say anything about our fiscal responsibilities. There'll never be another Henry Ford, for the simple reason that no one will have that clout again. We spent the equivalent of a billion dollars in today's dollars in '66 and then again in '67."

Another story of Henry Ford's reaction was quoted in *Remembering the Shelby Years*. In this story, Frey reports to the top floor of the Glass House and a conversation between him and the chairman ensued that went something like this:

HFII: "Frey, you lost your ass."

Frey: "Yes, sir."

HF II: "Have I made myself clear?"

Frey: "How much money can I spend?"

HFII: "I never said anything about money."

Still another story narrowing in on the specifics of why the Ford team failed in '65 is that Frey got an order from HFII that said to the effect: "I don't care if you have to make the gears out of solid gold. We don't want any more transmission failures."

As bad as these tongue lashings were, the good news was that HFII was willing to carry on the fight for another year. Maybe the European press would still portray the battle as David vs. Goliath but the truth was that after Le Mans '65, Goliath was seriously ticked.

One of Leo Beebe's memorable moments from back then—right after the '65 Le Mans race, was recalled in an interview conducted by Fred Beall, printed in *Shelby-American* magazine (Issue #43): "Everybody was beaten and tired and had been up all night, some of them for several nights," said Beebe, "which is usually the case in preparing for a race. I got the key people together (in) a little hotel in Le Mans...here these guys are sitting around, all of us dragging, work clothes on and some of them greasy-faced, and pretty dispirited because we had put a lot into that thing. And we were losers. And I've always remembered the thing I said to that group. I said 'Gentlemen, this is a victory meeting. We start this instant to plan our victory next year,' and we really did. In that room, still in our dirty clothes, tired, bedraggled and dispirited, we concluding saying that we'd gone in with the wrong purpose: thinking that it was a speed race when it fact it was an endurance race. If you don't know what kind of game you're playing, you may play the wrong game—and that's exactly what we did. The emphasis on our earlier Le Mans efforts were on speed instead of endurance.

"So we started with the simplest question: 'What average speed for 24 hours would it take to win this race?' Then we went back up from there and everything we would do from that moment forward would be aimed at achieving the average speed we figured we would need to go (in order) to win that race."

To Shelby, celebrating the following year's victory a year in advance was a little like the Allies celebrating victory in Europe during WWII when they had only just taken the beaches of Normandy. But, hey, it wasn't his money.

The Europeans loved that the Americans came to joust with the European automakers and loved the fact that those same Americans were subsequently humbled in combat. Le Mans was run by the Automobile Club de l'Quest (ACO) and they were attuned to the sensibilities that the Europeans saw Ford as the villains because their cars were heavy, loud, and clumsy compared to the svelte Ferraris. The cars were as despised as American tourists, often pictured in French cartoons as fat, clad in Bermuda shorts and Hawaiian print shirts, and bumbling about with their Brownie Starflash cameras. But on the other hand, the organizers of such races as Le Mans were businessmen. They knew having a worthy adversary to Ferrari present on the field of battle would make for a higher ticket gate, so they encouraged Ford to enter.

As one French race driver, Philippe de Lespinay, commented: "They weren't supposed to win."

The French could be really perverse. They would invite Ford, but then look at their cars with a fine tooth comb to find ways to disqualify them. Of course, they were up against American racers with vast experience in NASCAR, USAC, and USRRC and the Shelby crew managed to put a few by them, for instance, making the car pass the height test by putting wooden blocks in the springs and then, after the car was tested for height, pulling the blocks out so they could run at a lower height and be more aerodynamic, thus saving on fuel mileage and being able to reach higher speeds.

Shelby outfoxed the French by making a Ford GT available to a French team from Ford of France. That way if the French race organizers disqualified a Ford GT for some infraction, they might have to disqualify the French entry as well, a move which would not sit well with the crowd.

For the next season, Ford decided there would be a few changes. For one thing, they realized that the steel chassis they were using was strong but too heavy.

Ford began exploring a true lightweight design—an aluminum floorpan and a honeycomb aluminum chassis, using aerospace techniques involving glue baked in an oven. This new design was called the "J-car" because it was built to meet the dictates of Appendix J of the FIA rules. The body style was radical—a full "flatback" station wagon style similar to a one off nicknamed the "bread-van" that the Italian design genius Giotto Bizzarrini had built years earlier for a Ferrari owner who had crashed his short wheelbase 250GT. The J-car had two features Pete Brock would have liked—a "Kamm effect" tail and a rear roof spoiler that was adjustable for angle at speed. Not to mention its neat tank periscope...

Though the failure at Le Mans in '65 wasn't all the fault of Shelby (other than the GT40 small blocks he prepared failing to finish) at the top floor of the Glass House a note of dissatisfaction was voiced about Shelby.

So, for '66, Ford had made a few adjustments in their Le Mans game plan, not all of them to Shelby's liking. Ford had longer standing ties with stock car racing builders so they called Holman and Moody (H&M), some good ol' boys from North Carolina who had helped them in preparing NASCAR stock car racers for decades, and put them in charge of a full third of Ford GTs that they planned to race at Le Mans in June.

And then they added insult to injury (from Shelby's point of view) by hiring a third team, that of Alan Mann, a British racecar builder who had done Ford proud with the Falcon Sprints and Mustangs in the Alpine and Monte Carlo rallies plus was even running (improbably but successfully) some huge Ford Galaxies in European racing along with some unbeatable Cortinas. Shelby could hardly complain about them. They had done a good job running the European racing effort with the Cobra Daytona coupes in '65, even though they had to cope with two mutinous American drivers in the persons of Alan Grant and Bob Bondurant. So Shelby could hardly claim Mann wasn't qualified.

Each team was free to prepare the cars their own way as long as they met the rules.

Ford may have been hoping that, with three separate teams all running under the umbrella of Ford, they were fostering three times the inventiveness.

And, in hiring Holman-Moody they might have been hoping for some skilled cheating, for NASCAR teams were legendary for ingeniously finding their way around the rules.

The Shelby crew hated the idea of sharing the effort and in the book *Remembering the Shelby Years*, Ford engineer Bob Negstad was quoted saying "For the '66 race, all the good stuff went to Holman and Moody while all the garbage—the stuff nobody wanted—was shipped to Shelby."

Carroll Smith, who Shelby had named head of the team at Le Mans, is quoted in the same book as saying that, during the race, "Ford officials wanted him to send false signals to slow the Shelby cars down."

Both remarks support the contention some Ford officials wanted a H&M-entered Ford to win at Le Mans, not a Shelby-American-entered Ford. But the infighting never got serious enough to hurt the corporation's chances of winning.

The rivalry between the sub-teams, especially between Holman and Moody and Shelby-American was seen in driver selection as well.

In *Remembering the Shelby Years*, there's a story about Shelby's ace driver, British-born Ken Miles, going to Ford's Kingman Arizona test track to test a prototype J-car. When he arrived he found that the Holman-Moody guys had just run a hot lap of 180 mph in the J-car.

Miles strapped himself in and the first lap he turned was clocked at 204 mph.

His second lap? 212 mph.

The Holman and Moody guys were awestruck and were overheard saying: "Did you see that—that SOB never even lifted in the corners."

After his two laps, Miles rubbed it in by coming into the pits and saying to Bob Negstad, a Ford engineer, in a voice purposely loud enough for the H&M guys to hear: "This is a really nice car, Bob. Did you want me to go fast?"

Negstad, in on the joke, said "No, hey, Ken, I just wanted you to check it out for the boys."

Thus was the first meeting between the tarheels and "Teddy Teabagger" (Miles' nickname from his habit of always brewing a cuppa before any race to relax himself).

Occasionally Miles' overconfidence would come a cropper though. One time he thought, being as he was King of the Cobras on the racetrack, flying a small plane would be no big thing. He borrowed an airplane and flew out to Riverside to do a car test. He was aiming at landing on the main straight but landed badly, damaging the plane. He emerged unhurt but had to endure endless ribbing from Shelby employees as the plane was painstakingly dismantled and hauled back to a repair facility on a flatbed. After that, he never mentioned his flying career.

One of the funny incidents recalled was that the Holman Moody team insisted on bringing their own pit crew to Le Mans, the Woods brothers, so they could effect fast pit stops. The Woods brothers were asked at Customs why their suitcases were so heavy and freely admitted that they were bringing plenty of smoked sausage from home. Damned if they were gonna eat any of that suspicious Frog food!

Shelby knew that when he hadn't brought the bacon home for Ford in '65, there would be hell to pay, and sharing the budget with two other teams was his punishment.

In '66 Ford also planned to stack the deck, putting so many Ford GTs on the grid that, by dint of sheer numbers alone, one of them would have to win.

So the result was, at Le Mans the following June, there were no less than thirteen Ford GT's lined up chock-a-block on the grid, but none of them the J-car which still had not yet proved itself to be any faster in testing. Ford had so many GTs entered in '66 that they had trouble finding enough good sports car drivers and had to recruit some talent from the ranks of NASCAR stock car drivers, like stock car racer and Indy veteran Lloyd Ruby.

Ferrari sent only three mid-engine P3s—their top of the line endurance racer—to fight the massive Ford entry. Enzo was guilty of underestimating the longevity of the Ford 7 liter engines.

The pressure was on for the Ford team. Just before the race a note was given to Leo Beebe, the Ford racing czar, on Henry Ford II's stationary. It read, "You better win."

The Ferraris blew up and, despite several of the Ford GTs blowing up as well, enough of them were still running at the finish for Ford to stage a controversial 1-2-3 dead heat finish (Ken Miles had been leading but, when Ford management decided to stage a three-abreast finish, he was told to drop back so they could all cross the line together. Well it didn't work because the McLaren/Amon Ford GT had started farther back on the grid 24 hours earlier, and the New Zealanders were ruled the winners instead of Miles).

Doug Stokes, a racing historian of the first order, says "Miles would have won all three of the great enduros in the same year. It had never been done before and has not been done since. It's said that it broke his heart."

In many interviews decades later, Shelby said he regretted going along with the decision to stage a dead heat because all of Ken Miles' friends wanted to see him take the unofficial "triple crown" of having won at Daytona, Sebring and Le Mans. Shelby, like many fans, subsequently felt Miles was robbed of a victory at Le Mans by company politics.

One Ford official who defends the last minute decision to stage the three abreast finish was Jacque Passino. Quoted in *Remembering the Shelby Years*, he said that Ford management was worried that the team members—each wanting to be a Le Mans winner—would crash or break if they were allowed to race each other to the finish. Said Passino: "So we concluded the only way to prevent this was to have a dead heat finish." From a sponsor point of view, it made perfect sense.

One of the most astute observers in racing was *Road & Track*'s Henry Manney who commented in the Sept. '66 issue of *Road & Track*: "It doesn't matter that there was a lot of curious comment in the French papers afterward about Miles and Hulme being almost dragged up onto the winner's podium first and then suddenly shoved aside for New Zealanders McLaren and Amon. It doesn't matter about Miles being a bit choked, as why shouldn't he be, having driven a lot of the race in front and done a lot of the development work. It doesn't matter that an English pilot was heard to remark in jest (not Miles) that those flyin' Antipodeans shouldn't have been transported after all that trouble for an American win, Ford didn't have an American driver. All that matters is that Ford won Le Mans after three years of hard labor and thus at one fell swoop gave International status (even if by association) to a branch of engineering that needs it plus a good crack in the eye for De Gaulle."

Leo Levine put it best in his classic history, *Ford: the Dust and the Glory*. "Three Fords had outclassed the finest field in the world in the most famous event of all, and had done it at record speeds. It was the greatest triumph in the 65-year racing history of the Ford Motor company, and when they played the 'Star Spangled Banner' a few minutes later, with the rain falling gently on the hundreds of thousands of spectators, the small group of Americans at the Ford pits stood just a little straighter. Phil Remington was one of them. Bill Stroppe was another. It as a long way from the dry lakes of the Mojave, where they took their first Model Ts and flathead V8s. Muroc was three decades and 7,000 miles removed. It didn't seem that far away."

At last Henry Ford had the results he wanted in the 24 Hours of Le Mans. And it had only cost him between $13 and $16 million.

Just to make it crystal clear that their '66 1-2-3 finish hadn't been a fluke, Ford decided to come back in '67 and do it all over again. This time they would be using as their main racer the Mk.IV, a car based on the J-car with its aluminum honeycomb chassis, but with different styling and more stout construction.

This was not a popular decision back at the Shelby plant on Imperial Highway.

This because, in August of '66, Shelby's ace test driver, Ken Miles, had been testing the original J-car at Riverside, California when the car inexplicably crashed at speed, killing him instantly. Ford, unsure of the accident's cause, increased the strength of the chassis and redesigned the body to be a more conventional fastback. Historian Doug Stokes states that Carroll Smith, Shelby's team manager at Le Mans, thought the composite structure had not been fully cured for strength. One has to remember that this was one of the first applications of composites in a race car chassis and it was somewhat of a "black art" at the time. Shelby's erstwhile hot rodder, "Rem" (Phil Remington) was sent back to Dearborn and, working with Kar Kraft, they designed a new body in 10 days. The new car tested out to be as fast as the Mk. II, and was a few hundred pounds lighter.

The light weight was key because a lighter car would be easier on brakes and fuel meaning less pit stops would be necessary.

When Shelby told his crew that Mr. Ford had ordered him to win in '67 with the J-car. they asked: "What if we don't win?"

Ironically the Mk. IV was still several hundred pounds heavier than the Ferrari P3, but by that time Ford realized that light weight was not as important as strength, not when you were running 24 hours. Again there weren't enough American sports car drivers who could handle these speeds of over 200 mph so NASCAR and USAC drivers were recruited and one of the most famous Indy drivers was signed on—Anthony Joseph Foyt, the tough-as-nails Texan oval track racer who had never even seen the Le Mans track when he was drafted to drive there for Ford. His partner would be Dan Gurney who had already raced at Le Mans five times.

Some couldn't see Foyt as a sports car guy but in fact leading up to his Ford appointment he had been road racing a mid-engined Lola T70, the car made by Eric Broadley after he had left Ford and gone back to building his own designs. In fact, he told many that his Lola T70 embodied all the ideas for an endurance racer that Ford had rejected.

Long time racecar observers were wondering if Gurney—an inveterate tinkerer who had the reputation of never being satisfied with his car (and screwing up many wins by fiddling with the car, often tuning it out of contention)—could get along with Foyt but they both proved to be consummate professionals.

Shelby, in a 2005 panel discussion, summarized the combo: "Everybody thought it was the worst combination ever put together. Foyt had just won Indy and was so full of himself, like a peacock struttin' around. At Le Mans we knew the engine and gearbox could take it. But the brakes. You had to baby the car because of the brakes."

There was one frightening moment during the race when three of the Ford GTs, in one horrifying instant, crashed because Mario Andretti, in the lead Mk. IV, found out the hard way that a mechanic had installed a brake puck backwards—a front brake grabbed, he spun out, hit the bank, and his car lay motionless in the center of the turn. Two other Ford drivers, who had been tailgating him at 180 mph plus, had no choice but to kiss the sand banks in order to avoid hitting him. Andretti walked away from the accident but knocked out 25 percent of the Ford team in one fell swoop.

But a few of the remaining Ford GTs outlasted the prototype Ferraris and Ford won the race. That irrepressible California boy Gurney immortalized this race finish by inventing the "champagne shower" soaking one and all in victory circle, even his patrons, Mr. and Mrs. Henry Ford II. Mrs. Ford was not amused.

But Henry Ford II was jubilant. Now it was obvious that Ford could win whatever they set their sights on. He promptly yanked the plug on Ford's endurance racing.

And why not? He had achieved his goal. Ford Motor Company was put on the map of automakers in Europe as a result of the victories and for years afterward made various cars they called "GT" though they had little to do with the cars that had won Le Mans.

Shelby went back to California. For him the Ford GT era was over.

Ironically, after all Shelby had to do with the Ford GT, Ford up and sold FAV, the factory that made the Ford GTs. Not only did they "sell" it at a bargain price but immediately awarded some contracts to the buyers—in effect they paid the new buyers to take it over. The new firm was JW Automotive, owned by John Willment and John Wyer. They were paid to prepare cars and were shipped millions of dollars in Mk. II parts which would have been Shelby's, had Ford not had them shipped to H&M. They hired British and European drivers and ran the next two seasons under a new banner.

At first, the Europeans laughed—how could the new Gulf team even think the heavy steel-chassied Ford GT40 could still be competitive when Ferrari had, by the end of '67, progressed to running sports cars that were really just wide-bodied Grand Prix cars? Plus now Porsche—Germany's premier sports car builder—was in the game and their racing cars were becoming more sophisticated and powerful race-by-race. The 240-mph 917, for instance, could leave the Ford GT in the dust.

But the pundits were wrong. At first, the Porsches proved to be too delicate for the pounding of 24 hours.

The GT40s ran with the reliability of Japanese railroad trains; plus the Gulf team had a new secret weapon—a 5-liter pushrod Ford engine that had "Gurney-Weslake" heads, basically heads that breathed better, designed by British engineer Harry Weslake years earlier for Dan Gurney's racing cars. With these heads the 5.0 liter Ford V8 put out almost as much power as the 7-liter Ford V8s the year before.

Ford did furnish the Gulf team with a couple of engines here and there but for the most part kept their money in the bank and enjoyed the spectacle of the Gulf team winning Le Mans twice more for the Ford marque without them.

The irony was that the Gulf team achieved their Le Mans victories not with the glued-together aluminum sandwich construction Mk. IVs with their big blocks but instead with the "old" steel-chassied GT40 hulls with small blocks—literally direct descendents of the GT40 that Ford had started with four years earlier. OK, they were heavy. OK, so the technology was old. But damn it, the GT40 was a car with the soul of a champion, a car determined to prove its worth despite the high-tech competition.

In his autobiography Wyer crows he was able to win Le Mans "with a development of the original small engine GT40 against very severe competition, at a small fraction of the ultimate cost of victory to Ford Motor Company. I am content to let the matter rest here."

Just how much Ford had been holding back on the good stuff didn't become apparent to John Wyer until after he left Ford and set up his own company.

In *The Certain Sound*, Wyer wrote that Ford shipped them "parts for 50 engines—four bolt main bearing caps, forged crankshafts, everything we needed to build reliable racing engines. Because of the alacrity with which these parts appeared after Le Mans 1966 it was impossible to believe that they had not been available for some time before and impossible not to suspect that they had been deliberately held back until after the 7-liter engine had won."

As for Shelby, his involvement with the Ford GT program ended in '67. He was still on Ford's payroll and tried to get some less ambitious racing efforts going, including one in Trans-Am. The Shelby Mustangs were no longer a concern—having been farmed out to an outfit in Michigan to assemble.

He tried to rev up a replacement for the Cobra, the Lone Star, a mid-engined road car powered by a 351 Cleveland and named after the one-time Texas slogan (Texas was briefly an independent Republic), but Ford was not interested. Only one was built over in England to a design by Len Bailey and it was sadly kicked from one used car lot to another, not as a "has been" but a "never was." It not only didn't have a soul, but never even had a life.

Henry Ford II eventually divorced his Italian wife the year after he retired in 1979 and became more of an Anglophile, lavishly sideburned and increasingly rotund, living much of the time in England in the lifestyle of an English country gentleman. He still hit the scandal sheets by marrying a third time, to former model Kathleen King Duross, a lady more than 20 years his junior and she remained his wife until he died on Sept. 29, 1987 at age 70.

At the time of his retirement, Ford Motor Company was the fourth-largest industrial corporation in the world.

Many other marques have won at Le Mans since, even Japanese firms like Mazda. But the four year reign of Ford at Le Mans will always be remembered, and even though Carroll Shelby didn't invent the Ford GT, all enthusiasts have to recognize that it was he who helped it become a winner.

Chapter 11- Shelby's Mustangs

Willow Springs, California, 1964.

The racetrack maintenance man at Willow Springs stopped sweeping and leaned on his broom. There was someone out there on the course, driving a little red hardtop at 10/10ths, hell, not just drivin', they were flat drivin' the wheels off it.

He edged up to the man in the Ford-badged transporter.

"What the hell is it?" he asked.

"Mustang," said the Ford man, nervous that he was revealing a secret.

The maintenance man spat on the tarmac and resumed pushing his broom.

"Gonna take a heap of work to make that sumbitch a racecar," he said.

Shelby was doing all right by Ford in '64 but he was about to become a whole lot more important because of a car called the Mustang.

Even though the Mustang, made from a rebodied Falcon, was a roaring success with 22,000 sold the first day, Lee Iacocca, then General Manager of Ford, wanted to really ruin Chevrolet's prospects in the youth market even more than the Mustang already had (it took Chevrolet two years to respond to it with the '67 Camaro) so he called up Carroll Shelby and told him he wanted to hear Shelby's plans for making the Mustang into a racecar. His goal? To make a version that would humble the Corvette in B-production racing.

On the face of it, it seemed a preposterous proposition—the Corvette being a sports car that had been raced since 1956, while the Mustang was a four seater with humble family car origins, and almost zero track time.

Shelby resisted at first, mindful of the fact that, at the time, he was a wee bit overextended what with managing a Cobra race team, selling car parts and making personal appearances and buying and selling real estate.

Then he thought about it some more. It is a little known fact today that Ford sent the very first ten Mustangs ever built (back in '64) to Europe to be prepared by Alan Mann Racing as rally cars. They competed all through Europe, in events like the Tour de France, creating a lot of excitement just as the first Mustangs were coming onto the market in the U.S. So the little "secretary's car" had already proved it had the mettle to perform right from the beginning.

And Shelby knew that they not only had Mann's phone number, but worse yet, Ford had the phone number of Holman and Moody in their Rolodex, and damned if Holman and Moody wouldn't just love to swipe the contract for making the Mustang a sports car out from under Shelby's nose! H&M, in fact, had prepared three Falcon racecars before the Mustang ever existed, and even entered one in the 12 Hours of Sebring, so, considering the Mustang was built on Falcon underpinnings, they had most of the work done already, and would no doubt like to remind Ford of that fact. As far as building 100 cars, hadn't they just done that with the 427-powered Fairlane Thunderbolts for drag racing?

So Shelby called Ford back. "Send over the Mustang" he said wearily. There was no saying no to Lee Iacocca.

Shelby sent a stock Mustang notchback and a test driver out to Willow Springs Raceway (the test track) and received back a not so favorable report. The car was a little wobbley at speed. A "flexi-flyer" to put it mildly.

But it had potential.

So Shelby persisted and, in a few weeks, had the first GT-350, now based on the new '65-1/2 2-plus-2 Fastback.

The name "350" was a bit of a ruse as the car did not have 350 hp. Nor did it have 350 cubic inches. The name came about after a long meeting on trying to decide the name. Shelby finally interrupted the interminable wrangling by asking the guy next to him: "How many feet is it from here to the shop?" The man replied "About 350 feet."

Shelby said, "That's the name—GT-350."

Shelby would have to make it a two seater in order to qualify it as a sports car, so they replaced the flip-up rear seat with a package shelf and put the spare tire there.

Shelby was working with the SCCA's technical director to make sure they did it right, and it was downright handy that the inspector, John Timanus, was a former instructor at Shelby's driving school. Shelby was told exactly what to do in order to make the car meet the rules.

With Ford backing behind him, Shelby was by now thinking big. He called up the San Jose CA Ford plant and ordered a three day supply of Wimbledon White 2-plus-2 fastbacks sent down to him at the factory he'd set up in a rented hanger at Los Angeles International Airport but, like ordering sandwiches at a deli, told them to "Hold the hoods, hold the rear seats, etc. etc." He had his own plans for those parts.

Ford already had a high performance engine they could ship the car with—a 289 that came in a model internally coded as the "K" car. Shelby was able to push the engine from Ford's rating of 271 hp to 306 hp merely by adding headers and exhaust pipes that came out in front of the rear wheels in the form of side exhausts plus an aluminum intake manifold and a fat Holley four barrel carb. Inside, he used a Borg-Warner T-10 four-speed manual transmission also used in the Cobra and Corvettes. For better handling, he relocated the front Pitman steering arm. It was only an inch but it transformed the handling of the car.

The GT-350 got a fiberglass hood with a functional hood scoop that gave it a more macho look than the production Mustang.

The suspension had to be beefed up to get rid of the soft feeling the stock car had on the race track. A larger front stabilizer bar, a good one-inch in diameter across, was installed, as were adjustable Koni shocks.

Out back, there was still a solid axle with leaf springs, standard issue on most Detroit cars for the previous 60 years. To be fair, he had tried a independent rear suspension but that version couldn't lap the track any faster than the solid axle with the same driver so he reasoned, why build it? Rear traction bars were added, the latter to stop the rear axle from winding up on acceleration.

The interior was no-nonsense, exactly what you would expect from the man that built the Cobra. It came only in black with a 3-spoke wood rimmed steering wheel with aluminum spokes like you would expect from an English sports car, and 4-inch wide Ray Brown competition seat belts with a huge aluminum buckle like something you saw in an old Indy 500 roadster.

Atop the dash was a big housing added for the tachometer and a clock. The price of the base Shelbys ran about $4,000—a good thousand above the regular 289 Hi-Po Mustang 2-plus-2 but if you wanted a race equipped one, you had to add thousands more.

Cosmetics included a paint scheme dreamed up by Pete Brock, his in-house designer, a paint scheme similar to the racing Cobras, only instead of white stripes on blue, it was the reverse, blue stripes on white like Cunningham's Le Mans racers a few years ealicr. The big Le Mans stripes running nose to tail were optional but the side of every GT-350 got two small stripes holding the words "GT-350" between them. Also on the exterior, all the original Mustang emblems were removed, Shelby adding a little running horse emblem on the driver's side of the grille and a little aluminum badge out back that simply said GT-350 like you were supposed to know it was a Shelby. There were hood pins so you could lock your hood with tiny padlocks and keep the curious out.

Shelby only expected to make a few hundred but had unexpected success with 562 Shelby Mustangs rolling out the door that first year. Almost forty were "R" models; which had features like plexiglass side windows with aluminum frames and a plexiglass rear window. The bumpers were removed and there was a unique fiberglass apron in the front replacing the bumper, which also fed air into the grille. Very macho was the aluminum panels riveted on the roof, replacing the heavy ventilation louvers on the stock Mustang.

The engine in the racing model got all sorts of special parts: a 7 quart oil pan, reworked cylinder heads, an oversize radiator, an oil cooler and a high rise aluminum intake manifold holding a 715-cfm center-pivot float Holley that wouldn't starve out when you threw the car into a corner like most carburetors did. The gas tank was two regular Mustang gas tanks welded together to hold 35 gallons. Accounts differ on how many were made, 34 being the minimum and 36 the maximum.

Out on the racetracks, the GT-350 proved to be a booming success right from its first race, which Ken Miles won in Green Valley, Texas, in February 1965. The GT-350s quickly established that they were the match of the Corvettes in B-Production and, at times, even finished ahead of Cobras, which weighed almost 1,000 lbs. less.

A GT-350 R-model was even run at Le Mans, in '67, entered and driven by a Belgian Shelby dealer, Claude DuBois. It didn't finish but its appearance was enough to reassure Shelby Mustang buyers that, yes indeed, their car had the cojones to run with the big boys.

The next year began the inevitable taming of the Shelby GT-350, a car which, in 1965, *Car and Driver's* Steve Smith had likened to "a brand new clapped-out racing car."

In '66, the car lost it's "take it or leave it" attitude on color. Now you could order black, red, green, and blue in addition to Wimbledon White. At first, the car was offered with a fiberglass hood, but complaints about poor fiberglass materials made Shelby redo the hood in steel.

An automatic transmission was also added to the option list.

Actually, the first 252 '66 models were leftover '65s. These still had the '65 standard features like Detroit locker differentials, and early style dash pads and interior trim, but more important, they still had the lowered front upper A-arms and rear traction bars. Shelby had stopped installing those on the remainder of the '66s to save time and money in production, with the result that four decades later the early '66s are prized more than the later ones because they are more closely related mechanically to the '65 models.

Shelby had been itching to get into the custom wheel business and by '66 succeeded so that the '66 Shelby was available with the option of his beautiful 14-inch 10-spoke mag wheels, which gave the car a more sophisticated look. The rear roof vent panels were also replaced with plexiglass windows which gave the car different styling than the stock Mustang 2-plus-2 fastback.

The engine and trans were still the same but now you could order an automatic. And because the traction bars used in '65 had come through the body, allowing fumes into the cockpit, for 1966, they were below the body. There was a downgrade to heavy-duty Ford shocks instead of the more expensive European-made Konis, which were now optional. The '66 was no longer a two seater, with the spare now back of the flip up rear seat.

But there were other goodies that were new and worth celebrating—one a supercharged option using a Paxton supercharger. Shelby ads for this option claimed a 46% power increase but you had to take this claim with a grain of salt—those were the days before advertisers had to be able to prove what they claimed in advertising. Shelby historians say only a handful were built at the factory with this option, but Shelby sold many more superchargers over the counter.

Another memorable version created in '66 was the Hertz GT-350. This came about when Shelby sent his General Manager, Peyton Cramer, a buttoned down preppy from the East Coast, out on the road to see if he could find some unsuspecting rental firm that might buy a few cars. Shelby had suspected Cramer might be too polished to wheel and deal like himself, who had been in the trenches in car selling. But Shelby worried for nothing—Cramer came back from his first sales call beaming. Hertz, he said, would take 1,000, almost double the entire first year's production!

Of course they wanted some in the Hertz colors, which way back when, in the firm's early days, had been black with gold stripes. No problem. There was also four other colors added later to the Hertz fleet that included the gold stripes too.

There are many entertaining stories about the Hertz cars that illustrate how clueless the Hertz officials were when they agreed to start renting high-performance cars. One is told by a retired Ford PR man who says they got a shipment of them in New York, and, since it was a cold winter week in New York, there was suddenly a rash of smashed Shelbys as driver's discovered the brakes don't work unless they're properly warmed up. Hertz had to put a special decal on the dash to warn drivers to warm up the brakes first and eventually the Hertz models got their own special brake system.

Stories abound of Shelby owners renting a Hertz car at $17 a day and 17 cents per mile and taking it to the racetrack to serve as backup. If they lost the engine in their privately-owned Shelby they could then borrow the engine from the rental. Still other stories say Hertz personnel found weld marks where a roll bar had been installed in their rental car during someone's rental period. Hey, for Hertz, it was an education.

An off-shoot of the '66 models that was a reminder that Shelby-American was still a one man company and not Ford Motor Co. making the cars (though Ford paid all the bills) was four (some say six) convertible GT-350 cars, which Shelby had made as special gifts for friends and relatives. Today these are among the most valuable of the '66s.

After seeing the success of the '65 and '66 Shelbys, Ford opened their purse up a little bit more and gave Shelby enough budget to create his own styling for the '67 model, which had a new floorpan. The goal was to not only make it more distinctive than a regular Mustang but to "preview" future Mustang styling. Shelby insisted on having a nose about four inches longer for a muscular look.

But the purists were miffed. The new car was heavier and none were prepared by the factory for racing. There was a lessening of the macho content, for instance, it no longer came with Tri-Y headers, but now came with stock cast iron exhaust manifolds which were heavier and less efficient. The 289 cubic-inch engine rated at 306 hp was still under the hood but now had a heavier load to haul around. One could praise the two hood scoops though, as they were functional, but the secret no one admitted was that they were located too far back to actually catch much air. To be praised, though, was the rear spoiler, functional at adding downforce to the rear in a nose-heavy car.

And in the new car, Shelby was creative in several ways compared to the '66. He followed the suggestions the Ford designers sent out to the coast to work on the clay model and put the high beam headlamps in the center of the grille, which gave the car a distinctive look like it had road lamps. The Ford rep assigned to the plant hit the roof when he discovered that this was not only against California law but violated the laws of several other states as well. Shelby was forced to move them further out after over 200 had been shipped with the first design.

Another Shelby gimmick got shot down as well. Turns out racecars often have a colored light on the side to tell the pit crew that their car is coming in. So Shelby had a red light put in the upper scoop on the car's roof. It was very distinctive but Shelby didn't know that in several states the only cars that can legally run a red light viewable from front or side is a police car or ambulance, so after a few were run off the line with the red lights, that disappeared as well.

Another innovation that even Ralph Nader should have thanked him for was making shoulder harnesses standard in front. The American auto industry had always lagged in innovating with seat belts, but Shelby, having put more than one racecar upside down in his time, thought if we don't try to innovate with seat belts in a Shelby, then what car should we do it with?

Out back there were huge Mercury Cougar taillamps, the Cougar being a fancier car than the Mustang but also built on a Mustang platform.

The big news for the '67 Shelbys was found under the hood. Gas was still cheap in those days and since the 289 was now hard put to make the car perform, Shelby offered the big block option—the monster 428 cubic-inch Police Interceptor engine, which though it was in fact one inch larger than the 427, was not nearly as powerful with 355 horses as opposed to the 427 side oiler's admitted 425 hp (real horsepower was more like 520!). Both engines were from the FE family but the 428 was not designed for racing like the 427 side oiler that had been the hero of NASCAR.

Rumors persist decades later that one could order a 427 side oiler in the Shelby in '67 but the only fully documented one is a car that passed through Mel Burns Ford in Long Beach, a car ordered by Shelby himself for tire testing. But odds are that any such cars were dealer installations or maybe "specials" built for friends of Shelby, among them a San Francisco cardiologist (when you have a bum ticker, it is not at all a bad idea to choose heart doctors as some of your friends). The 428 had a medium-riser aluminum intake manifold.

Shelby beat the Chevrolet offering of a big block engine in their ponycar (the Camaro SS 396) by one year and in the car industry a one year lead was significant. (Chevrolet was to respond two years later by bending the rules enough to make it possible for Pennsylvania car dealer/race driver Don Yenko to build a run of Camaros with 427 cubic-inch aluminum block V8s, of which 69 were made. Shelby never built an aluminum big block Shelby to match that challenge...)

Because the '67 Shelby was heavier, you needed that power steering and power brakes.

By '67 Shelby-American were selling a lot of the C-6 automatic transmissions as opposed to the Ford "toploader" 4-Speed manual. The Shelbys were now being marketed as a luxury sports models rather than as a pure rough-and-ready, barely-disguised racer.

Ford had taken over the creation of the ads, and in the process sadly lost much of the exciting flavor of the original ads created by Pete Brock for the '65 and '66 models. Now Shelby ads looked like all other Detroit automaker ads, all beach bimbos or mountain cabins. Still, Brock had lit a lamp that influenced muscle car ads for years to come. His factual recitation of all the ingredients that made up a Shelby was used by Chevrolet in selling the Z/28 Camaro in 1967 with great success.

The '68 looked much the same as the '67s but there were some subtle differences. Somewhere along the way, Ford had bought the name "Cobra" from Shelby (for one dollar, Shelby's worst business deal ever) and since the real Cobras were now no longer in production, Ford felt free to plaster the Cobra name all over the '68 Shelby. The official name of the car was even changed from "Shelby Mustang" to "Shelby Cobra," which no doubt grinded owners of the genuine A.C. Cobras, with their car's name being used on lesser Detroit iron.

And the 289 was gone, replaced by the 302, an even milder engine than the Hi-Po 289. But Ford no longer made the 289 so you had to take that the 302 if you weren't ready for the big block. Again, the Shelby was listed as having a 427 option but finding documentation of any of those being built is near impossible. Later when Ford offered the energetic big block in the production Mustangs, known as the 428 "Cobra Jet," that engine, when installed in the Shelby, saw a new model created called the GT500KR (the initials alluding to a popular song entitled "King of the Road.") The story at the time was that Shelby reportedly leapt on the name first only because he heard Chevy was planning to use it on the Corvette.

The Cobra Jet engine was rated at a mere 335 hp, ironically the same as the previous 428, though it had much more power. The reason for this is that Shelbys were becoming hard to insure, and Ford thought de-rating it would enable some buyers to still afford insurance.

One small improvement on the '68 was the moving of the hood scoops farther forward where they would stand more of a chance of actually scooping air.

One good innovation for safety was the use of the '65 T-bird sequential taillights where one square of the four on each side lit up sequentially, creating in effect a moving turn signal, making them a lot more noticeable and thus improving safety.

Fresh air fans were rewarded for their patience in the '68 which finally came in a convertible. Again in the '68s, Shelby's good intentions ran afoul of the law. He loved road lamps, had raced many a racecar with them. When he speced some Marchals from France, there was some question if they violated the law in some states so there was a change to weaker-beamed Lucas Square 8 models from England. American automakers were forced to wait another two decades until the obsolete headlamp laws were changed so that in the new century there were great strides in automotive lighting.

Shelby also had the chrome snake badge redesigned. When Ford designers didn't get his drift he commissioned a jeweler to sculpt it.

By 1968 the Shelby Mustangs were no longer made in California though the publicity pictures were still shot there, making fans think they were still coming out of a factory that had gone back to airplane use. Instead Shelby had farmed out the building of the Shelby Mustangs to a Michigan auto industry supplier A.O. Smith, the same firm who had been building the '67 Corvettes for Chevrolet. All he had to do now as far as Shelby Mustangs were concerned was pose for pictures and sit back and collect the checks.

In the final Sixties iteration of the Shelby Mustang, Ford continued to have the Shelby Mustang preview upcoming Ford styling. The Shelby styling was previewed by a show car as well, one called the Milano that had a full-width grille cavity similar to that on the '68 Dodge Charger.

Despite the new model design, Shelby sales were down and with that news all plans for future Shelbys beyond the new body style were cancelled. Fred Goodell, the Ford official designated to liaison with Shelby, told an interviewer from *Shelby-American* magazine that at the time Ford was even planning a "family" of Shelby cars including a four-door sedan, a fastback and a two-seater. Ford also diverted a few Shelbys off the line to experiment with various and sundry devices including both Lucas and Conolec fuel injection systems. Both would have delivered better fuel mileage but, hey, in retrospect, what were they worrying about? Back then gas was probably a buck a gallon.

Since they knew they were near the end of the Shelby line, Ford designers figured this was the opportunity to use every gimmick they had failed to use before. The result was that this last Shelby Mustang body style is considered by purists to either be the most gooped-up Shelby or the most distinctive, depending on your point of view and whether you own one.

The whole nose treatment was totally different from regular Mustangs. The fiberglass hood boasts no less than five openings, three flush-deck NASA scoops pointing forwards and two air exhaust vents pointing backwards. Two other scoops were put right behind the door on the rear fenders to cool the brakes. The front grille was large with just a small little Cobra emblem blocking any air. The fog lamps were now under the front bumper. The side stripes used a reflective tape, again a safety feature ahead of the rest of the industry.

Shelby, a big fan of cast aluminum in any form, had long yearned to have cast aluminum exhaust tips and finally was able to offer them as standard on the '69 Shelby. Beautiful works of art they were, too, being rectangular and cast in heavy alloy. Only trouble was, due to improper gas tank cap venting, the beautiful exhausts lit a few Shelbys on fire and Ford had to do a recall to change the gas caps.

Under the hood was a standard 302 with no pretense that it was a high performance engine. But at least there was an optional 351. The big block was again the 428.

The '69 must have been a losing year because the '70s were actually leftover 1969 cars with a black front spoiler added, and two black stripes. Reportedly Ford issued new VIN numbers to update the model years so no one buying a '70 would realize that they were in fact getting a leftover '69 (later, American Motors would be fined heavily for advancing the model year designation of some unsold cars but Shelby's up-dating act wasn't thought illegal because Ford had informed the FBI of the re-numbering in advance).

The poor sales of the '69 showed Ford that ol' Shel's string was just about played out. Ford cut off production after the '70 model year.

The plain and simple fact was that Ford didn't need the Shelby anymore. They were already shipping another new high performance Mustang to put in showrooms in its place, and this time they wouldn't have to pay a royalty to any spokesman like Shelby. The new car was the Boss 302, a last hurrah of the earlier days of high performance, a car with a lusty deep breathing small block V8 that was an even better performer than the Hi-Po 289 had ever been. And Boss Mustangs were winning races. Hey, now that they had a new winner, who needed Shelby?

Actually, the cut-off of Shelby production cars didn't mean they didn't need Shelby, the man. Ford still needed him when it came to racing and, from '66 on, had him running Trans-Am teams. The Boss 302 cars were the most successful of the Trans-Am cars, but finally were defeated by the Penske team's Camaro Z/28, a car that sold more cars in the showroom in 1969 than Shelby had sold out of Ford showrooms in five years!

In total, in five years, Ford had moved roughly 14,000 Shelby Mustangs.

With Shelby there was always the inevitable side deal. One was actually spawned by Ford, stealing a little of Shelby's magic. That was called the "California Special" and came about when the Ford rep assigned by Ford to the Shelby plant, Fred Goodell, built his own little notchback Mustang complete with big block, Shelby '67 rear end styling, a vinyl top and a Paxton supercharger. The car was nicknamed the "Little Red Wagon." A sales rep from Ford saw it, borrowed it and presented it at a district sales meeting. Immediately dealers wanted to sell this car too. A second notchback called the Green Hornet (green with black vinyl top) was created and that was shown to the dealers too. It wasn't long before a special model, the California Special, was being sold by California dealers. Colorado dealers also bought almost the same notchback model, dubbing their's the High Country Special. They are not Shelbys and there were no restrictions on what engines you could order with them. There was some worry at Shelby's end at the time that these may water down the Shelby image, but from Dearborn's point of view, hell, why worry, it was more Mustangs out the door!

Another project that Dearborn might not have found out about until it was already in the works was the Mexican Shelbys. That came about when a Mexican car enthusiast named Eduardo Valazquez began buying Shelby parts in 1965 and taking them back to Mexico. On one of his buying trips, he met Shelby and Shelby even invited him to stay in his house in Playa Del Rey. The two hit it off famously, and in one conversation, the subject worked around to just who Valazquez knew in Mexico. Well, before you could say "boo," Shelby had hornswoggled a grand expedition to Mexico where he and his party (which included an astronaut and some beautiful ladies) would stay in Valazquez' friends beachside house, his friend who happened to be Adolfo Lopez Mateos, the President of Mexico! The upshot was that upwards of a thousand Shelby de Mexico's were made, on notchback bodywork because those were the only Mustangs made in Mexico, and some were even raced. But decades later Valazquez would rather talk about that great time they all had down in Mexico, scuba diving and partying in el Presidente's mansion, than talk about the cars he built.

Then there was the Shelby d'Europa. Those came about through an old racing friend, Claude du Bois of Belgium. Du Bois was a Shelby dealer, selling at least one Cobra and several Shelby Mustangs. He recalls contacting Shelby after he had ordered several Shelbys and complaining that he had paid for the cars but never received them. Shelby checked on the order and, swearing a blue streak, told Du Bois that the cars had been sitting on the tarmac outside his plant for months and that, from then on, Du Bois was strictly to order directly from him, not Ford. Eventually Du Bois wanted to make some Shelbys in Europe out of regular Mustangs. Buying a raft of parts from various year Shelbys, he put his own Shelby d'Europas together. Whether they can be considered real Shelbys is up to the collectors, but they remain a little known footnote in the Shelby Mustang saga.

There was even a Zagato Shelby, or two of them, rebodied (mostly in roofline) by one of Italy's most famous carrozzerias. Who paid for them? Who ordered them? No one seems to know, but the cars still exist. Perhaps Shelby was returning to the idea he had started with the Italian bodied Corvettes, hoping that the magic of a great Italian carrozzeria could make a Shelby even more special. Evidentally the costs didn't work out and the two cars remain one-offs.

The reason for the Zagato Shelbys was not fathomed. Neither was the reason for a one-off Mustang rebodied for a firm called OSI. None of the three, 40-plus years later, can be connected with Shelby. But you never know. Shelby's business style was always run on two levels—the part you saw and the part you didn't see. His business style has been compared to that of a grand master chess player with each piece on the board representing one of the many businesses he runs. In hearing that analogy, Rick Kopec, co-founder of the Shelby-American Automobile Club, commented, "He knows exactly where each piece is going. He sees three years down the line, and doesn't tell anybody about it. But he gets there."

As time went on and he was no longer an automaker, Shelby missed the Shelby Mustangs. In fact he made at least two aborted attempts to bring back the Shelby Mustang—once with the owner of a firm called Beverly Hills Mustang, another time working with a TV producer in Marina Del Rey. Each time a few replicas of his orignal '65 body style cars were made, showed off to the press and, as part of the deal, Shelby drove off in one, but Shelby is a man who never gives up on a profitable idea. Decades later, in 2006, Shelby was offering continuation models of various Shelby Mustangs through participating vendor partners, and, given the track record of the originals, there is reason to believe that even these might someday approach the values of the originals.

There have been other modifiers who have tied in with Ford to build special Mustangs since the Sixties—such as Steeda or Roush—and Ford welcomes all such builders as each of these special cars represents another car out the door for them and there's no doubt that they build showroom traffic.

But to the purists, the Shelby fans, the '65-'70s are the solid gold investments and the ones most worth remembering....

Chapter 12- From Snakes to Big Cats

Coventry, England, the early Sixties.

The British Lord walked down the steps. The air was nice, a good day for a drive. Ordinarily he didn't like to be bothered with driving a prototype, but this car was said to be something special.

It was from Shelby, in America.

It looked like one of their Sunbeam Alpines but when he started it up, he knew this car was serious. It had a gruff, meaningful no-nonsense exhaust sound.

He let out the clutch, and the car leapt forward. He steered down to the highway and then upshifted and floored it again. Again it leaped forward. It was, as they say, a beast straining at the leash.

He came back ten minutes later, his aides visibly relaxing their expressions when they saw him beaming.

He climbed out and threw the keys to an aide. "Geoffrey, call Mr. Ford."

When Shelby succeeded with the Cobra, it opened the door for others to try to follow in his steps. One such effort actually involved Shelby; an effort which, in retrospect, would have to be categorized as nothing more than a "side deal." But not to worry—in this case Shelby had Ford's approval to participate because if he succeeded, the result would be more Ford V8s being sold.

The candidate for "Cobraization" in this case was the Sunbeam Alpine, a pleasant little British sports car that had been introduced back in 1959. It was actually quite luxurious considering the rudimentary nature of British middle class sports cars before that, with a standard soft top, roll up windows and an optional hardtop.

The engine was a 1494 cc four cylinder mated to a 4-speed manual with optional electric overdrive. Brakes were disc/drums and steering recirculating ball.

In four-cylinder form, they were raced with some success, one of the most notable entries in its logbook being in 1961 when an Alpine with a Harrington fastback body modification won the Thermal Efficiency Index at Le Mans. This doesn't mean that you are the fastest, but that you were the most fuel-efficient.

Over in Blighty, after the Alpine was getting a bit long in the tooth, its maker Rootes, run by Lord Rootes, began to search for another engine. Developing an all-new one from scratch was impossible—that took years and labor disputes were already threatening to put the company under. They had to come up with something fast. They considered the Buick/Olds/Pontiac aluminum 215 cubic-inch V8 but alas Rover beat them to it.

The savior, or rather creator of the idea of the Tiger was a Brit posted to that savage land of American's west coast, Ian Garrad, officially Rootes West Coast Manager. Having observed the runaway success of the Cobra with its formula of British chassis and body combined with an off the shelf Ford V8, Garrad arranged for a meeting with Carroll Shelby and John Panks (Director of Rootes Group America). The meeting probably took all of an hour, the upshot being, yes, there was a development budget at Rootes, and yes, Shelby was interested if it didn't take too much time.

Some accounts also suggest the famed race driver and car constructor Jack Brabham for inspiring the Tiger. According to those accounts, Brabham was doing some work with the Alpine and lamenting the inadequateness of the powerplant to Garrad. Garrad thereupon dispatched an underling armed with a tape measure to various American car dealers to see what V8, if any, would fit under the hood. Damned if a 260 Ford engine wasn't the ideal candidate.

A prototype would be made. Budget wise, it was a real low-cost deal, almost cigar money to Shelby, with a potential commission per each car sold for Shelby should it reach production.

Accounts vary but the general consensus is that there were two such prototypes. The first was done by Ken Miles, the British race driver who was, at that point in time still an independent shop operator/racecar driver. (His shop eventually being closed by the IRS, who had taken a dim view of his bookkeeping.) His conversion was your typical "quick and dirty" engine swap, jamming in the engine without making any additional room in the firewall. His car also used a Ford automatic trans. There was no room for an engine-driven fan so he used two electric fans. His labor price was a bargain—a mere $600.

After seeing how undriveable and thoroughly unpleasant Miles' budget prototype was, reportedly Shelby took delivery of a second Alpine and directed Phil Remington to do a more thorough conversion in which the firewall was moved back to make room for the engine. This car was more civilized, yet barely.

The Cobra's Borg Warner T-10 was also installed, connected by drive shaft to a Salisbury rear end. They didn't make the same mistake of keeping the original steering like they had originally with the Cobra, but went right to rack and pinion, and, because they knew a V8 would run hot in a body designed for a four, they went to a larger radiator.

Of course, a V8 had to have good exhaust and dual pipes were routed through the frame rails.

The Shelby-built prototype was test driven in California and then shipped to the Olde Sode, not air freighted as the Cobra had traveled in its early days but as steerage on a Japanese fruit freighter where, according to Bill Carroll, a mere $20 bribe insured the car would be well watched over. The decision to green light it lay in the hands of the Chairman, Lord Rootes. The story is that he roared off and came back with a broad smile on his face. Never mind the fact that he drove his entire session with the handbrake on!

Ambitious, Rootes put down an order for 3,000 V8 engines, an extremely positive sign considering that Shelby had yet to sell more than a few hundred Cobras. But then this car—at $3500—would be only a little more than half the price of a Cobra. No doubt the good Lord figured he could underprice Shelby by using a bit of his own snake oil!

Ironically, Rootes didn't have production facilities large enough for the project and Tigers were built by Jensen Motors at West Bromwich, a firm which had been making British chassis with American engines since before WWII.

The Sunbeam Tiger was a commercial success. For one thing, its performance took Sunbeam out of being compared to MGs and Triumphs, and put it in a class with Jaguars and Corvettes, which sold for several thousand more.

Originally the Tigers came with a two-barrel carburetor equipped 260 motor rated at a mere 164 hp at 4400 rpm as standard equipment, but high performance options were studied for adaptation by Shelby-American, then those judged suitable offered for sale through Sunbeam dealerships just as Cobra hop-up kits were already available through mail order and at Ford parts counters everywhere. Super lightweight factory mag wheels were available, as well as four-barrel Holley carburetors on Edelbrock F4B manifolds, traction bars and scattershields to protect you should the gearbox blow up. Once treated to some of the Cobra items, Tigers really screamed.

Shelby's grinning visage was featured in at least one of the ads, one with the headline "You don't just start it—you unleash it."

Again, paralleling Cobra history, as the Cobra engine increased in size from 260 to 289 cubic inches so did the Tiger. The so-called Mk. II Tiger was rated at 200 bhp at 4400 rpm.

While 200 hp at 4400 rpm doesn't sound like much compared to the power of the Shelby Mustang GT-350, it was still 22% more power than that offered in the Tiger Mk I(A)'s 260.

One problem that had been there with the 260 but became more aggravated in the 289 was the fact that the tires were just too small compared to those on the Cobra and Mustang. You could get a 7.5 second ET but think of what you were throwing away because you didn't have adequate tires. With its relatively low weight and oodles of torque, it felt faster than it was.

The first Tiger racecar made its debut at an SCCA divisional race in Tucson in early April 1964. Later, in the Pacific Coast Divisional Championships at Willow Springs, Lew Spencer made history by being the first man to win a race in a Sunbeam Tiger, finishing 12 seconds in front of his nearest rival who was driving an E-type Jaguar. Humbling a Jaguar, that was something! (In fact, dozens of owners installed Ford and Chevy V8s in their E-type Jags, all with indifferent success as there was a heap of difference between a professional conversion and your average backyard conversion.)

Lew Spencer was a name that loomed large in Shelby history. He did double duty—he was also Shelby's sales manager besides being a capable race driver.

But the racing revealed the car's major flaw—the weight distribution was not anywhere as near as good as it was in the Cobra, perhaps due to the steel body being much heavier than the Cobra's body, which only weighed 50 lbs. all told. That led to suirrely handling. According to Doug Stokes, a racing historian, the culprit was the car's short wheelbase. "It was a major problem on turn-in," says Stokes.

Spencer had one of his biggest crashes in his racing Tiger. In a SCCA B Production race at Laguna Seca in May 1964, he lost control on the approach to turn 2 and went off the track, injuring himself. That was the last time he raced the Tiger though it went on to be raced by others more foolhardy.

Garrard then found another man to race the official Tiger, Doane Spencer at Hollywood Sport Cars who won many events, though you might say his car was a bit tweaked, at one point being rated at 349 hp with a two-barrel carburetor!

Tigers were also rallied in Europe, taking first in class at the 1964 Geneva Rally, the 1965 Monte Carlo Rally, the 1965 International Scottish Rally and 1st in class and the overall win in the 1965 International Police Rally held in Belgium.

When Shelby went to a coupe body style for his race Cobras in '64, the Tigers did likewise, with two fastback coupe-bodied Tigers competing at Le Mans. The Lister-bodied cars were clocked at over 160 mph at Le Mans, 10 mph short of the Daytona coupe, but alas, during the race, both engines blew. Rick Mueller, a Tiger historian, says that Tiger owners suspect skullduggery. The group preparing the cars had asked Shelby for two racing 289s. What they got when they opened the box from California was two 260 inchers. Shelby reportedly told them not to worry, that the small block was more durable but in the end both engines blew up during the race. Was Shelby sandbagging them so his 289 Cobra Daytona coupes wouldn't be beat by these other British hybrids? We may never know, but some Tiger owners claim, in retrospect, they were "snake-bit."

The Tiger was a mere footnote in Shelby history but there's an amusing twist in the chronology that occurred when Chrysler, one of Detroit's Big Three, bought Rootes just when the Tiger was proving popular. They originally thought they would drop in a Chrysler 273 incher but found that it would cost too much to re-engineer the car. They said "What the hell" and continued to offer it with the Ford V8, even helping to develop the 289 Mk. II model.

You have to admire the skill of the Chrysler ad agency copywriters who managed to write the ads for the Tiger, and make it sound good without ever letting you know it, ahem, had a *Ford* V8. Really painful was the fact that they had to warranty the Tiger's Ford V8 for two years or 24,000 miles!

Chrysler eventually dropped the car rather than continue to live with the embarrassment.

Looking back, you have to say that the Tiger, no matter who was selling it, did damn good considering the paltry funding that went toward their development. Ironically, there were more than six times as many Tigers (over 7,000) than there were A.C. Cobras made in the Sixties. And the Tigers were sold only over a three year period, not five like the Cobra. They were marketed in several countries, though in some countries they were called the Alpine V8.

The most developed ones, if you believe that the last of a line is always the most developed are the Mark II models, which number only 536 of the total Tigers built. These came stock with 289 c.i. V8s, all the revisions of the Mark IAs, plus a new eggcrate grille. They had a beautiful wood veneered dashboard, making the Cobra's interior look downright utilitarian by contrast.

About 80% of the Tiger production was originally sold on the US West Coast and most of the rest in the U.S. It wasn't popular in Europe since they were priced about twice as much as an Alpine Mk IV/MK V and were considered impractical because of their fuel appetite. If they had enjoyed a racing success record like the Cobras, which only could have been done with a team run out of Shelby-American and funded by Ford, maybe they could have done better but the fact was that, for Carroll Shelby, the Tiger was no big deal. More like a passing fling, a car he remembered barely more than some of the stewardesses he squired in his jet set travels around the world....

Chapter 13- The Trans-Am Wars

Dearborn, Michigan, 1966.

The Ford executive sat back in the bar. He had snuck out of the office during a break. He liked it over here at the Dearborn Inn, an old watering hole restored by the first Henry Ford. It was a place full of antiques and dark little corners you could relax in.

He opened a copy of Competition Press, *a raggedy auto sports weekly. There was a headline: "Bob Tullius Dodge Dart wins in over 2.0 liter class in Trans-Am."*

He caught the waitresses eye, holding up his drink to signal he need a refill.

"Trans-Am," he tought. "What the hell did that mean?"

He looked at the picture. It was a rather ordinary looking car; it shouldn't take much to beat that! He finished the drink and signaled for his bill. "Goddam it," he thought, "when I get back to the office, I gotta get a hold of Shelby and find out why the hell we don't have a horse in this race?"

In 1966 Shelby already had Ford bankrolling production of the Shelby GT-350 Mustang. Ford was also backing up Cobra production. And paying Shelby to shape up their International racing effort for the Ford GTs which had fallen flat in their initial racing season in 1964. That was three full time jobs right there. But when Ford saw the publicity potential in Trans-Am, they wanted in.

"Trans-Am" started out with a touch of Internationalism, the "Trans" referring to drivers from both Canada and America participating. The first race in the Trans-American Sedan Championship Series was staged March 25, 1966, at Sebring International Raceway in Florida. Future Formula One World Champion Jochen Rindt took the overall victory and Bob Tullius won the Over 2-Liter class. Other first-year entrants who are now famous names included A.J. Foyt, Richard Petty, Jerry Titus and Belgium's Jacky Ickx. It is hard to believe now when you imagine Trans-Am cars of the Sixties that the original heroes and cars in the sport were people like European drivers Horst Kwech and Gaston Andrey in Alfa Romeos, Bob Tullius and Tony Adamowicz in Dodge Darts, and Bob Johnson in a Plymouth Barracuda.

Ford was a little slow in picking up on the fact the series existed, so the first Mustangs in Trans-Am were amateur-built cars. The first appearance of a Mustang in Trans-Am was in a four hour long support race for the 12-Hour, at Sebring in 1966. An Alfa won, while the two most watched Mustang drivers, Dr. Dick Thompson, the racing dentist, and A.J. Foyt, finished out of the top ten.

Back in Dearborn, they didn't like the fact that the Mustangs weren't doing well. Hadn't Shelby proved the Mustang a winner in sports car racing? Someone in the Glass House in Dearborn dialed Shelby.

When Shelby got the call from Ford, his first thought was "hey, duck soup." The Shelby GT-350 was well dialed in. But he was soon apprised of the fact that he would not be allowed to run a GT-350 in Trans-Am. That was because the GT-350 had already been homologated as a two-seater sports car so it could race against the Corvettes in B-production. Even if they put the back seat back in, for some reason it would not considered a sedan. So the Shelby-American team began to prepare notchbacks, which was not such a biggie, because in fact Ken Miles had used two '64 notchback Mustangs as mules in developing the GT-350. Those cars were still around.

Ford actually liked the fact that the Mustang notchbacks were to be their weapon of choice this time 'round because it was better for show room rub-off. Not everyone could afford a Shelby—averaging $6000 at the time—but notchback "plain" Mustangs were half the price so if their racecars could be identified with a road car that was more affordable, then it stood to reason that they would move more Mustangs out the showroom doors.

Another key point was that, by racing Ford-branded cars, any points won would accrue to Ford Motor Company, not Shelby, and Ford kind of liked the idea of the Ford brand winning races because they were in it for the long run, where Shelby, conceivably, might someday fold his tent and steal off into the night.

The class the Mustangs would compete in was the over 2 liters class where maximum displacement was 5 liters, or 305-cid, with a maximum wheelbase of 116 inches. The series would consist of seven professional races to be held at different tracks across the US and Canada. The manufacturer with the most points at the end of the series would win a Manufacturer's Trophy. The races ranged from 200 miles to 2,400 miles. The races ran from 2 hours to 24 hours and required pit stops for gas and tires. Dr. John Craft, in his book *Mustang Racecars*, points out that the series was deliberately called a "manufacturer series" instead of a "driver's series" because then automakers would come in and support it. The SCCA was right. Shelby-American built sixteen 1966 Group 2 Notchback Mustangs, all for sale to independents. The theory this time was that they didn't want a factory team to be defeating their own customers as had happened with the GT-350, but rather have private teams run cars they prepped after starting with a basic racecar built by Shelby.

Shelby assigned Chuck Cantwell (who had done the suspension of the GT-350) to be the Project Engineer and Jerry Schwartz, Shelby-American's ace fabricator and mechanic, to develop and prep the cars. Though they didn't look like the GT-350, the Mustangs were built to GT 350R-model specs, though stricter rules required that they have more stock parts than the R-model Shelbys, such as steel hoods (with no hood scoops) and front ends where the old GT-350 R models had fiberglass hoods and front aprons, and plastic side and rear windows. But the Shelby Team was still able to use lots of Shelby R-model bits including locking devices on the hoods and trunks, American Torque Thrust-D racing magnesium wheels, lowered A-arms, 34 gallon fuel tanks, trunk mounted batteries, electric fuel pumps, six gauges housed in a special instrument housings including gauges for fuel pressure, oil pressure, and water temp oil temp, a tach reading to 8,000 rpm tach, a four point roll bar, 3-inch wide competition lap belts with shoulder harness, an 18 quart Ford Galaxie radiator, an oil cooler with remote oil filter, tube headers with straight pipes dumping out just in front of the rear wheels and the famed "Monte Carlo" brace running from one shock tower to another in front to strengthen the front end.

Brakes were discs up front, and drums in the rears.

Under the cars you found Koni shock absorbers, and the noisy but effective Detroit "No-Spin" rear ratcheting differential that had been part of the original GT-350 package. Steering was quick steering and the gearbox a Borg Warner T-10 close-ratio four speed.

The engine was straight out of the Shelby Mustang R-model—a 289 small block with an aluminum hi-rise intake manifold and a 715 cfm Holley carb. The engines developed over 350 horse power, about 40 hp lower than the 289 in the Cobra racecars but sufficient for the task at hand.

Ford's participation came so late that only one car of the three cars they were building was completed in time to make the Trans-Am race at Sebring in 1966.

Shelby-prepared Mustangs finished in five out of the remaining six races. Independent teams drove non-Shelby Group 2 Mustangs to wins at Mid-America Raceway, the Virginia 400 and second at Briar 250. Ford and Chrysler fought for the lead in points up to the last two races. At Green Valley, Texas, Brad Booker and John McComb driving a Shelby Group 2 Mustang beat out the "Team Starfish" Barracudas and Group 44 Dodge Darts to win tying the standings at 37 each for Chrysler and Ford.

That first season's last race took place at Riverside in California. Shelby hired Jerry Titus to drive a Shelby Group 2 Mustang. Titus was an intense man who worked during the day as an editor at Petersen's Sports Car Graphic. In a racecar, he was a tiger, but hard on the equipment. But Shelby kept him behind the wheel because, when he was on a winning streak, nothing could stop him.

During the qualifying on Saturday, Titus set a track lap record of 1:41.9 at an average of 91.854 miles per hour to earn the first spot on the grid for the race on Sunday. The race started with the traditional "Le Mans" type start where the drivers line upon one side of the track while their cars are lined up opposite them. When the starter drops the flag, the drivers sprint across the road, jump behind the wheel and take off. This type of start was later outlawed because too many drivers, trying to save a few seconds, took off without fastening their seat belts. Some of them crashed trying to fasten them later at 100 mph!

In his eagerness to take off, Titus flooded his Mustang leaving him next to last to move off the line. A later broken oil filter cost him almost two laps while it was being replaced. Titus then put on a Herculean effort, fighting his way through the mob of 34 cars to finish first, over half a minute ahead of the Tullius Group 44 Dodge Dart. Mustang and Ford won the first Trans-Am Manufacturers Trophy.

With the taste of victory in their mouth, Ford opened their pocket book and doled out money for preparation of more Trans-Am Mustangs for '67. Shelby had to start over again, homologating a '67 model Group II car. This time the cars had full interiors, rollup windows, door panels and dash pads. Roll bars were mandatory, suspension modifications and even R-Model over-rider bars were allowed. Because the race teams all wanted to run wider rubber than road cars, it was permitted to radius the wheel wells to accommodate them.

The big news in the engine department was that twin four-barrel, Holleys were allowed for '67 even though you couldn't order a small block Mustang with them out of the showroom. The SCCA allowed it because the twin carb set-up was available on Ford's parts list at every dealer. Shelby built 25 Trans-Am cars for '67 but only kept three as Shelby team cars, the rest going to independents.

Firmly separating the Shelby-American Team name from the Ford name, the teams Shelby ran for '67 were listed as entries by David Witts, his lawyer friend and partner in the chili cook-offs, and Grady Davis, a Gulf Oil executive who had earlier been a big supporter of Duntov's Grand Sport Corvette effort.

One bit of Shelby humor was evident on the sides of the Shelby Team Mustangs—an odd crest on the fenders for what was called the "Terlingua Racing Team." This was an inside joke. Terlingua referred to a river that was on 200,000 acres of worthless desert scrubland that Shelby owned in Texas near Big Bend National Park along with Witts. One time, years earlier, when Shelby asked some buddies at one of his cook-outs, how they could unload the god-forsaken piece of land, a friend who was an experienced PR man suggested, "Maybe we should hold a chili cook-off?"

The result, once Shelby got to working on it, was a world class wing ding with beautiful startlets flown in from Hollywood, gourmet cooks and oceans of tequila. The event became an annual event and soon there were chili cook-offs being held everywhere worldwide. Shelby even became a manufacturer of Original Texas Chili, a mix so potent that Alka Seltzer was included in the brown paper bag of mixings. To further promote the land among the racing fraternity, Shelby started a fictional racing team, commissioned a team emblem and that badge, featuring a yellow and chrome crest with a very combative-looking rabbit, went on many a racecar, some of the decals even finding their way onto GT40s at Le Mans, Indy 500 winners and on cars that won at Sebring, Riverside, and Laguna Seca. But in Trans-Am the Terlingua Racing Team graced the side of the Shelby Trans-Am Mustangs during the '67 season.

Ford was so gung-ho for Trans-Am in '67 that they funded a second team, the Mercury Cougar team, with NASCAR car builder Bud Moore running the operation. Moore had signed up two of Shelby's former Cobra drivers, Dan Gurney and Ed Leslie, plus Indy favorite A.J. Foyt. Shelby was miffed that his team would be competing with another Ford team, when it would be nice if all the Trans-Am money would be coming to him. But that's the way Dearborn was playing it. If it hadn't been for Chevrolet, the Mustang might have dominated Trans-Am. But Chevrolet, miffed that they had misjudged the potential of the ponycar market and gotten into the market two years too late to go toe-to-toe with Ford, came out with three high performance Camaros right from the get-go in '67. They had a big block 396 in addition to their 327 but the Chevrolet that would eventually torpedo the Mustang in Trans-Am was an option innocently called "RPO (Regular Production Option) Z/28." Chevrolet officially adhered to the GM Corporate policy of not promoting racing, but behind the scenes had a man named Vince Piggins serving in the role of Chevrolet "product promotion manager." Piggins thought of a way to get the bow tie brand back on the track. He saw NASCAR and NHRA not as good for that as Trans-Am, especially when the goal was to establish an image for the Camaro in the ponycar class. Even though the SCCA's required displacement limit, no larger than 305-cid, which was inconvenient since Chevy's smallest V8 in the Camaro was the 327 there were ways. By merely taking their 327 block and putting in a 283 crankshaft, that gave their new powerplant a displacement of 302.4 cubic inches, just under the SCCA's 305-cid limit.

The engine with this optional package was rated at a mere 290 hp but probably put out closer to 400 hp. It sort of crept into the market on cat's feet. It was so little known that even many Chevy dealers didn't even know of its existence in 1967. As a result, only 602 Camaro Z/28s were built in 1967. To promote it, a single car was sent to Riverside to race in November 1966, just in time for the '67 Trans-Am racing year.

Chevy might have come late to the party but they came with the right team, one run by Roger Penske, a former racer himself who had once raced against Shelby when he was a driver and who was, by all accounts, one sharp cookie when it came to business. He proved perfect to campaign the Camaro Z/28. He came with an existing racing organization, a sponsor with deep pockets in Sunoco, plus a great driver, Mark Donohue, who also happened to be a graduate engineer. Donohue, it should be pointed out, had his own reason to have it in for Shelby. He had once raced his own GT-350 as an independent but was passed over for the job of team driver for Shelby-American. He relished the opportunity to show the chicken farmer what a mistake that was! Donohue could be infuriatingly clever. At one point, he took out his slide rule and calculated cold fuel takes up less space than warm fuel so he rigged the Sunoco team's refueling tank with a surrounding layer of dry ice to cool the fuel and was thus able to squeeze in an extra gallon of fuel, one more than the car's gas tank officially held.

The Penske/Donohue Trans-Am Camaro program hit the track in the 1967 season debut at Daytona with Donohue piloting a Sunoco blue '67 Camaro Z/28. They didn't win that race but soon scored their first Trans-Am victory at Marlboro, Maryland. The '67 Camaro of Team Penske would score 2 more victories in the '67 season, but those were not enough to take the championship away from Ford.

One of the yeoman jobs done by Shelby's pit crew during that '67 season occurred when Titus snagged a haybale in practice at Green Valley, Texas, and put the Mustang on its roof. Undeterred, the crew went into town, bought a new Mustang notchback out of the Ford showroom, brought it to the track and used most of the parts to rebuild Titus's racecar. The next day, Titus was able to field a car, but the wind wing was broken and it was so hot in the car that, during the race, he passed out in the pits and another driver had to take over. The car finished third but still kept Ford ahead in points.

At another race that season, at mid-Ohio, Titus showed some luck when he finished thirty seconds ahead of the second place car, and had the engine torn down only to discover it had no oil left in it. He lucked out!

Accusations continued to fly throughout the season of cheating, but the NASCAR unofficial rule was "If you ain't cheatin', you ain't winnin'." It was even suspected that the Bud Moore Cougars had been cut down somehow in size or someone had dipped the chassis of Titus's car, losing a few pounds each time it took another swim through the acid tank.

The last race of the '67 season was at Kent, Washington. Donohue, in the Camaro, led from start to finish but the insiders were all watching which Ford team won because that could determine who got the bags of money from Dearborn the next season. Fortunately for the Shelby team, the Mercury Cougar team had bad luck, Gurney's Cougar having a broken windshield he had to hold in place with one hand and another Mercury was black-flagged because someone forgot to close the gas cap. Bucknum won in a Team Shelby car, and the Bud Moore Team were the losers.

The next two years, though, the Penske-prepped Z/28s would dominate the series, and Chevrolet would reap the rewards in the showroom, selling more Z/28s in 1969 alone than Ford sold Shelby Mustangs in five years total! Ford's response to the Z/28 engine was to come up with a new engine themselves. They were now allowed to go up to 305 inches but ended up with a 302, however, unusual because of the 302 "Tunnel Port" which was a pull-out-all-the-stops effort to maximize the flow of the heads. The head had straight intake ports with the pushrod tubes running through the port. In the past the ports would twist around the pushrods. Each port feed an individual cylinder. On paper this combination of the head design with the new 4 bolt main 302 looked unbeatable.

Although SCCA rules required 1,000 of a car be built with the same equipment to qualify the parts as production, for some mysterious reason Ford was allowed to run the Tunnel Port engines the whole season without ever getting around to offering the engine in any Ford car. The new engine pumped out more than 50 horses more than they had ever got out of a 289, so things looked promising.

When Ford decided to run the Tunnel Ports, they told Shelby to ditch the non de plume of the "Terlingua Racing Team" and simply run them as products of the mundane sounding "Shelby Racing Company."

Five new Group II Mustangs were built for the Shelby team for '68 and two '67 cars upgraded as backups. Kar Kraft, Ford's semi-secret race shop in Dearborn, was involved in the building of the cars as well. The year before Kar Kraft had been involved in the building of the MK. IV Ford GT that had won Le Mans.

The first Trans-Am race of the 1968 season was the Daytona 24 hour endurance race. This was good for exposure for the series because the Trans-Am cars were being included the same weekend as the main event. Trans-Am races were held prior to the main endurance races in 1967.

The Mustangs dominated the Group 2 race. Jerry Titus and Ronnie Bucknum finished 64 laps ahead of the nearest Group 2 car, Donohue's Penske Camaro. The Titus/Bucknum entry really stood out. At the end of the race, it rolled to the finish in third overall just behind three Porsche 907 prototypes—cars capable of nearly 200 mph. Though he was far from being on the same lap, the photo of that finish impressed a lot of people who were amazed to see an essentially stock-looking Mustang keeping up with the exotic hand-built Porsche prototypes.

But the victory at Daytona gave Ford false hope in a way because, for some reason, the same Tunnel Port that performed so well at Daytona proved to be a dog for the entire rest of the season. Worse yet, after Daytona Ford insisted on building the engines themselves and the Shelby teams suffered for it. The Mustangs blew engines left and right—over fifty in all. Mechanics used to bet not only on what race you would blow in but also on what lap of each race!

Shelby's mechanics during that year still tell horror stories of engines arriving from Dearborn that were missing vital parts like pushrods. The long simmering belief of the Shelby crew that Ford Dearborn favored the NASCAR racers was fueled by Ford's sending of bum engines to the Shelby team in '68.

That left the way clear for Penske's Camaros to roll right over all the other Trans-Am teams in the '68 season. Penske's lead driver, Mark Donohue, nicknamed "Captain Nice" by the press because of his cheery demeanor and preppy looks, drove the Sunoco Blue Z-28 to victory in eight consecutive Trans-Am races, beginning with the second event of the season, the 12 Hours of Sebring late in March 1968. "Captain Nice" walked away with first in 10 out of 13 races that year.

The Shelby team, hobbled by bum engines, won only two races—the 24 Hours of Daytona in February, 1968, and Riverside at the end of the season with Horst Kwech driving. The Tunnel Port's problem was eventually diagnosed as bad oiling at the top end range of rpm. The engines were so badly preprared that, at one point a Shelby-American mechanic remembers that they had to dump 30 quarts of oil into a Trans-Am engine built by Engine & Foundry in order to get it through a single race. Reportedly, the Shelby Team pleaded with Ford to let them go back to the tried-and-true 289s but Ford wanted the 302s to win because they weren't offering the 289 anymore. After all, what would a switch back to 289s tell buyers in the showroom? "Don't buy our 302—it's not as good as the engine we used to build?" According to historian Dr. John Craft, Ford did relent near the end of the season and let Team Shelby build its own engines for the last couple of races, such as the Mission Bell 250 at Riverside. At that event, at least Titus had qualified only tenths of a second behind Donohue, proving Shelby could build a good Tunnel Port 302. But his jubilation didn't last for long—ironically, both Titus and Donohue were out of the race with engine problems and Kwech won in another Team Mustang.

The real irony of the Tunnel Port disaster is that before the season started, Ford had commissioned a test of head designs that showed an alternative had been available that would have solved the problem. Shelby had used a Gurney-Weslake head in the test, using the head design Dan Gurney had once commissioned from famous engine designer Harry Weslake in England, Ford had come with a Tunnel Port. The Tunnel Port had lacked torque but Ford still nixed running Gurney-Weslake heads in Trans-Am, feeling that they were too expensive to make in case they followed through on their plan to offer the same engine as the racecar had in a showroom model.

In the final race of the '68 season, at Kent, Washington, Titus showed up in a Firebird, having earlier quit the Ford team because Ford refused to produce the Tunnel Port 302 for the showrooms of America. But at Kent his Pontiac engine blew right away and that gave Peter Revson, who had filled Titus's spot on the Shelby team, a chance as well as Kwech in another Shelby Team Mustang. But, Kwech was bashed by Folmer and went out, and Revson's Tunnel Port let go in the 24th lap. Donohue won and Camaro took the championship for the '68 season.

Even while their Tunnel Port engines were failing, Ford was already working on a replacement, this time a 351 for the 1970 model year. The 351 heads had huge canted intake and exhaust valves and ports. Someone looked at them and decided to try those heads on the 302 block. With some slight modifications to water passages, they found that the heads would fit the Tunnel Port block. This became the Boss 302 engine, which proved to be streets ahead of the Tunnel Port in reliability. Plus, during 1968 SCCA lightened up and allowed some "non stock" parts to be fitted, including floating rear ends, four wheel disc brakes and wider tires.

Wheel and fender flares could be added to accommodate the eight inch tires. Fuel cells were mandatory. Just in time for the racing season, Ford introduced a new Mustang body shell for the new engine. The '69 Mustang body was completely redesigned to make the car more aerodynamic. The previous body styles were far too boxy to slice through the air. Many of the previous Shelby Mustang features were incorporated in the new design including a rear spoiler.

The 1969 season was successful for Ford with the Boss 302s doing well against the Camaro Z28s. And best of all for Ford, they could make Boss 302 Mustangs for the showroom cheaper and faster than Shelbys which, by 1969, required their own separate body panels to be installed front and rear, a job which had to be farmed out to a non-Ford plant with huge costs in shipping. And, best of all, they didn't have to pay to use Shelby's name with the car.

Dissatisfied with the way Shelby handled money, Ford had sent a "hatchet man," the white haired and urbane executive Jacque Passino to be in charge of the Ford racing efforts in 1969 as well as act as head of Ford's Special Vehicle Activities. Also selected was Homer Perry who had been with the GT40 racing effort at Le Mans. Perry's contact at Shelby Racing was Lew Spencer. Bud Moore was the Moore team contact. Dr. John Craft points out in his book, *Mustang Racecars*, that though Shelby-American was building and racing Ford Mustang racecars, Bud Moore's effort was accorded the lesser status of a semi-independent team, i.e. second in line for putting their hands into the kitty. Perry also worked closely with Kar Kraft's lead Trans-Am engineer, Lee Dykstra, who designed the suspension for the Mustangs.

The Boss 302 Mustangs raced during the '69 season were shipped from the factory to race teams as 4-speed 351 fastbacks, not as Boss Mustangs per se. A change in the SCCA rules allowed the fastback body to be raced, prior to this only the notchback coupes could be used. The racecars for the '69 season were started in late '68, even though production cars weren't scheduled to come off the line until April '69. Seven Mustangs were shipped. One car went to Kar Kraft, Ford's own semi-secret racing shop in Dearborn.

Three went to Shelby-American and the last three were shipped to Shelby's rival for Ford dollars, NASCAR race preparer Bud Moore. (The Moore team raced Mercury Cougars in '67 and '68 but the Cougars were dropped for 1969.) At least the Shelby team was allowed to build its own engines for 1969. The cars were all stripped and rebuilt to the specifications used on the prototype Trans-Am Mustang built at Kar Kraft. All special parts came from Kar Kraft.

There was copious cheating in Trans-Am, but creative cheating nonetheless. In the *Shelby-American* magazine, in an interview of Lew Spencer, a key Shelby employee, Rick Kopec quotes Spencer recalling: "Bud Moore was caught cheating when the inspector couldn't lift Dan Gurney's helmet off the seat—there was so much lead weight inside of it." When the helmet was removed the car was underweight. Moore pointed out that the weight was supposed to be the car as fielded, complete with gas, coolant, and fresh tires. His argument for fresh tires was that, if the tires were worn, they would weigh less than if they were fresh. The inspectors indulged him and a few minutes later the car reappeared at the scales with a full tank of gas, fresh coolant and new tires. It passed the weight minimum. Moore took it back to the pits and changed tires again. That was necessary because one thing he had neglected to tell the scrutineer was that the tires he had used for the weigh-in had been filled with water.

In an odd twist, a famous Florida mechanic long associated with GM cars was consulted for advice on the Boss 302, much to the consternation of everybody else concerned. That was because earlier Henry Ford II had hired Semon "Bunkie" Knudsen, a second generation GM man to be Ford's president, this in the vain hope that he would learn some of GM's secrets about upcoming product. Knudsen, a car buff (it seems incredible that we have to point this out but the truth is that a surprising number of Detroit automaker car executives are *not* in fact car buffs), was a friend of "Smokey" Yunick a famous racecar mechanic based in Ormond Beach, Florida. Yunick had once prepared Pontiac NASCAR racers when Knudsen had headed up Pontiac.

A Boss 302 was sent to the outspoken Yunick, Knudsen perhaps secretly hoping Smokey would think of a creative way to "cheat" the car. But if Smokey thought of a way to "cheat" the Boss, it didn't get found out by the public.

The level of preparation on the Boss 302 Trans-Am cars surpassed anything Shelby had done on the GT-350. It took the Shelby team six weeks to take their cars apart and rebuild them to Trans-Am specs. Each car cost about $20,000. The car's weight was restricted to 2,900 pounds, which meant shaving 350 lbs. off the road cars. The distribution of the weight of the cars was shuffled around so that they were 50/50 front and rear, that being considered the ideal weight balance. The interiors were removed completely, although the dash pad was saved and reinstalled. The windows were all replaced with lighter glass. The windows had to work, so the regulators were fabricated from aluminum to replace the heavy cast factory units. A mandatory roll cage was extended to stiffen the body. The factory seats were replaced with one racing bucket seat. A safety harness secured the driver in place.

The Shelby team replaced the stock Ford shifter with a Hurst four speed, the Moore cars used the stock shifter. Ford then had to offer the Hurst shifter on the showroom models so the part could be labeled "stock" (thus proving once again the truth of the old saw that "racing improves the breed").

The suspension of the Trans-Am Mustangs was pure racecar. Trans-Am rules prohibited moving the suspension mounting points, so the roll cage was welded directly to the car suspension mounting points for strength. The cars were aligned perfectly to the computer specifications developed by Kar Kraft for the production Boss 302s. The A-arms were replaced with heavy duty Boss 429 pieces using metal bushings instead of the stock rubber. The 11.96-inch disc brakes from Lincoln Continental replaced the stock front discs. The stock rear discs were modified and replaced with larger discs. Thicker front stabilizer bars were used. Different front bars were used depending on the track and the conditions. Heavy duty forged spindles, racing coil springs and leaf springs installed. The leaf springs had a Watts linkage added that restricted the side to side movement, allowing the spring to move vertically only. Traction bars were welded in above the leaf springs.

Adjustable Koni shocks were put at all four corners. The mounting points were moved slightly for better control, contrary to Trans-Am rules. Single or twin radiators mounted just in front of the both sides of the rear axle used the cool air under the car to cool the rear end differential fluid. The modifications dropped the car about 3 inches from the stock height. A front spoiler hung under the front of the car made of ABS plastic with scoops just above to channel air to the front disc brakes.

The 1969 racecars did not use the rear spoiler. The doors had to open and latch, but they were held in place with click pins instead of the stock door latches. Twelve-inch wide Goodyear racing tires were mounted on American Racing or British Minilite mags. Every racing part was heavy duty to stand the rigors of the upcoming season. Each team was in a ferocious hurry to race the car, but first they tested the waters by releasing photographs of parts they intended to use. Ford released pictures of a huge intake manifold that would carry two giant Holley carbs. This was called the "Cross Boss", similar to Chevy's Cross Ram intake.

But when the Holley carbs were finally available, the manifold runners proved to be too long to produce power in the 5000-6000 rpm range. A single plane manifold was built with shorter runners. The intake had a runner for each of the Holley carbs eight barrels, one for each cylinder. The distributor was still in the way so a special offset distributor was made. Since all parts used in racing had to be available as production parts, the Cross Boss intake was produced even though in the end, it wasn't used in the races.

There was also a six-barrel inline carburetor produced by Autolite that flowed an incredible amount of air, but this also was never offered on a street Boss so it couldn't be used in racing though it seems to have been available over the counter. Parnelli Jones tested it but never could dial it in to his satisfaction.

The valve cove breathers were stock Cleveland 351 valve covers that emptied into a collector to keep oil from blowing out on the track. The racing engines cranked out over 470 hp at 9,000 rpm.

The Bud Moore team signed on two firecracker drivers, Rufus Parnelli Jones and George Follmer. Shelby signed on movie matinee handsome Peter Revson, an heir to the Revlon cosmetics empire, and the Australian driver Horst

Kwetch. Lew Spencer was the team manager. But a problem would be that they lost Cantwell, who was working for Penske on the Sunoco Camaros.

Chrysler came back into Trans-Am in 1969, with the E-bodies built off a shortened B platform. There were two varieties, the Challenger and the 'Cuda, the name shortened from Barracuda. Both brands competed in Trans-Am. The Trans-Am Challenger was the race version of the normal street Challenger. About 2,400 Challengers were built to comply with the SCCA (Sports Car Club of America) rules—the AAR Cuda was built for similar reasons. Sam Posey, a genteel Connecticut yankee who had Lime Rock racetrack practically in his back yard, drove the real T/A. It had a destroked 303 cubic-inch LA motor with a four barrel.

The stakes were high for 1969. It was one Detroit manufacturer pitted directly against another. There was absolutely no doubt winning on the track could result in more sales in the showroom. (Even if you didn't win, it might not matter, for ironically the Pontiac Trans-Am did poorly in the Trans-Am series but Pontiac eventually was to sell over one million Firebird Trans-Ams, so the truth was that creating the right image had everything to do with sales and winning nothing.)

Winning was going to require more sophisticated methods than in the past. Though these were clumsy cars in comparison to the low-slung GT40 racecar, the Boss 302 cars still got such GT40 treatment as wind tunnel testing and this time Shelby was determined to run engines built by his own team in '69!

Lots of other new ideas were used that hadn't been legal before—front air dams, wider tires, fender flares and rear wing-spoilers all of which had to be offered on the same model in the showrooms to be legal for racing.

On the track, the Boss 302 Mustangs were winners from the first race, which took place at Michigan International Speedway in Irish Hills, Michigan. That one was won by Parnelli Jones on the Moore team. The win was originally given to Mark Donohue in a Camaro with Jones in 4th. The Ford team protested and the SCCA realized that Jones' laps had been undercounted and a couple of hours after the race Parnelli was given the win. The Jones' Mustang was the only Mustang that finished. Revson got stuck in the mud after running off the track. Follmer lost his clutch and Kwech crashed.

The second race, held at Lime Rock, Connecticut, on Memorial Day was won by New Englander Sam Posey in a Shelby Mustang. Sadly, that was to be the Shelby team's only victory during the 1969 season. Three of the drivers skipped this race to drive at the Indy 500 race, which you couldn't blame them for, as winning Indy could instantly make you a millionaire. Posey was driving Revson's car #1, John Cannon piloted the #16 car of Follmer and Parnelli's #15 Mustang was driven by Swede Savage. Kwech dropped out after 19 laps with brake problems after leading the race. Posey took the lead and stayed there.

The race was between Posey and Savage. Posey broke a valve near the end of the race slowing him down. Swede put forth a huge effort to catch him, but cut a tire on debris from the track, and came in second. In June at Mid-Ohio even though the Mustangs ran a good race, the Bucknum Camaro slipped by finishing just ahead of the Jones' Mustang. All the Mustangs finished. George

Follmer was third, Revson came in second and Kwech was 10th.

At Bridgehampton, New York, Penske put Donohue in the Bucknum Camaro after his engine blew while warming it up. Even though Donohue had to start at the rear of the race since he did not qualify in the car, he fought his way up to the front to challenge the Mustangs. Follmer and Jones fought for first place for 29 laps which must have burned Moore because the last thing a race team manager wants is his own team members breaking their cars racing against each other. Jones went in for fuel leaving room for Donohue and Jerry Titus in a Chevy powered Firebird (Chevy-powered because the Firebird engines weren't strong enough to race). Follmer won, Revson came in 5th. Jones went out with a broken shifter, a wiring fire and a flat tire. Kwech lost his transmission.

Following Lime Rock, the Shelby Team was plagued with problems, starting when Horst Kwech wrapped his Boss around one of the few trees on the Donnybrooke course in Brainerd, Minnesota, in July, after running a great race. (Follmer's car went out in an accident in that race as well). Parnelli Jones won at Brainerd, his fourth win out of the last five races, and Revson came in 3rd. Donohue blew the engine in his Camaro. The Ford Boss Mustangs held 42 points to Chevy's 30, the Pontiac team had 13 and the AMC cars had 8.

The sixth race at Loudon, New Hampshire, was Donohue's second win of the season. Jones gave him a run for first but went out with an overheated engine. Kwech's engine broke early in the race. Revson came in third and Follmer fourth. The Mustangs had a six point advantage over the Camaros. There was hope that Captain Nice would stub his toe.

But the wheels came off Ford's train at Ste. Jovite, Canada, in August 1969. The Mustangs did a tremendous job during the 3 hours of the Le Mans Circuit Trans-Am that warm day in Canada. Jones, Follmer and Donohue fought for the lead until the ninth lap. Jones' shift linkage jammed, taking him out of the race. But Ford's effort all came apart in Lap 14. Follmer's Boss blew an engine and spewed oil all over the track, causing him to hit a guardrail. He had just gotten out of the car when a Mini plowed into his Mustang. Kwech slid into the fence, pinning a marshal, breaking his arm. Revson came around at speed, piled into the mess, sailing his car aloft until he landed his car on the hood of a Firebird. Three Mustangs were involved as well as a lot of the other cars in the race. Revson even received an embarrassing injury. Opening the door to step out, he failed to realize that he was ten feet off the ground and fell out, dislocating his shoulder.

The Mustangs weren't damaged that badly in the pileup. But after the tow trucks were finished you could say so were the cars. A tow truck driver looped a steel cable around the roof of Kwech's Mustang to lift it over the guardrail doing serious damage to the car. All three Mustangs were all but destroyed. Donohue, with the luck of the Irish, managed to miss the accident and went on to win the race.

Camaro now led the series, 49 to 46. All the damaged Mustang racecars were taken back to Detroit to salvage what was left. They did it the cheap way—instead of building all new cars they pieced together two Boss racers from the wrecks of the three Bosses in the week between races.

But when they got to the next race, they found that the pieced-together bodies just didn't work as well as the original ones had. At Watkins Glen, only three Mustangs made it to the track. Kwech's car was out of the race. Jones took the lead early in the only original Boss but went out with a bad tire. Donohue took the lead. Both Donohue and Jones were black flagged for passing under a caution flag. Their punishment was that they had report to the pits to be reprimanded by the track steward. Donohue got there first and got back on the track while Jones was still getting toasted by the officials. Parnelli never caught up. It was Donohue's third straight win. Follmer and Revson did not finish. The Camaro team now had 58 points to the Mustangs 52.

In August, at Laguna Seca in California, Shelby put his old friend and some-time partner Dan Gurney into one of the Shelby cars, replacing Horst Kwech, who had only finished one race the whole season. Gurney brought his own mechanics from his own shop, All-American Racers (AAR) in Santa Ana, California. It didn't make any difference. Jones and Follmer traded first place until the sixth lap when Jones went out of the race with rear end problems. Follmer led until a brake line broke. He went out of the race with a cracked wheel. Donohue won his fourth race. Gurney finished third, Revson fourth. The Penske Camaro team now had 67 points to the Ford team's 56. So, even though Gurney was universally acknowledged as a great driver, he wasn't an immediate star when on the Shelby team.

After Laguna, Gurney complained that the Shelby team wasn't getting the best parts—that they were going to Shelby's rival, Bud Moore, instead. But Lew Spencer said the Shelby team's problems were worse, going way back to when they lost Chuck Cantwell, Shelby's ace suspension man, to the Penske team. Spencer's opinion was that—without Cantwell—the Shelby team couldn't match the Moore team. At Kent, Washington, the Ford team needed to take first and second in order to catch up in points with the Camaro team. Ford rented the track prior to the race to try and sort out the problems in advance.

During the race, Parnelli Jones held the lead for Ford for the first 74 laps. Donohue blew his Camaro's engine, raising the hopes of the Ford team. Jones pitted with a stuck safety valve in his fuel tank. Ronnie Bucknum took the lead. Jones got back in the race and gave it another valiant effort. During the last lap, he blew a tire and crossed the finish line with a shower of sparks coming off his tireless wheel, finishing second to Bucknum. Revson finished fourth and Gurney tenth. Follmer had an accident in lap 129, almost at the end of the 135 lap race.

But Ford was now the underdog. Five straight wins for the Camaro team gave them 72 points to Ford's 62.

The September race at Sears Point in Sonoma, California, gave the Penske team another chance to outperform the Ford team. Revson was out of the race with carb problems. The Jones pit crew was a lot slower than Donohue's. Even though Jones led most of the race, Donohue's pit crew was putting his Camaro back on the track faster. Donohue's team could do three pit stops in the time the Jones' crew could do two.

Some races are won in the pits. In the final seven laps. Jones was forced to drive like a wild man, sliding around corners, locking up his brakes, speed shifting in the straightaways, to make up for his team's slow pit crew. The season ended with Mark Donohue outdoing the Mustangs again to win the 1969 championship. But Donohue hadn't had it easy—he had to win six of the last seven races in order to beat Parnelli Jones and the remaining Mustangs. Moore's team proved to be faster and more dependable than the Shelby team, earning Ford's full support by the end of the season. The race wasn't just to win with the Mustangs. It was also to see which team would be awarded the contract to carry the Ford flag into battle next season.

The Shelby-American team was subsequently left out in the cold for 1970. Ford failed to renew their contract. Shelby tried to put a good face on it by saying "Ford's takeover of the racing team took the fun out of it."

Shelby further severed his relationship with Ford. He didn't say: "From now on you're the enemy" but the raft of lawsuits he filed against Ford in the years that followed showed he wasn't exactly nostalgic about their former good relationship.

When you ask, "How is it that a guy who could help Ford win a major world class event like Le Mans could lose in Trans-Am?" the answer has to be that the Shelby-American company that had built the Cobras and Ford GTs in the '60s wasn't the same company—man for man—that the Shelby Racing Co. was in Trans-Am. A lot of the good people had left. And you have to factor in the fact that Trans-Am, though an entirely domestic series, was incredibly competitive—Shelby was up against GM and Chrysler's engineering staffs and some great drivers.

Shelby went on to other forms of racing, and sponsored futile efforts, buying a couple of Can-Am cars, including a McLaren made by the same young driver he had hired years earlier to test the GT40 for Ford, Bruce McLaren. He also bought a Lola T-70 roadster built by Eric Broadley, who had been Ford's first partner in developing the GT40. Shelby's Lola had one significant victory—in Japan! And he even commisioned a racecar of his own over in England, one designed by Len Terry that was powered by a 351 Cleveland. That car, which had unorthodox pushrod-activated horizontal springs, used up months in getting sorted out and never reached its potential. (Even 40 years later vintage racers who own it are still trying to sort it out!)

A try at Indy as a car owner in '68 also proved disappointing. Shelby had seen the potential in Andy Granatelli's STP turbine cars and come back to Indy with his own turbine car designed by British engineer Ken Wallis, one complete with 4WD. Doug Stokes, racing historian of note, says, "The car was a dead nuts rip-off of the Granatelli sidewinder car, and I believe it led to a lawsuit." His drivers were Bruce McLaren and Denis Hulme, two Le Mans winners.

But the Shelby turbine car proved to be pitifully slow in practice. Indy observers say the problem was that Shelby's turbine supplier, GE, didn't supply him with a turbine with the power that the Pratt and Whitney-powered Granatelli cars had. Plus there was the politics. The Indy track officials were worried that turbines would take over Indy racing, and throw a lot of the traditional teams out of the running if they couldn't compete with cars powered by essentially what were jet engines. So in defense of keeping the status quo, the officials kept coming up with more and more restrictions on the size of the air intake that could be used in turbine cars, basically choking off their horsepower.

Shelby could see the writing on the wall. He had launched a doomed ship. Then, too, there was a personal side to Shelby's decision to pull out. A dear friend, Mike Spence, had been killed in practice testing a turbine-powered Lotus. He wasn't part of the Shelby team, but Shelby, knowing the general public would think there was something wrong with all turbine cars, seized upon Spence's crash as a good reason to depart. Al Dowd, Shelbys right hand man at the time recalls: "Shelby looked at me and asked 'Is there any reason we should still be here?' and we couldn't think of any."

The Shelby Indy team pulled out of Gasoline Alley in the middle of the night, leaving a sign on the door that read something about having to further develop their car. Some felt it was a face-saving gesture but other feel that the car had some fundamental problem, making them unsteerable in traffic.

After Shelby's efforts with the Lola and the McLaren, in 1969 Ford cast their lot with the Agapiou brothers, two ex-Shelby American mechanics, funding a Can-Am car effort based on the Ford G7A, essentially a Mk. IV with the roof cut off. It had a large engine nicknamed "Calliope" because of all the pipes sticking up in the air. The G7A was doen without Shelby but at least used the lighter Mark IV's honeycomb chassis. It was a failure which never did get sorted out.

Ford also tossed some money to Shelby's "enemy," Holman & Moody, funding them to run a car called the Honker II in Can-Am, driven by Mario Andretti and sponsored by Paul Newman. It was built by Alan Mann in the U.K. but it was a very unsuccessful car. The Honker II was lightweight, 225 pounds lighter than a Lola T70, but the trouble was that it had a small block in what had become a big block world.

A lost era began in Shelby's life then, one that has never been fully explored by car historians who, after all, center on Shelby's relationship with cars. The story will be told someday, involving a game ranch in an African country, one that fulfills "every boy's dream" (back in the Thirties when Clyde Beatty had a lions-and-tiger show) of being a big game hunter.

In a nutshell, the game ranch existed, and Shelby led safaris, but it was in one of those countries that changes names and dictators like restaurants change menus and eventually what Shelby built up there was summarily taken away, the prime hunting concessions granted to someone else—a local who was in tight with the country's ruler who, had some point decided to appoint himself Emperor, always a bad sign in Africa.

Shelby could generally get along with all kinds of folks but this Emperor was, as they say in Texas, "meaner than a skilletful of rattlesnakes."

So he returned to Texas.

Return to racing? Shelby had no incentive (and no sponsor, having burned his bridges with Ford). Still plagued with heart problems, he was tired of racing, that much was for sure. He told the press all he wanted to do was go home to his ranch in Texas. With his heart problems he thought maybe that pulling out of racing would help reduce the strain.

Back in Texas he began raising appaloosa horses, and claims he became so good at it—and won so many awards—that an Appalossa horse breeder's association somehow banned him. He never really retired from ranching and as late as 2006 was releasing press releases about his latest breeding program—forming a syndicate to import Tuli cattle directly from Zimbabwe first to Canada and then to the U.S.

The cattle, says Shelby, can take the heat of Texas and then some. Always the superlatives. (But if he's right, is a Tuli-burger far behind?)

A funny story from that time when Shelby drifted into relative obscurity is when he was selected to be part of a judging committee at a concours d'elegance. At a party afterwards he was seated next to a lady who didn't know cars from Adam and she looked at his name badge that read "Carroll Shelby, Ford mechanic."

"Oh," she said, "Can you tell me what's wrong with my Pinto?"

After he left both racing and car making, the car world thought they had seen the last of Carroll Shelby.

They thought wrong.

Highland Park, Michigan The late '80s.

The auto executive looked out the window. The view was bleak. Snow was falling and the trees were bare of leaves. If you took a color picture, he was willing to bet it would look like a picture taken in black and white.

He had just gotten the 10-day report on sales and, while things were looking up, he could tell they were still too much on the bread and butter side.

Ma-and-pa cars. Puddle jumpers.

What Chrysler needed, dammit, was some goddamn excitement—some tire burning cars with engines that could wind to 7,000 rpm and beyond.

Who ya' gonna call but Shelby?

When Shelby had worked for Ford, it was with Lee Iacocca. Iacocca, who, as seen by his success with the Mustang, had the reputation of being a man who could turn a sow's ear into a silk purse (the Mustang, after all, had started with the dull-as-dirt Falcon).

When Iacocca went to Chrysler, he was determined to use every arrow in his quiver. One was to start Chrysler on the minivan, an idea that had been jelling at Ford but which management had tarried on (much to their regret when they saw Chrysler premiere it first).

Iacocca would bring that concept to reality. And he would add some excitement to the Chrysler brands, by livening up the product line by associating various models with various personalities from Frank Sinatra to Carroll Shelby.

The Sinatra connection was dubious at best. Iacocca brought out an "FS Imperial" which had a discreet badge that alluded to the famous crooner's initials but everybody who knew Frank (whose nickname was "The Chairman of the Board") knew that out in Palm Springs Ol' Blue Eyes drove at minimum a hand-built Corniche, not a production line Detroit car. So that promotion went nowhere.

Almost all of Shelby Dodges in the beginning were based on the Omni/Horizon, which was designed by Chrysler Europe (a merger of Simca and Rootes Group). It had unibody construction, with an independent iso-strut front suspension using coil springs. The Omni/Horizon basically saved Chrysler. Consumers were eager to buy an All-American economy car and snapped up 189,000 total in the platform's first year.

Before calling Shelby, Iacocca attempted to develop themes that would "resonate" with buyers, sporting names like the Dodge 024 Turismo and Plymouth TC3 but these cars made virtually no impression on the public. "Turismo" was Italian for "touring" as in "Gran Turismo."

But Iacocca was stretching it very thin.

Names did not make a memorable car, people did. The enthusiast press yawned, bored stiff with this tomfoolery.

Then he tried calling Alejandro DeTomaso, his pal from the days at Ford when DeTomaso had made over 6,000 mid-engined Pantera sports cars for Lincoln-Mercury. The resulting Omni 024 DeTomaso had no more DeTomaso content than DeTomaso floor mats and a decal or two.

What a sad joke and dilution of the Italian brand's name! So after all these shameless hypes failed, Iacocca called Shelby, with whom he had worked hand in glove during the Cobra and Shelby Mustang days.

Shelby was done with Africa. He hadn't been booted out of his stint as game preserve owner, but let's just say that because of politics on the continent, Africa was not the safest place to be, even if you had a Weatherby, a good eye, and hand-loaded magnum cartridges. Shelby had decamped and was open to opportunities.

Shelby as a spokesman for Dodge was more believable than the weak DeTomaso tie-in. But looking back, it seems as if it was a bad idea on the face of it at first. After all, Shelby's reputation had been built entirely on building fast rear wheel drive cars powered by hulking V8s.

But Iaccoca was hoping that the buyers of the 1980s would be more educated than they had been in the '60s. After all, the buyers of America had now been exposed to fast front wheel drive cars like the turbocharged Saabs and the VW GTi (a model so desirable, that when VW's U.S. distributor refused to import it to the U.S., buyers would sneak them over from Canada). Iacocca hoped that they had reached the point where they realized that speed wasn't the only parameter where you measured a car's performance. Real racers went around corners, he reasoned, and it was about time America built cars that could do that too.

You had to have the handling to cope with speed, so Iacocca set the goal with Shelby to make front wheel drive cars that would have European-type handling. Plus Iacocca had no choice—Dodge had to try to promote fast front wheel drive cars because they had inadvertently let all their rear wheel drive high performance cars fade out a decade earlier. Front drive cars were all they had. The question was: would Shelby's magic work on those?

Iacocca was willing to take a chance. Iacocca had one thing going for him—the other Detroit cars, due to the automakers struggling to meet emissions laws, had become woefully emasculated. Shelby alluded to this when he was interviewed in the Detroit Free Press where he pointed out that, in his learned opinion, "The Pontiac Firebird Trans-Am is one of the most beautiful cars ever designed but it couldn't pull a greased string out of a dead cat's ass." Chrysler PR officials cringed at Shelby's colorful language, but some GM engineers called Shelby to thank him for saying what they couldn't say.

Overall the media treated Shelby, according to Carl Goodwin, an executive at K & E, Chrysler's ad agency at the time, like a "returning hero bringing renewed excitement to autodom."

Goodwin says that Chrysler was just beginning to wake up, because up until Shelby came along, "our market consisted of the fat ladies wearing turquoise stretch pants at the supermarket."

Goodwin remembers having a couple of strategy meetings with Shelby. "Of course he has always had an outstanding sense of what the market wants and likes," recalls Goodwin. "One of the first ads we did involved not the area of motorsports that made him famous—road racing—but drag racing. He had an idea of running an ad about the Chrysler Hemi V8 engine being used in Ford and GM funny cars. I wrote an ad with the headline 'Thanks GM and Ford for using Chrysler engines in your funny cars.' It created somewhat of a flurry on the drag racing scene and underscored the superiority of Chrysler engineering."

The NHRA hated the ads, which in effect dropped the mask that a lot of marques could only go fast with a Chrysler V8. The campaign was dropped.

The next campaign was to promote the entrance of Chrysler's four-cylinder into road racing. Unfortunately they didn't have a winning car yet but the agency did field an ad where it showed a Dodge front drive racecar with the good parts highlighted as in the '65 Shelby ads and the headline "How to Build an IMSA Charger" with a little picture of Carroll Shelby, performance Guru, up in the corner, with his famous signature. The ad for enthusiasts' magazines had the headline "Only Chrysler will give you a direct connection with Carrol Shelby."

By the time all the prints ads ran—directed to various sub-groups like autocross fans, off-road fans, etc—sales of Direct Connection performance parts shot up 150%.

So like Shelby in the sixties, Chrysler was making money selling performance parts associated with Shelby while they were still grooming a Shelby car to sell.

A modest budget was created and Shelby showed up and got down to business, setting up his own engineering team operating out of Sante Fe Springs, California a suburb of Los Angeles, ironically the same town where, several decades earlier, he and hot rodder Dean Moon had first installed a Ford V8 into an A.C. to create the first Cobra.

Chrysler nicknamed Shelby's facility the "Skunk Works" in honor of the famed Lockheed facility in Burbank where Lockheed had created their top secret spyplanes like the U2 and SR-71 Blackbird.

Before Shelby could actually develop any cars, Chrysler announced the Shelby Charger—a more or less tapes and stripes job that didn't have much improved mechanical content.

Later, when Shelby had enough time to develop special models that would carry his own name first, and have Shelby's own serial numbers, he made several that are considered worthy of note. Among them:

—'86 GLH-S, based on Dodge's Omni GLH, with Koni adjustable shocks and struts, 15-inch tall Goodyear Gatorbacks and powered by a 175 bhp 2.2-liter Turbo II turbocharged engine with air-to-air intercooler.

—'87 CSX, based on Dodge Shadow, Turbocharged, air-to-air intercooler,a tuned intake system, modified electronic fuel injection controller, powered by a 175 hp four.

—'87 Shelby Lancer based on the ES T1, a luxury performance 4-door sedan with 175 hp, integrated Marchal foglights, and a leather option.

Chrysler also shamelessly used Shelby to "shill" the press, i.e pump them up when there was not much coming up in new product to promote.

One such memorable incident was when two outsiders came up with a custom designed mid-engined sports car based on the A.C. ME3000 platform, which must have caught Shelby's attention, as the Cobra was but an ol' A.C. sports car that he had juiced up with a Yank powerplant. Shelby talked them into loaning it to Chrysler as a test car and had it repainted to look like a Chrysler car. He then would leave it parked near a slalom course that journalists were invited to drive on, in little contests with Chrysler front wheel drive cars (first prize: a Rolex watch—shameless, those journalists). Naturally journalists would see the prototype and say: "What's that car?" and Shelby would act all surprised and embarrassed, saying "Oh, that wasn't supposed to be there," and have it promptly whisked away. The press would then rush to their typewriters and write that Chrysler was experimenting with a mid-engined car which momentarily added a little luster to an otherwise bleak picture.

Eventually Shelby gave the car back to the young designers, the car only slightly the worse for wear. They weren't miffed by the rejection of it for production—after all, they had had their 15 minutes of fame working with a legend in his own time.

And we can't forget Shelby's side deals. Shelby and Iacocca's right hand man, Hank Carlini, imported five DeTomaso Panteras through Chrysler (automakers being allowed to bring in non-conforming cars as test vehicles) and had Chrysler V8s installed. Perhaps they were thinking Chrysler could re-body the now aging Pantera for a whole new audience but, after a couple clay models were done at the new Chrysler design center in California, the plan died and the imported test cars were sold off, the only Chrysler V8-powered Panteras ever made. Shelby kept one to drive in Europe.

But not all the Shelby back door projects got shot down. One that actually came to be and had full support from the corporation was a club racer called a Can Am Spec Racer, using a Chrysler V-6. The idea of this was to have a racing series composed of identical cars so that it would be the drivers' skills tested at each race, not the cars, mechanics, or engine builder's skills. A few dozen were made but the series died due to the high cost of the car—close to $75,000. An interesting note is that Shelby called upon his old protégé/competitor Pete Brock to design the car. Brock did his best but after he was done, Chrysler redesigned it without consulting him. The last straw for Brock was when Chrysler designers added side intake scoops big enough for an F-16!

Still, Shelby calling back a member of his old crew was in line with one of his lifelong character traits—if you did him good once, he never forgot you.

He also sought to replicate some of the famous moves he had made while at Ford. In a move reminiscent of the days when Peyton Cramer arrived back from his first sales call to announce that he had sold 1,000 Shelbys to Hertz, in 1988, Shelby scored a coup by selling 1,000 of this new generation of Shelby cars to Thrifty Car Rental. Known as CSX-Ts, the 1988 models weren't quite up to regular specs in that the stock T1 engines were retained for durability. The differences from the previous year were 15 x 6.5-inch Shelby wheels, and the colors were all the same, white with blue and silver trim.

Shelby's sojourn at the Skunk Works was not easy. One would think that Chrysler would, after inviting him into the tent, given the maestro of speed carte blanche to select any items he wanted from Chrysler's parts bin such had been the arrangement he had with Ford when building the Shelby Mustangs. Alas, this wasn't the case. Shelby could ask for it, but might not get it.

For instance when he was making the CSX, Shelby wanted to use the powerful Turbo 2 engine in his new project, but Chrysler couldn't spare them. So he changed the Turbo 1s to T2 specs—cheaper than swapping the engines. The production line installed T2 intake, turbo, throttle body, intercooler, and the associated parts.

Again when Shelby asked for the more expensive German-made A555 Getrag transaxle, the answer was "no" so he was forced to have the American-made transaxle computer re-programmed to limit torque to assure durability.

In 1989, Shelby finally was able to go whole hog on the last CSX. He got more aggressive styling out of the Chrysler and finally wrested from them some better hard parts, such as the tougher Turbo 2 engine and the stronger A555 Getrag transaxle. In addition, Shelby modified the engines with a Variable Nozzle Turbo, which eliminated the turbo-lag and upped the torque by over 25 ft-lbs. This model was called the VNT. Finally Shelby was pushing the envelope, making "pocket rockets" that could keep up with the Euro imports.

He was also continuing to experiment with new materials. The CSX VNT, for instance, was also the first car ever built with plastic wheels. They were called "Fiberide" and were 15 inches by 6.5 inches and much lighter than aluminum counterparts. Tires were standard Goodyear 195 x 60R15 with optional 225 x 50R15 Gatorbacks. The car had an aggressive front air dam, rear wing, and side skirts.

But cars Shelby created for Dodge had a problem with image as far as durability. They were true 'nickel rockets'—impressive for a brief while before fading out. It didn't help that the warranty on the Shelby-branded ones was shorter than the regular Dodge offerings, a dark indication that even Chrysler thought they were dicey on longevity. Plus Shelby always seemed to get a late start on getting his entry for the year ready so by the time they came along each year, the hoopla over new models was long gone.

The idea of small two door coupes was the first generation cars Shelby modified for Chrysler but Shelby also yearned to show that Dodge had potential in the family sedan area as well. The Shelby Lancer was his touring sedan entry with turbocharged performance equaling that of the European competition such as the BMW 3-series. In every interview with a journalist, Shelby would point out it handled and performed like a German car and was ideal for those but who didn't want to pay German car prices. (Ironically, less than two decades later, Chrysler was bought lock, stock and barrel by a German automaker, Daimler-Benz).

Shelby's first Sojourn at Chrysler was disappointing to Shelby and to the fans. Chrysler was so greedy to make money off every possible use of the Shelby name that, at the same time they were paying Shelby to make Shelby-branded limited editions, they would continually undermine Shelby by selling Dodge-branded

Shelbys that had some better parts than the Shelby-branded Dodges, inexcusable when, if they were touting the influence of a world acknowledged tuning expert like Shelby, his cars should have had first choice of the best parts.

A case in point was in 1987, after Shelby brought out the Shelby Lancer. Shelby's version was a one-year only model run, but then in '88 Dodge came out with the Dodge Lancer Shelby. They were using the name "Shelby" but there was no numbered dash plaque in the Dodge version and Shelby's name was nowhere on the car except on the outside. The Dodge version was a blend of what Shelby had offered and the Lancer ES. The stiffer springs were used, the power steering was offered, but the Monroe Formula GP struts and shocks Shelby had used were replaced by lower cost units from the ES. Dodge also failed to offer the rear disc brakes that Shelby had used on his version, instead mounting cheaper drums. Then, in a weird reverse move, Dodge offered a true Turbo 2 engine rather than a converted Turbo 1. It didn't have more power but was more robust than the converted engine Shelby had used. So, they had denied Shelby the engine he needed for his version only to offer it in their own.

From Chrysler's point of view, though, the tie-in with Shelby was golden. After all, they sold many more cars with the Shelby name on them than Ford did in the Sixties. But are the Shelby Dodges collectible? Dodge nixed the chances of that ever happening by muddying the waters between which ones were Dodge Shelbys and which ones were Shelby Dodges, so that anyone outside of a dedicated marque collector's club is hard put to affix a ranking or value. Tom Corcoran, the historian, says in recent years Shelby Dodges have been somewhat 'ghettoized.' "You won't find them in the Shelby-American world registry or see them selling for six figures at the Barrett Jackson auction," he says. Corcoran figures that Shelby purists look down their noses at four-cylinder and front-drive cars and consider the only proper Shelby to be one with a Ford oval on it.

Consequently, the Shelby Dodges and Dodge Shelby's remain a little known secret—if you find one on a used car lot and the salesman doesn't know the name "Shelby" from Adam, you might be able to pick up a fun to drive car at a very attractive price. Each true Shelby Dodge had only a one year run, received a numbered dash plaque and was only titled as a "Shelby" but even that doesn't provoke anywhere near the same interest that's shown in Shelby built Fords. For a ranking of which Shelby Dodges are the most desirable, we quote Steve Thorton, of the Shelby Dodge Club who says "The '86 GLHS and the '89 CSX-VNT are the best deals for the money while, while the SL is unique as Shelby's one foray into the world of high performance touring sedans."

There were indications that Chrysler had planned to go up-market with the Shelby name. In 1990, there was a plan for a 16-valve car, but that was cancelled. According to Dan Fitzgerald, a Dodge dealer who was able to sample a prototype, the 16-valve may have had too much power— "It had more torque steer than you could hang onto," he recalls (torque steer being the tendency of front drive cars to veer off to one direction on acceleration). It might have also been canned because it was thought it would diminish the luster of the 16-valve being offered in the TC by Maserati, a pet project of the Chairman which turned out to be another Italian-American misadventure like the Pantera program Iacocca had instigated at Ford, a program equally fraught with problems.

Shelby's only role with the TC program was simply to submit a DOHC head design for the four cylinder, and it was said he was in competition there with Cosworth and Maserati, but, wouldn't cha' know, it was a set-up from the word "go" with the winner already determined—Maserati—so that Chrysler could stretch the truth a bit and say the car had a Maserati engine (they knew that the common public didn't much know the difference between engine blocks and heads) but the twin cam head in truth ended up being made by Cosworth.

Iacocca's choice of builder of the TC was Maserati, then owned by Alejandro DeTomaso. Shelby managed to steer clear of the project, understandably wary because of a previous deal with DeTomaso going South, but it wasn't a total turkey.

In fact, you could say the TC accomplished Iacocca's goal—over 6,000 were made and every one sold, and it served Iacocca's purposes in beating the Cadillac Allante (also bodied in Italy) to market, though it wasn't on the market much longer than Caddy's two seater. Ironically only a handful of the highly tweaked four cylinder DOHC versions were made while the bulk of the TCs went out the door with a Mitsubishi-supplied V-6, leading one to ask "Exactly how Italian can an Italian car be if it's got a Japanese-made engine?"

The brutal answer? Not very.

One of the last cars created during Shelby's first tie-in with Chrysler was the Shelby Dakota pickup truck. Chrysler couldn't resist it. Their trucks were selling better than their cars and they wanted to see if the Shelby touch could help pump up truck sales. But the truck had a mere 175 hp 318 cubic-inch V8 when anybody would expect a truck carrying the Shelby name to have a Godzilla engine, something like the Viper-powered pickup Chrysler made a decade or so later. The point Chrysler never grasped was: Why were they hiring a gunslinger and then equipping him with only a piddling 22? Shelby was the magnum load and should have been saved for ultimate muscle cars. Shelby later offered a kit that added 25 hp but it didn't save the Shelby Dakota.

Car companies have a tendency to do that—starting out with a name that adds luster to their products but then over-using the name just as Ford did the "Ghia" name. In 1969, Ford bought Ghia Carrozzeria in Italy and at first only used the coveted Ghia badge on cars legitimately designed by Ghia like the Pantera, but eventually began plastering it on any Ford with a fancy interior.

The result: they devalued the name to zero.

During the time Shelby was being promoted in Dodge ads, a new image was groomed for him, sort of a combination of his standard old cowpoke look with a dash of Johnny Cash black. The 10-gallon hat was there and a jeans jacket (you dare not look too rich for a middle class market). Fan clubs for the products sprung up.

But the clock was running out. The demand was falling to the point where dealers were refusing to take the new Shelby Dodges because they still had last year's models sitting on the showroom floor.

Chrysler cancelled the program. By sheer numbers of cars out the door, though, you had to say it was a success. More Dodges bearing the name Shelby were sold than Ford had sold Mustangs bearing the Shelby name in the sixties.

The truth is that, Chrysler at that time, for all the vaunted success of Iacocca (touted in his own books) sold Drek. On the other hand, you could agree that Shelby improved the Drek.

Thinking long term now, Shelby succeeded ever so incrementally in moving the mindset of American car enthusiasts a few millimeters from their old way of defining what performance was. Now the old hot rodders were willing to concede that, yes those front wheel drive puddle jumpers could be fun, even if they would be blown off the road in the propwash from a passing Cobra.

In fact, one could build a solid case for proving that the modern-day Chrysler Neon SRT/4 became popular because of the groundwork laid by Shelby for Dodge almost two decades earlier—Shelby proving front wheel drive cars could be as fun to drive as the rear wheel drive musclecars of the Sixties. You have only to drive a modern Neon SRT/4 for ten minutes on a winding road to realize that it is indeed a car with "soul," the kind of front wheel drive car Shelby had been trying to build for Chrysler but never quite got there because of lack of quality and technology.

Eventually, even Iacocca realized he had been using Shelby wrongly, associating him with the wrong cars. Sometime in the late '80s, Iacocca called in Shelby for a little set-to. He knew the topic would be something Shelby would warm to: an all-new Chrysler sports car.

A rear wheel drive sports car, something mean and nasty and totally outrageous, in fact something built very much along the lines of his legendary 427 Cobra...

Chapter 15- Chrysler's Cobra: The Viper

Ann Arbor, Michigan, the late '80s.

It was a nice summer evening. The executive decided to wear his leather bomber jacket, and pulled on his stringback driving gloves as he strode out to the barn where he kept his stable of machinery. He looked over the row of cars and decided, as long as the weather forecaster was promising that it wouldn't rain, the Cobra would do.

He delicately opened the eggshell-thin aluminum door and sat down. He started the engine which emitted a satisfying roar. He backed out, put it in gear and headed down the driveway.

A few minutes later, he was parked outside the pseudo German bratskeller.

He liked this place because they not only had good German Schnapps, but would allow him to smoke his Macunados out on the veranda.

"Is that your car?" an attractive waitress asked, nodding in the direction of the Cobra. The executive smiled. He was always noticed when he drove up in the Cobra.

"Yes," he said. "Like it?"

"I love it," she gushed. He smiled and inspected the ash of his cigar. The trick was to get the ash burning evenly or it was no damn good.

Forty five minutes later he was home. He walked to the phone and called out to his wife. "Dear, do we have a number for Carroll Shelby?"

He had an idea.

Chrysler would make its own damn Cobra.

The man with the cigar was Bob Lutz, then a Chrysler executive (now at GM) who qualifies as one of America's most true blue enthusiasts. Born in Switzerland the son of a banker but educated in the U.S. (UC Berkeley) Lutz has cultivated the reputation of being somewhat of a renaissance man. He is among other things: multi-lingual, holder of a Masters in Business, a former U.S. Marine fighter pilot, a best-selling business book author, owner of his own jet fighter trainer, a sports car collector, a former executive for major automakers in the U.S. and abroad, a cigar afficienado, a chronometric watch collector, etc. And he no doubt makes a pretty good cheese fondue.

Some thought him dictatorial but at least, in an industry full of sheep, Lutz has always been a lion. (He even wrote a book chronicling his approach to executive decision-making, unabashedly titling it *GUTS*.) Lutz says he conceived of the Viper one evening when he was tooling around the environs of Ann Arbor, Michigan, in his A.C. Mk. IV, the car that picked up the Cobra after A.C. left off.

Shelby, upon receiving the call, was thumbs up. Make a new Cobra? "Hell, yes," said the Snakemeister. "But dammit, the name 'Cobra,'" he informed Lutz, "is tied up."

That was a sore subject with Shelby. One author says that Shelby thought he could get the name back from Ford for Chrysler. But it was nothing doing. However, that didn't deter Lutz who, after more thought on the subject, was building up a head of steam to go ahead on the project. The Cobra was a snake. At one point, he grabbed the thesaurus and looked up the word "snake" and pretty soon came across the even meaner sounding word, "viper."

The first step was to make a show car—sort of let's-run-it-up-the-flagpole-and-see-who-salutes thing.

According to Bob Hubbach, who had a many years of design involvement with the Dodge Viper program, "The Viper RT10 show car was created from a series of theme sketches by a designer named Craig Durfey. It was a running show car. That's all it was. But, after the sensational response it generated at the Detroit International Auto Show, it was green-lighted as a production model and it then became my assignment to re-design it for production."

In short order, a show car called the Viper was made. It followed what one Chrysler executive called a "take no prisoners" design approach, basically the same formula as the big block Cobra—long hood, short rear deck, monster engine, fat tires, mag wheels and side exhaust pipes as thick as a weightlifter's biceps. Under the hood was a V-10. Actually it was a mocked up engine. Chrysler didn't have a V-10 engine. But they didn't let that stop them from showing the car with a V-10. It was a little bit like the philosophy in the film *Field of Dreams*— "If we build it, they will come." It proved wildly popular at its unveiling January 4, 1989 at the North American International Auto Show in Detroit, with showgoers taking out their checkbooks and writing checks for deposits.

This was where Shelby came in. The whole auto industry knew he had an "in" with Chrysler's Chairman of the Board, Lee Iacocca. Shelby had accomplished great things during Iacocca's tenure at Ford. Shelby was briefed on the package and dispatched by the fledgling Viper team on the delicate mission of schmoozing the Chairman in place of Lutz, who not only didn't have the same kind of credibility with Iacocca, but, some thought, was even resented as a rival by Iacocca who was being edged unwillingly into retirement and forever sniping at any would-be successors, the leading and most qualified one of which was Lutz.

Shelby was quoted by Dan Carney in his book *Dodge Viper* as saying "I had to meet with him and tell him we were in budget until we got enough money into it that he couldn't back out." That's what happened. Shelby assured Iacocca that getting a production version ready would only cost $20 million. He was a good $50 million off in his estimates and maybe Iacocca knew that, but if he did, he never admitted it. You don't have to when something is a success.

The Viper was justified to the Chrysler Board on two counts: first, Chrysler needed a halo car to show they were still the best at building a low-cost vehicle of any type (Even though it would still be the most expensive Chrysler product ever built, ironically was relatively inexpensive for a 170-mph sports car). And they needed a high quality car to counter the public image that was coming from a line of cars that were being recalled for product flaws as fast as they were being built, Iacocca's philosophy being along the lines of "build them with flaws and sell them all. We will repair them later." Secondly, the Viper was to be a testbed for new methods of manufacture and assembly to lower the cost of a vehicle. The thought: "We'll build them for a year or two then come out with a newer more refined model."

The first generation Viper was exciting to look at, particularly with the outside pipes reminiscent of the 427 Cobra S/C, and the way the front fenders flared out from the body, as if it were a giant insect that needed to lift its wings in order to breathe. But that first generation was a quality-control nightmare, not any better than the Cobra replicas being built across America by amateurs.

But in all fairness, the goal at that time was never to make a car that was perfectly flawless like a Lexus. With the Viper, Chrysler wasn't out to win the J.D. Power award for customer satisfaction. What they were after was to create a car with a take-no-prisoners attitude, a car with raw animal performance—a brute of a car that would go from 0 to 100 back to 0 in under 15 seconds like a 427 Cobra, cruise at 160 mph plus and above all, look outrageous and scare the women and children. They didn't even design roll-up windows at first—hey, why bother, when this car would be bought by rich people who would only drive it on Sunday mornings in the sunbelt states like Arizona, California and Florida. In short, bought by the very same type of people who owned the original Cobras.

Alan McPhee of *Car Guide Magazine Online* reported Carroll saying of the first Viper, "In my opinion, the Viper is more just-plain-fun to drive than a $500,000 Ferrari. It's not supposed to be the world's most sophisticated sports car, just a '60s-style all-American performance car that'll put a grin on your face when you drive it."

An independent cross-functional team was created, making its own rules and creating its own supplier base. The team leader sifted through scores of volunteers to find appropriate people for what was called "Team Viper." After a brief flirtation with a mid-engined design (one clay was built) they decided to continue on the Cobra route, going front engined but at least balancing out the weight by moving the engine far back.

Chassis prototypes, called "mules" in the automotive industry, were developed to study vehicle dynamics. Initially, Shelby designed his own frame, a sort of spine frame similar to that of the mid-engined 70P Can Am car he had ordered from DeTomaso back in '65 but never picked up when he withdrew funding from the project. Chrysler rejected his concept and designed their own frame, but still consulted with him every step of the way.

According to Bob Hubbach, there was some tussle among Shelby and Lutz over the size of the car. Shelby wanted a smaller, more nimble car that would have been V8-powered, although maybe with twin turbos. Lutz wanted an awesome engine; a torque king, something the emotional equivilent of the late lamented 426 Hemi engine of the Sixties. Lutz prevailed.

Once they had the team and a place to build the car—a section carved out of the floorspace of the aging Conner Avenue plant—they began working hard, sometimes around the clock. "Work" also included the pleasure of renting race tracks like Nelson Ledges and Road Atlanta so that they could, fine-tune the chassis and powertrain under performance conditions.

This was a far cry from the way Detroit usually does things. Only the Corvette group at GM do anything close, but their car was becoming fat and complacent compared to the outrageous Viper which was by contrast cheeky, rude and in-your-face. It was like Chrysler saying "While Chevrolet worries about the shape of the stereo buttons on the Corvette dash, we're gonna make a car that lays rubber a full block when you dump the clutch." If anything it was a throwback to the L-88 Corvette, a 650-hp Beast Chevy made in limited numbers by GM from '67 to '69. One had even been raced at Le Mans by ex-Shelby driver Bob Bondurant its debut year.

In order to make a sports car with such brute performance, the Viper engineering group had to lean on the suppliers to develop super-strong parts. For a car with such power you needed tougher parts that could take the stresses, the high g-loads in cornering, for example. Or rear axles that wouldn't bend like spaghetti when hit with over 500 foot-pounds of torque when you put the pedal to the metal. For an engine, Chrysler was hurting. They had shown the car with a mocked up V-10 but in reality all they had in car engines for rear wheel drive cars was a 360 cubic-inch V8. But that engine was a boat anchor with less than 200 hp. And with not much tuning potential. Lutz, going whole dog, advocated a V-10 because, in his view, in the consumer's eye, the Viper would be measured against the original Cobra. It wouldn't be faster (with safety bumpers, catalytic converters, etc. etc.) he told a reporter but "we have to build a better car than enthusiasts remembered the Cobra to be." In other words, they were competing with an actual car but with a legend!

Fortunately, Dodge had a V-10 scheduled for the Dodge Ram pickup truck. While this seems a crude American solution, a truck engine for a sports car, one has to remember the Ford GT40 in point of fact used a 289 which came from, guess what—a 221 cubic-inch V8 developed as a Canadian Ford truck engine. Engineers would say it doesn't matter where an engine starts, its where it finishes.

They were even able to use the new gearbox that had been developed for the new pickup. In May 1990, Chrysler announced that the Viper would be made with an aluminum V-10; a block designed in the Lamborghini plant (which gave it an etheral exotic quality) and in May, 1991, there was a Viper, rootin', tootin' and ready to serve as the official pace car of the Indianapolis 500, with none other than the Snakemeister himself, Carroll Shelby, at the wheel.

Shelby's turn at the wheel as pace car driver was a miracle in itself because less than a year before—in June 1990—Shelby had been dying. But a 38-year old gambler had dropped dead at a craps table in Las Vegas of a brain aneurism and somehow Shelby's heart doctor got to him in time. There was trouble with his body rejecting his new heart but no more trouble than Shelby had been in before. This was a guy, you must remember, who had been through the ringer on race courses all over the world! We're also talking a guy who had more than once put one of Uncle Sam's perfectly good airplanes deep into the dirt. According to a story in the *Las Vegas Sun*, after removing his original heart the doctors told Shelby, "we've never seen a heart that's had at least 40 heart attacks—your heart was one big piece of scar tissue."

Shelby worked his way out of it, just in time to be behind the wheel of the Viper at Indy, on the start line waiting to pace the race. Shelby's appearance at the Brickyard had a touch of irony about it, too, considering his two previous official appearances there—one to try to qualify in '58 and the other as a car owner in '68. Both times he bombed out.

There's one funny incident worth recalling from Shelby's Viper Pace Car stint. Chrysler flew dozens of journalists and celebrities to Indy to take a ride in the Viper with Carroll Shelby. One of the passengers was the same Army General who had been in charge of the invasion of Iraq in the first Gulf War— "Stormin" Norman Schwarzkopf. Schwarzkopf was once interviewed years later by a reporter who asked him if he had ever been scared. "I wasn't scared in combat," he said, "but one time someone arranged mc for me to have a ride around Indy in a new Dodge Viper. The driver was a pretty old guy and while we were cruising around the track at 140 mph, he told me had just come back from the hospital where he got a heart transplant."

In December of 1991, the first Viper RT/10, a 1992 model, rolled off the assembly line—exactly three years after the concept car's 1989 auto show triumph. There was a scary moment during an early private preview, one scheduled expressly for *Automobile* magazine founder, David E. Davis Jr. Davis had once been an amateur car racer (and like Shelby, had crashed hard, requiring extensive plastic surgery) and was considered a world-class connoisseur of sports cars. He drove the prototype briefly and then jammed to a stop and leapt out when he realized that the ugly smell was the plastic doorsills on fire! An alert PR man threw some cold water from an ice bucket on the pipes and the rocker panels were changed to aluminum for production, but the car almost got off to a bad start as Davis dutifully reported on the malady in his column.

But that problem was forgotten months later as group previews were scheduled for the buff books. Chrysler broke all the rules by first inviting reporters to sit in on engineering sessions while the car was still being developed. Shelby, health permitting, appeared at one or two early Viper press functions but it was Lutz who took the lead when Shelby's health failed, relishing in his romantic role as test pilot/test driver, such as the preview at Sedona, Arizona, where he would arrive in front of the hotel for each journalist's appointed test ride, smoking a foot long cigar. After strapping a journalist in the passenger seat, he would put the pedal to the metal and head for the hills. Even veteran journalists following him in other Vipers had a hard time keeping up with him. Lutz understood that, in order to recreate a legend like the Cobra, you had to have a car that first and foremost delivered the goods. The Viper most certainly did. (And for those journalists who couldn't keep up with a guy in his late '60s on the back roads of Arizona, shame on them!)

The demand for the car far exceeded supply at first, and that first year only 285 cars were made. Some dealers were able to sell them for as much as $200,000, a mere four times the announced price! There were changes throughout the years, such as having to drop the side exhausts, and coming up with a hardtop lid that would stay in place (the first design, a cloth top, famously blew off when *Road & Track*'s European tester, Le Mans winner Paul Frere, was driving a Viper across France at 170 mph plus).

The biggest model change came when they tried to echo Cobra history again by coming up with a coupe concept car in 1993—this one called the GTS (even though in Europe the "S" usually referred to a spyder, an open car). While the GTS and the RT/10 looked like the same car except for the roof, more than 90 percent of the Coupe was new. They had managed to take weight out of the car by going to an all-aluminum suspension system and re-engineered frame. It reached the showrooms as a 1994 model.

This time Bob Hubbach was in charge of the design from the beginning. He recalls "I was the given the assignment in February of 1991 to design a coupe version of the Viper along with a more radical roadster version as a companion car. I took the liberty of adapting the Cobra Daytona stripes and color scheme to re-enforce the spirited impact we were after. But when the sketches went to Tom Gale and subsequently Bob Lutz, it was the coupe sketch which got the enthusiastic approval. It had all the 'right stuff' from day one; Gurney blisters (roof humps for drivers with helmets--Ed.) air dam, wrap-around rear spoiler, NACA hood air scoop and out board exhausts. The GTS Coupe model was started but then shelved for later development as the RT10 roadster was just getting itself established in the marketplace. When the GTS show car was finally was completed in '93 it was a big hit at the 1994 Los Angeles auto show and subsequently approved for production. During the following year we fully developed the body aerodynamics at the Lockheed wind tunnel and incorporated these features into the production car."

The coupe preview, organized by Tom Kowalski (who later went to GM), was a model of how to generate ink. American journalists were flown to France, and got to drive the Viper coupes on racetracks all over France, including at Le Mans. Then, on a spur of the moment whim, Kowalski proposed they run eighteen Viper coupes, three abreast, down the Champs Elysee, the main drag of Paris. They did that, and had crowds cheering—fans who were glad to see Americans back with such a robust enthusiast car, one that recalled the Cobra Daytona coupes that had run at Le Mans almost thirty years before.

One small worry Chrysler PR had about the coupe was: "What would Pete Brock say about it?" Brock being the designer of Shelby's original Cobra coupe. Tom Gale, then heading Chrysler Design, even paid Brock a courtesy visit, showed him the drawings and asked him point blank: "Would you mind if we made a coupe similar in concept to the Cobra Daytona coupe?" Brock was generous, saying "I think your design stands on its own." (A decade later, Brock would be introducing his own Brock coupe, a larger copy of the original Cobra Daytona coupe and a Viper competitor.)

Chrysler showed sheer genius in promoting the Viper, creating a fan base out of nothing. They started a fancy magazine for owners and then helped start a Viper Club of America and made sure that—at events like the Monterey Historic vintage car races—there was a special hospitality tent expressly for Viper owners, each of whom was seen strutting around wearing name badges like "Bob Smith, Roanoke, VA, Viper no. so-and-so." Bob Lutz once shocked some Chrysler stockholders at a stockholders meeting by saying "I would stay longer but I have to go to a Viper Owner's Club event." Viper owners were made to feel special, almost like the owners of the 1,000-plus original A.C. Cobras do today. (The average original A.C. Cobra now being worth 40 to 50 times its original price.)

Only there are a lot more Viper owners. By 2005, over 15,000 Vipers were cruising the world's boulevards and racetracks, making for a very strong and extremely enthusiastic owner core. Currently there are more than 1,700 members of the Viper Club of America and 27 Viper Clubs throughout the United States.

Following in the footsteps laid by Shelby in the '60s, Chrysler even developed a racing version, the GTS-R, announcing it at the Pebble Beach concours, with Bob Lutz doing the introduction and attempting to link the "instant history" of this high powered Chrysler with his early Fifties Chrysler-powered Cunningham racecar.

That was a bit of a stretch, as few reporters at Pebble were old enough to remember the original Cunninghams but the fact was that the race version of the Viper went on to do well in its class at Le Mans (including 10th place finish in GT-1).

Bob Hubbach recalls the moment the race car was introduced to the Viper fans. "In 1995, at Monterey, California, the 1996 production coupe was presented first to the Viper Club owners at a banquet dinner along with the prototype GTS/R race car by Bob Lutz, both resulting in a standing ovation. When the race car's engine was started in the dining hall, some enthusiastic Viper owners were loudly cheering and began jumping up and down on the dinner tables! The next day at Pebble Beach, It was presented again to the public and to the press core along with a rousing dissertation about Chryslers racing heritage."

Hubbach remembers, "It was during these events that I first met Peter Brock. We talked a lot together about design; both the evolution of the Viper coupe into the GTS/R and of his design challenges with the Cobra Coupe and his experiences with the racing development. We became fast friends and I have the utmost respect for him. He's the real thing."

For various reasons the GTS coupe did not adopt the concave rear end of the Brock design of the '64 Cobra Daytona coupe but overall the car has the same presence—a kick-ass attitude that says, "I take no prisoners."

Particularly pleasing to Chrysler was how a French team, ORECA, took to this American monster and raced it, finishing 1st and 2nd in the GT2 class at Le Mans. And this during an era when the French were supposed to be solidly Anti-American! Just over fifty Viper racecars were built, far beyond the days when Shelby-American built just six Cobra Daytona coupes and refused to sell them to outsiders while they were still competitive.

Eventually Chrysler did a full convertible version, called the SRT-10, its chassis all new and even the body shape was different. This, they thought, would make for a Viper more competitive comfort-wise with the Corvette. They thought wrong. The convertibles built up an excess supply on dealers' back lots and in 2006, Chrysler was forced to bring back much of the old body design in a new fastback coupe. (Like the Cobra, the fans had fallen in love with one shape and wanted no updates, thank you very much.)

The only way Shelby got in on making money on the Viper personally—aside from being on Chrysler's payroll as a consultant—was to make a deal with a dealer in New England to sell personalized Shelby versions. Carroll Shelby collaborated with Fitzgerald Motorsports (Laconia, New Hampshire) to create 50 CS model Vipers. For a price of $79,000, you got a Wimbledon White paint job with Guardsman Blue stripes. Plus a composite hardtop, a removable rear window, and a rear deck spoiler. Plus *beaucoup* badges on the rear bumper, behind the front wheel wells, just over the grill, on the top of the windshield, and even on the all-new three-piece wheels. The interior had a CS logo, blue four-point racing seatbelts, and a dash personally signed by Shelby plus a serial number showing where the car came in the series. Although smog laws prevented a really hot engine, it was advertised with more horsepower. These were snapped up. Chrysler, wary of having the Viper be "appropriated" by Shelby as his own car, stopped short of making their own Shelby-badged version and were miffed when Shelby did it himself.

In truth, Shelby really didn't have much input. "Carroll's only request," says Dan Fitzgerald, the dealer who created the car, "was to have his name on the seat backs. The rest was up to me." There's some indication that Chrysler might have considered having their own CS model but Fitzgerald says, "Shelby kept his word to me and told Chrysler they had missed the boat."

To the Cobra purists, it was bad enough that Chrysler stole the concept of the Cobra, but even worse when Chrysler stole the '65 Daytona coupe livery—a dark blue paint job with dual white "Le Mans" stripes. But, hey, could Chrysler really be accused of "stealing" when the fact was that it was der Snakemeister himself helping them? (And, one could argue that they had earned those "Le Mans" stripes, after all.)

Shelby left Chrysler when his patron, Lee Iacocca, retired. It was high time. He had more than accomplished his mission by creating a new icon in American musclecars, one which, in contrast to Chrysler's expectations, proved to have "legs" far beyond the original projections. So far the Viper has been in production over three times longer than the original Cobras.

Why? It is a car with soul. But even Shelby probably couldn't define exactly what the elements are that made it so. Lutz, despite his pivotal role in the car's creation, remains just as puzzled. He told reporter Dan Carney (author of *Dodge Viper*): "What I didn't foresee was the degree of commitment, enthusiasm and almost religious fervor and fanaticism for the Viper among its owners."

Gee, that sounds awfully familiar...

Northern California, sometime in the '70s.

The man rolled up the garage door and then went back to the car and started it up. It was a sound that commanded respect, like a B-52 dropping a string of daisycutters beyond the horizon. You couldn't see it but you could feel the ground shake.

He eased it into gear and moved it out into the sun.

The muscular bolide was in gleaming blue, the better to set off the bits of chrome and polished aluminum.

And, to Jim Arntz, what he had created was a good thing—a grand tribute to the 427 Cobra.

Back in the early '70s, when Jim Arntz first unveiled his Cobra 427 replica, he might have thought he had done a good thing.

He saw it as a tribute to the master. But Shelby didn't see it that way. He saw it as a rip-off.

Not that the Cobra was exactly an original shape. It had sprung, after all, from the A.C. Ace, a sports car introduced in England in 1953, which in turn had been copied off some specials (one-off cars) made by a man named John Tojeiro, whose coachbuilder had used as their inspiration for styling the Ferrari 166 MM spyder which in turn had been styled by Carlo Felice Anderloni of Carrozzeria Touring over in Italy.

When Shelby had created the Cobra, it was merely by dropping an American made V8 into an already existing A.C. Ace.

Then, as the Cobra developed to meet Shelby's needs, his ace mechanic, Phil Remington, had adapted the A.C. chassis and body here and there, dropping some features here, adding others there.

Shelby hadn't actually applied for a patent on the body shape, something which is apparently seldom done in the auto industry. He saw no future in the Cobra once he shuttered his factory. He had given away the name "Cobra" to Ford and after Shelby left the building, Ford subsequently whored out the name, using it on various Shelby Mustangs, a Fairlane, a Torino, and numerous parts. The name was dropped for a time, then used again by Ford on the Mustang Cobra in the '90s, an upmarket version of the Mustang offering more style and performance than the regular Mustang.

Shelby had left Ford's employ but the Cobra wasn't forgotten, not by a long shot.

Over in England, someone remembered it.

Brian Angliss, a British Cobra enthusiast, had quietly been helping UK-based enthusiasts keep the Cobra alive by reproducing parts that they needed—a fender here, a windshield there.

Gradually he had enough parts to where he found he could build an entire Cobra—the whole car. He went to A.C. Cars Ltd., who had gone on to other models and still made invalid carriages, and found that over in a dusty corner they had the Cobra's original wooden body formers, which could be used to guide the shape of the alloy body panels pounded out by hand and then compared to the formers. They were willing to sell him their tooling and bless his project as they still had hopes of making it with another new car someday. He began making replica Cobras, choosing the 427 body shape because it was much more popular in America than the 289 body shape.

At first the replicas Angliss made didn't have a name but gradually he evolved them into a standardized model he called the A.C. Mk. IV because he too discovered that Ford had a lock on the name "Cobra."

In the 1980s, a Chicago-based distributor partnered with Angliss to import the car, originally planning to make it the spitting image of the 427 Cobra. They quickly found that, in order to do so, their dream of offering a big block was impossible. First because Ford didn't make either the 427 or 428 anymore and secondly because even if they did, those old engines didn't have a prayer of meeting emissions. The auto industry had gone to fuel injection.

So in order for the A.C.-built replica to be sold in the U.S., it would have to have a standardized EPA-approved engine. An off-the-shelf Mustang 5.0-liter fuel injected V8 was chosen. This choice wasn't anywhere near in character to the rip-roaring engine in the 427 Cobra or even 428-powered 427 Cobras but at least it was a Ford V8. And the car even came with a warranty. A franchise system was set up through participating Ford dealers and at least sixty were sold at approximately $65,000 each. Among the customers was high-powered auto exec Bob Lutz, who claims that it was while on a Sunday drive in his Mk. IV near Ann Arbor, when he was struck with the thought that Chrysler, his present employer, should build a Cobra-like car (which became the Viper).

The Mk. IV's very existence riled Shelby. In an interview by Paul Lienert, Shelby was quoted saying, "Brian Angliss, he's a friend of mine," but insists, "Derek Hurlock screwed me by sellin' Brian Angliss my design and chassis jigs. I never wanted the car built again, and that was my way of keepin' it from being built. But Derek Hurlock decided to give them to him. I don't blame Brian for seein' a good thing and latchin' on to it. And I have no gripes at Ford for lettin' him use the Cobra name."

But in *Motor Trend*'s May '86 issue Shelby grumbled to writer Rick Titus, son of the famed Shelby Mustang racer, "Hell I've got nothing against the man's car. It's a nice piece of work. But it ain't a Cobra...Shelby-American built the Cobra and I just don't feel right about the name being on the car."

And even though one would think that Cobra fans would have welcomed with open arms an aluminum-bodied Ford-powered fully legal clone of the 427 Cobra, it turned out that the car was rejected in favor of the kit Cobras, customers preferring the replicas to the Mk. IV. First because the kit cars were cheaper, roughly half the price. Second because with a replica you could put in a big block and dispense with catalytic converters because most were registered as "home-builts" or kit cars, their model year based on the year of the engine block (ironically the law is written so that you could buy a brand new aluminum block and have it stamped with the serial number of an old pre-smog engine as long as you had a receipt for that old engine). That also meant you could install the side mount exhaust pipes which gave your kit 427 the macho appearance of a rip-roaring S/C, semi-competition Cobra.

The Angliss-built Mk. IV, alas, while well intentioned and arguably the legitimate hier to the mantle of the 427 Cobra DNA-wise, was far too tame. It didn't have the side mount exhausts, it didn't have the hood scoop, it wasn't the 427 Cobra the fans wanted. And, because it had to meet current noise regulations, it was way too quiet. It was a pussycat, a Cobra light.

There is photographic evidence to the effect that there was indeed a Comp version of the A.C. Mk. IV, one with flared wheel arches, outside exhausts, and an FE-series big block, in short all the acoutrements of a 427 S/C. But, due to the way the car was being type approved for the U.S., the importers couldn't bring in a MK. IV with these features unless a buyer were to swear that they would only use it on the racetrack. So with the A.C. Mk. IV, it was a case of promising a lot more with the looks than they could deliver into a U.S. showroom legally.

So, in the U.S., the kit Cobras thrived, and multiplied.

After Arntz rolled up his operation, other replica builders rapidly filled the gap. In America the biggest volume makers were Factory Five and ERA and in Germany there were at least two makers, plus even makers in Mexico, Australia and New Zealand (famous countries for fabricating what was too expensive to import) spawned half a dozen Cobra clonesters.

Eventually there came to be as many as fifty Cobra clonesters worldwide, all thriving much to the chagrin of Carroll Shelby who, at that point, wasn't making a dime off any of them.

Shelby's first response was to complain to the media; in fact, to anyone who would listen. "Why can't they make something original?" was his mantra. And he had a point.

But the trouble with making an all new design, as many a kit car maker had found, was that the result was just one's man's vision of the perfect car. Whereas—if you copied the Cobra—you were building a car with (albeit stolen) heritage.

Even if you put a small block Chevy under the hood (demonstrably cheaper and more durable than a small block hi-po 289) you had a car with presence, the automotive equivalent of the .44 magnum revolver. Pull up to a drive-in restaurant in any other kit car and there were always snickers, derisive mutters of "kit car," but pull up in a 427 Cobra replica, especially one with unmuffled side mounts, and you soon have the whole restaurant throbbing with the pulse of the engine. (One favorite prank of Cobra replica owners is to blast through a parking garage and set off all the motion detector burglar alarms in their wake.)

Eventually there were rumors that Shelby was thinking of re-entering the Cobra manufacturing business. The first hint was when he appeared at RAM, a company in England making high quality clones and announced in the English press that he approved of their design. He also licensed them to produce it.

Later Shelby announced that said he would grant permission for anybody to clone a Cobra if they would donate to his charities, most of which revolved around children's heart funds. But the kit car makers in America saw no need to co-operate with what they viewed as "blackmail." To their collective minds, the Cobra design was one that had been free and clear for decades. Shelby had ignored the production of replicas for the first ten years, so he had, they argued, in effect abandoned his claim, the same principle as in land ownership where a "squatter" can come along and occupy land that has been abandoned by its owner for a certain length of time and eventually be ruled the legal owner.

Shelby also fought a war of words with Brian Angliss in the British and American auto press, saying he had never granted permission for Angliss to continue the reproduction of Cobras. Gamely, as if to prove he was a real automaker himself, Angliss bought A.C. entirely and sank millions into coming up with an all new modern A.C. car, also called the "Ace" like the predecessor to the Cobra, but the reception to the new Ace was tepid at best and it sank without a trace. Ford Motor Company actually bought A.C. about this time, but their analysis of the new design was that it was a loser. Ford did use two mid-engined A.C. chassis as the basis for show cars but that was only because they needed some mid-engined chassis and could get those free. They didn't think the mid-engined A.C. ME3000 had any potential either. It didn't help that A.C.'s manufacturing facilities were stone age and totally obsolete.

They sold the company back to Angliss. Eventually Angliss ceased producing Cobras, and went on to other ventures.

In the late '80s, Shelby then shocked the sports car world by announcing that he had "found" a number of unbuilt Cobra chassis. All 427 S/C's, wouldn't cha know. (If he had found some 260 Cobras, maybe nobody would have cared.)

Never mind that it was unlikely he wouldn't have noticed—in the previous 20-odd years—a pile of rusting frames, but those who were quick to criticize weren't reckoning with the life style of a multi-millioniare with far flung business interests. It was just possible that he had these chassis tubes buried under something at one of his factories or warehouses or ranches and had just discovered them. You have to know that guys like Shelby have homes and cars and ex-wives scattered worldwide, some they haven't been seen in years. Despite the criticism, he began reassembling them, assigning chassis numbers that hadn't been used in the original Cobra era. (The Cobra Register, published by the Shelby-American Automobile club, revealed there were in fact a sequence of chassis numbers assigned back in the Sixties to cars that were never completed). Buyers clamored for these continuation cars, though there may have been as few as three sold before Shelby ran into trouble.

Part of the thinking of the buyers scrambling to buy them might have been shameless greed—the hope being that, if they bought the "last 427" from Shelby himself, and Shelby up and died, well, then they would own something valuable—the last 427 Cobra—sort of like buying the last painting by Picasso as he lay on his deathbed. But Shelby continued to live on, no doubt leaving some of these speculators disappointed. Some of them reportedly paid as much as $500,000—or more than they could have bought a "real" CSX-3000 series 427 Cobra for at the time, a car that today would be worth $500,000 to a million dollars depending on if it came with a documented racing history.

The trouble Shelby ran into, after an expose by Paul Dean in the L.A. *Times*, was when the California Department of Motor Vehicles had some questions about the actual dates of origin of the chassis and Mike McCluskey, a car restorer who had restored Shelby's original Cobra CSX2000, and built the bodies for the rediscovered chassis, made it clear that he wasn't willing to go down with the ship and state on record under oath that the cars were original.

One way out would be to call them "racecars" for the track only. That way, whatever year the cars are titled would be reduced to a moot point, because if the cars were merely trailered from racetrack to racetrack as many racecars are, then what it is called isn't important, since it isn't licensed. But at the point the tires touch the public road, a license plate has to be affixed, and to get that somebody has to first state what model year it is in order to have the plates issued. That was the rub. You couldn't count on buyers not wanting to take it on the road someday. And so it is that some of these "continuation cars" are on the road today.

Shelby, without admitting any wrongdoing, up and moved to Nevada. He began building Cobras in the Nevada Territorial Prison, again showing his PR skills were unparalleled. Everybody wants prisoners to learn a trade and what more exciting project can you imagine for employing prisoners than building Cobras?

The State of Nevada needed tourism and could see any tie-in with a real automaker an exciting prospect. They welcomed Shelby with open arms. The cars built in the prison were called replicas, with rapidly diminishing mention of the "continuation cars."

Then Shelby moved most of his operations out of the prison and set up shop next to the brand new racetrack, Las Vegas Motor Speedway.

This shop was much bigger and he wouldn't have to worry about "lockdowns." That was the trouble with operating in a prison—every time some fight started, the whole place would be locked down, with Shelby executives suddenly caught in a place with hundreds of angry men, some of whom had sharp-edged tools in their hands just when the lights went out.

At the new facility, the first car to go into production was again a 427 body style, this time with a new series of serial numbers, but after a few years, Shelby added a 289 body style, even racing versions of the small block with the "cut back" door of the FIA cars that had raced as team cars in Europe. If the proliferation of Cobra replicas continues, it's entirely possible that buyers may eventually be able to order their Cobra clone in the exact configuration and paint scheme of a specific car in a specific race, say, phoning in an order for a "289 FIA/Gurney/Grant Targa '64."

There was still the nagging problem of who owned the name "Cobra?" Shelby sued Ford over the rights to the Cobra name in 1992. Before any resolution could take place, Shelby and Ford settled. Ford would retain world rights to the Cobra name, and Shelby obtained exclusive rights to use the name in association with the cars he developed in the 1960s and any reproductions of those vehicles.

But, even with his own factory churning out replicas, Shelby couldn't keep ahead of the clonesters who had preceded him into the field, so he finally forced a confrontation by taking two of them to Federal court in Boston, claiming he and he alone had the legitimate claim to sole ownership of the Cobra name and body style. He first sued Force Five, and then Superformance. But each time Judge Rya W. Zobel looked at all the evidence she came up with the same conclusion—that Shelby had, in fact, abandoned the Cobra body style for too long in order to be able to come back and claim it.

The major thing Shelby won out of the lawsuits was that he and Ford could continue to claim the name "Cobra" jointly as their own, though one wonders what Ford plans to do when they finally bring out a two-seat Cobra and Shelby is still making his two-seat replica Cobras.

Shelby also won exclusive right to the model names "427 SC," and "GT-350."

At his new facility, Shelby makes an ever-expanding variety of clones. Among them a 427 body style, and two different versions of the small block 289 body style, the latter of which has tremendous growth potential since Cobra connoisseurs are finally beginning to realize that most of the Cobra victories won by the Shelby-American team from '63-'65 were in fact won in small block 289s, not the thundering 427s, which, ironically, because they did not receive homologation in 1965 as production sports cars, failed to be budgeted for racing program by Ford.

There was briefly a time in 2005 when it looked as if the hallowed name of A.C. Cars Ltd. would be coming back into the picture, at Shelby's plant. This was because South African entrepreneur Alan Lubinsky had bought A.C. and fired up the assembly lines.

Lubinsky is a fast talking glove hopping promoter who some feel is a bit longer on words and follow-through. Gee, sounds like early Carroll Shelby!

Although Shelby at one time announced that Lubinsky would be supplying a aluminum-bodied A.C. Cobra replicas both in the small block FIA car body style and the big block 427 body style, both made in Surrey, England, Lubinsky informed this author in late 2006 that the contract has been terminated.

More's the pity, as Shelby would have loved to have been able to sell the A.C. Cobra again, even though at one time, 40-plus years ago, he did everything in his power to try to separate A.C.'s name from the Cobra.

Lubinsky likes to infer that his cars are the real Cobras. "Every year, approximately 1,500 copies of the cars A.C. built in the 1960s are sold in America," he told Edmunds.com, an automotive website. "Why would anyone buy a replica when they can own an authentic A.C. roadster that is lighter and better for the same cost?" In the U.K., the Mk. V costs $94,000 U.S.D. at 2006 exchange rates.

A.C. now makes a carbon-fiber bodied Cobra look-alike on the island of Malta.

As of Nov. '06 Lubinsky was still talking about making cars in Connecticut but hadn't yet opened a plant. Lubinsky says, "the heritage and appeal of the Cobra body styles will always be there...[but] as an automaker who has been in existence since 1901, it does not have to always be simply replicting its 1960's products."

One thing that made Shelby's production of aluminum-bodied 427 Cobras possible, thus getting one step closer to re-creating the magic of the raw aluminum 1965 originals, was the activities of two Mormon brothers in Utah. The Kirkham brothers had inspected a friend's Mig fighter, which had been bought in Poland, and realized that any factory that could build that plane could easily build a Cobra. And with the end of the cold war, the former Soviet Bloc fighter factories in Eastern Europe were hurting for business.

Shipping a real 427 Cobra to Poland, the Kirkham brothers eventually made a deal to produce 427 rolling frames and replica bodies in a former jet fighter plant. At first Shelby fought them, but when he realized they could supply him aluminum bodywork cheaper than he could get it anyplace else, he tolerated them and today they are a Shelby supplier besides selling Cobra replicas on their own, though of course the ones from Provo, Utah are badged "Kirkhams" in the engine department.

A crystal clear example of the sheer power of a famous personality is seen when you go to Provo, price a Kirkham with a big block and full 427 S/C accoutrements and then go to Las Vegas and price the exact same car from Shelby. For the Shelby version you will pay roughly $40,000 more. Enthusiasts who opt for buying the car from Shelby justify the additional expense by stating the fact that they preferred to buy their Cobra from The Man himself—using the Picasso example again, would you rather buy a Picasso print from Picasso or a print that looks like a Picasso done by a guy no one ever heard of? The fact that the Shelby replica might actually have been built in Provo (the Kirkhams have supplied Shelby with complete cars) notwithstanding, there's no more unique selling proposition than being able to buy a Cobra from "the man himself." (Still, it is charming to call Kirkhams and have the Kirkham brother's mom answer the phone. How many automakers can you name that do that?)

In the end, the future of Cobra replicas isn't one you can bank on. At any time, the ecologist lobby could discover that Shelby and that army of imitators in his wake have been driving completed cars that defy all emissions laws through the kit car loophole for years and shut it all off. On the other hand, maybe there will always be kit cars—and legislators willing to allow them. This is America, after all, where we allow private citizens to own all sorts of things, from jet fighters to 50-caliber handguns.

One of the stranger appeals of the Cobra kit cars today is that they are in effect Luddite dream cars, containing no computers, no catalytic converters, no air bags, no anti-slip regulation ("that's your right foot" joked one one builder), no navigational system and best of all no stored memory that, in a modern car, can nastily be subpoenaed after an accident and used by the opposing attorneys to separate you from your money. The classic two-seat Cobra may be rude and downright uncivilized compared to a modern car but at least you know, should some fracas occur, it's not going to be like a modern car and rat you out.

The first person to make a Shelby Mustang clone was—Carroll Shelby! This came about because back in '66 Shelby had made a run of four to six (accounts differ since these were "off the books" cars) GT-350 convertibles that were either given to valued employees or friends (again accounts differ). Shelby left his parked at the office while he was off in Europe running part of the Ford GT racing effort and when he came back, he found much to his consternation that his ever-efficient secretary had sold the car, sticking to the rule of selling company cars that had reached six months' service. Shelby missed that car somethin' terrible and 20 or so years later tied in with a man named J. Orion Brunk to make a run of new Shelby convertibles out of standard '65 or '66 Mustang convertibles. Apparently this effort was not profitable and about all Shelby got out of it was a car for himself to drive. A few years later Shelby and a TV producer tried to get a replica Shelby Mustang program going but again only a couple of cars were built. The market was not there yet that could cover the cost of buying a donor car, buying all the new old-stock parts, including a "K" engine, then building a car to original Shelby specs and still return a profit.

All that changed with the dawn of the new century. By then the legend of Shelby had seeped into the mythic lore of America and new Shelby fans were coming out of the woodwork, many of them "baby boomers" who were updating themselves on what they had missed back in the Sixties. The new entrepreneurs began making Shelby clones, on two distinct paths. First exact copies of the originals, with a few minor updates to make them even better cars. By now, a $60,000 price tag was not so unreasonable.

Then came the customs. At first the idea of customizing a Shelby seems anathema to a purist but what happened to change all that was a single movie, a remake of the classic film *Gone in 60 Seconds*. In the original film, the protagonist drove a Mach I Mustang but in the remake Nick Cage lusts after a customized '67 Shelby coupe called "Eleanor." Soon after the movie was released, there began a demand for Eleanor re-creations and soon they were in production with Shelby's permission. "Eleanor" freed Shelby fans from having to stick anywhere close to original because it was a highly customized car, offering features that weren't designed back in the Sixties. Shelby then tied in with a company that makes replicas of his '66 models but with fully modern drivetrains, in effect "restrorods" in which the outside of the car looks more or less original but under the hood you have the latest big inch alloy block engine and the whole works. These cars easily cost over $140,000 but meet the needs of the new breed of Shelby fans who want the styling of the originals but also can't live without the latest hot rod technology under the hood.

Fueling the frenzy to own a Sixties-era Shelby Mustang or a modern retrorod version is the collector car auctions. The most popular one is the Barrett-Jackson that takes place each January in Scottsdale, AZ. There, in recent sales, even cloned Shelby Mustangs have fetched over $100,000, proving that there are no holds barred now—no longer any need to stick to authenticity, no reason to search out old parts.

Like the movie *Field of Dreams* in which the hero builds a baseball stadium in a cornfield because a mysterious stranger tells him "If you build it, they will come," the proliferation of Shelby variants proves the same is true of Shelby Mustangs.

Still a later variation besides the restrorods is the recent announcement of the availability of reproduction of new sheet metal to create brand new clones of '65-'70-style Shelby Mustangs, available as a complete rolling shell or even as a complete car. On the website ShelbyAutos.com in late 2006 appears news of Shelby's Mustang replicas, er, recreations, as he prefers to call them…Among the ones pictured on the site in Nov. 2006 were a model called the "CSX 4000 Series 427 S/C component vehicle." About these the site says they "are everything the 1965 models were and more…Improvements include a stronger steel frame and better alloys used in the components, plus better cooling and additional heat shielding to make these cars safer and more drivable without losing any of their original character. With 0-60 mph under four seconds, and 12 second quarter mile performance, you'll know exactly what it's like to drive a true American legend. Bodies are available in fiberglass, carbon fiber and aluminum." The presence of these will necessitate bidders to do deep research in advance into what separates a genuine Sixties Shelby from a modern clone before they do any bidding, though arguably, the clones will be built better if all you want is the image and the driving pleasure.

At another place on the same site are pictured two other series. To quote the site: "The CSX 7000 (289 FIA) and CSX 8000 (289 Street) are authentic recreations of the Shelby Cobra 289 models that started it all...CSX 7000 bodies are available in fiberglass or aluminum, while CSX 8000 bodies are available in fiberglass only."

The last wrinkle in the Cobra clonester wars as we go to press is the Daytona coupe. There, arguably, Shelby would seemingly have more of a leg to stand on regarding his claim of ownership than he does to the open Cobra body styles, for it is indisputable fact that it was Shelby who commissioned the Cobra Daytona coupe. But again, some 30 years went by before anyone built a replica, and Shelby didn't act immediately to stop it when they did.

In fact, in an odd twist of fate, it was Shelby himself who commissioned at least one Daytona replica, with Mike McCluskey building the body, to replace the real coupe that he had sold for a million to cover debts he owed to a Las Vegas money lender. Shelby talked about adding the Daytona coupe to his stock of replicas but was beaten to the punch by his old employee/erstwhile rival Peter Brock, who made a deal with Superformance of South Africa to design a new coupe with all the improvements he had once envisioned if the original had been a road car. At this writing over 100 Brock coupes have been built and sold, so Shelby's chance to stake out a claim that he and he alone had the right to make coupes withered in the face of reality.

But Shelby, true to his traditions, once he realizes he's been dealt a bad hand, has been known to compromise. He not only kissed and made up with Superformance, but is now selling the Brock Coupe himself though of course his is called the "Shelby Daytona coupe." Poor Brock, 40 years on, and he's still being aced out by his mentor.

In addition, once Mike McCluskey, who had restored Shelby's original coupe, the one Shelby had bought back from Japan, had the tooling to make an aluminum-bodied Cobra Daytona coupe—all the hand-built formers. He began taking orders from others, and he has built at least sixteen more, four of which went on genuine A.C. Cobra chassis and others of which went on replica chassis. Some racing organizations will allow a replica body if the chassis is real, others don't give a damn—they are just happy to have a Cobra out there.

And so it goes. The kit car loophole may be closed someday. Maybe one lucky kit car manufacturer will have their designs brought "in house" and legalized by big time automakers, but this is increasingly unlikely as cars get more complicated.

On the other hand, even if the U.S. closes the kit car loophole, there's still those other countries which welcome them and there are not only Cobra enthusiasts everywhere but there are new fans waiting to be won over the very first time they see a 427 Cobra tooling down the avenue at speed. Shelby lit that fire back in '62, and has since found out it's not a fire you can easily put out...

Chapter 17- Seducing Oldsmobile

The Midwest, 1999.

The Oldsmobile dealer looked at his watch. It was just past noon.

He looked out into the showroom. The car was there—the car he had just paid an arm and a leg for.

He called his secretary and checked if the ad had come out in the paper. She checked and called him back to assure him it was.

It couldn't be the car. It was low. It was sexy. It had all the good stuff—alloy block, four overhead cams, fuel injection,

And the name SHELBY on it fore and aft.

A single drop of sweat rolled off his brow and onto his pristine desk, marring the shiny surface.

If this guy Shelby was so goddam popular, he thought, where the hell's the crowd?

It was in the late 1990s that Carroll Shelby finally succumbed to the temptation to do an all-new car to carry his name—a car with no link to Cobras, Ford GTs or Fords in general.

The idea for the new car, says Eric Davison, an ex-Detroit ad man who chronicled the history of the Series 1 in a book called *Snake Bit*, says that the idea came from the man Shelby (then in ill health because of kidney problems) had appointed as his firm's President, Don Landy.

Landy had discovered that Oldsmobile was developing a new model car, the Aurora, and that it would have a four cam V8 originally developed for Cadillac.

Naturally there was a certain amount of money set aside for promotion of this engine, and the good news was that the head of Oldsmobile, a man named John Rock, not only knew about racecars, he had even already approved a tie-in with open-wheeled cars where some would race with a version of the Olds Aurora engine.

In an article in a 2006 issue of the magazine, *Motor Trend Classics*, Rock tells a *Motor Trend* editor that the impetus came from him. "I called Carroll and told him Olds was in a hell of a mess," recalled Rock. "I told him we had just made a deal with Tony Hulman to get the engine in a North-South configuration and go racing. If we could take that concept and spatter it over a car, steal a few Corvette parts to keep it going, and get an engineer who knows half-assed what he is doing I think we could come up with one hell of a sports car."

The only trouble was, Olds, whose sales had been falling precipitously, didn't have the budget to develop an all-new platform. Rock told *Motor Trend*, "I told Shelby we had a budget for a concept car," but Rocks days were numbered at GM. He told the *Motor Trend* interviewer that, when Ron Zarella took over as CEO at GM, Rock had explained to Zarella all his plans for the future, including those for some enthusiast cars, but Zarella didn't see the same future, so Rock exited stage left. "I got my ass thrown out," Rock told *Motor Trend*. "I don't think Shelby ever paid for his engines but then I don't think he ever got paid for his prototype either. But, by that time I was in Mexico, just watching the waves roll in."

In his book *Snake Bit*, Davison goes through what happened step by step, starting with Shelby's right hand man, Landy, making an appointment with Rock. When Landy walked into his office with his proposition, Rock saw an opportunity to make Oldsmobile sports cars. Landy's idea was to do that and go one step further. Shelby would not only build a concept car but if there was any interest shown by Olds dealers, then Shelby would put it into limited production. Olds would have their own four-wheeled traffic builder. All Olds would have to do is supply their Aurora V8 and kick in a little development money to get the project going.

Rock, an enthusiast, liked the idea, but according to Davison, didn't much like Landy. Landy, realizing that few are immune to the charms of Shelby, arranged for Rock to meet "the man himself." Rock met with Shelby and they bonded immediately. Both are take-charge guys. Both hunters. Both fishermen. Both car enthusiasts. Rock approved a program where Olds dealers would chip in $50,000 each to fund the development of a running driving concept. Twenty-three dealers signed-up with Davison hitting the hustings to find even more dealers who believed in the concept of an Olds-powered sports car.

A designer was hired, Michael Mate of Colorado. Mate recalls doing some preliminary drawings but it was kind of difficult in that he had no information on the wheelbase, the engine or what size of car they wanted. "I came back with some drawings and then [Don] Landy asked me if I could build a one-fifth scale model. Well, again it was kind of difficult—I still didn't know how big the car was going to be—though they did say 'Make it smaller than the Viper.' So I went ahead and built a scale model…and the next thing you know Landy was asking me to 'scale up the model to make full body drawings.'"

Things looked promising to the Shelby folks. They had a design now to build on.

And then, just as quickly, it all started to come undone.

Mate recalls: "It was about that point that I saw the whole project going awry. My understanding was that my drawings I had done, and even the scale model, were all preliminary, that at some point in the future we would meet with the chief engineer and have a session where we lay down the mechanical parameters and I would get chassis drawings and so forth and I would do the real drawings. I couldn't believe that here they were steaming ahead wanting a final body design when I had no information on the power train or chassis.

"Well eventually they hired a chief engineer, Peter Bryant, and he started on some chassis designs, but I think he was in the dark as to what they wanted as well."

Picking up the project after Mate left was Lavin Cuddihee, a designer currently residing in Tryon, North Carolina. Cuddihee says, "Originally I was called in to redesign the face; well into the project. I also submitted revisions for the side and rear of the car. Shelby liked the progress of the redevelopment so I was retained to do the interior. I did like Mates' original design, but it didn't translate well to full scale. Most likely this had to do the modelers trying to match

Michaels' lithe roadster styling to a frame that was much larger than even he anticipated. Since the frame had not been locked in by the time I arrived, I suggested that the frame dimensions be reevaluated, but that was not to happen. We also explored a coupe version and built a prototype removable roof, but after all was said and done the roadster won out as the hands-down favorite."

To hear Bryant discuss his sojourn at Shelby's Las Vegas plant is to hear a horror story. Bryant, who was well known in racing for his Can-Am cars went into the project thinking his sole task was to engineer a concept car. "Concept cars aren't reality," he told the author. "They don't have to meet any real-world rules. They are useful though in gauging public reaction and in seeing how the seating position works out, etc."

When he started on the concept car program he was presented with a full size fiberglass body mock-up at the prison where Shelby was getting Cobra Parts made. So he dutifully tried to design a chassis that would go under the already-designed mockup. One problem was that the tires would have to be Z-rated," he recalls (Z-ratings mean the tire can take sustained 150 mph), "and there was only one Goodyear tire available that would do that, but when we put it in the wheel wells it looked too small. So for the show car we used much bigger tires."

"Another problem was that the design of the body had no consideration for chassis strength and was not modern in terms of aerodynamics." So he did away with the rounded rocker panels to enable a chassis to be built that had beam strength and allow the doors to open and close. He changed the hood to exit the radiator air out of the top ahead of the engine (as used in the Daytona coupe) and he put a big vent on the sides of the front venders to exhaust the air that got under the hood and from the wheel arches.

He eventually completed two concept chassis, having to make them of steel because there wasn't time to build them out of aluminum, which takes longer to weld and requires complex fixtures.

As soon as he saw the Aurora Northstar engine that was proposed for the car was used in a front drive application by Oldsmobile, he asked Shelby if he could redesign the car to be a mid-engined car because it would be much easier to pick up the transverse engine and put it with the Automatic transmission in the back behind the driver, much as had been done in cars like the Fiat X1/9.

But Shelby was adamant—it had to be front-engined.

Finally in January of 1997 He got the two cars done, and they were shown to the press at the LA Auto Show and Detroit Auto Show in January '96.

The building of the prototypes had been financed by corralling some 23 Oldsmobile dealers to put $50,000 deposits ($25,000 a car) down in advance. At another point, Shelby, hard pressed for ready cash, opened his garage, and rolled out a Cobra Daytona coupe out of his collection, one of six in the world that had contested the World Championship in 1964 and 1965. There were buyers waiting in line but he put it up for collateral so he could borrow a million dollars.

It was going to be Oldsmobile's 100th Birthday and the idea that the concept car could be used as a pace car was still being toyed with. After all, in this particular Indy race, the field would be full of Olds-powered cars. It would be a perfect tie-in, even if, historically, the pace car had always been a production car.

Bryant was hoping that there could be a limited production run, say 50 cars, but only as race cars to avoid the costly certification required for street legal cars. The cars could be sold for a premium price, the owners would send their own mechanics to build them, there would be no warranty problems and you could get more for the cars. They would eventually find there way onto the street anyway.

But Rager thought he was thinking too small. Bryant was invited to a meeting in Las Vegas, and was surprised when two ad men, Eric Davison and Vic Olsen, were making a presentation on putting the car into production. They weren't talking a small limited run, but 500 cars!

Bryant was grilled by Olds officials on his credentials who were relieved when they found that besides being a race car designer he had been director of Engine Development and emission certification for the Yugo car. That meant he had real world experience with cars that had to be certified for production, not just race cars.

Bryant was a little leery at this point. He assumed that now that the car had been greenlighted for production, there would be a transfer of funds from Oldsmobile to fund the drawing up of production car plans, funds to buy tooling, buy parts, etc.

He waited in vain.

Meanwhile back at his home office, he began adding up what it would cost to produce a modern car with all the expensive materials they wanted in the car, including a carbon fiber body. "The total came out at over $84,000," he says, "which was above their list price." That did not include labor, in what was a high-tech car. That did not include profit for Shelby-American or profit for the dealers, or shipping or insurance and a hundred otherthings. It was evident that each car would be produced at a loss unless the projected list price was raised.

"Oldsmobile did generously say you can use any GM parts you want in the concept cars and GM will give you a special price for those parts for production cars," recalls Bryant. But there was a small but significant stipulation: "You can't use anything from the upcoming C5 Corvette."

That dismayed Bryant who was planning on using a great many Corvette parts (because) after all it was GM's only high performance rear wheel drive car. It was the Corvette group once again protecting themselves from Shelby, as they had in 1960, when Shelby's Italian-bodied Corvettes surfaced.

It gradually became clear to Bryant that in Las Vegas the people at Shelby-American were doing a lot of wishful thinking that money would be coming from East Lansing. But back in East Lansing, at Olds' headquarters, they thought their commitment was merely to supply engines and even those would end up being at a hefty price.

In an interview Bryant said "I told them that I had seen an article in Ward's *Auto World* that said that Chrysler was proud that the Plymouth Prowler was able to be built using 75% of its parts off the Chrysler parts shelves, and yet the car had still cost them $75,000,000 to tool up (and that was spread over at least 10,000 cars)."

"But whenever I told Rager (Shelby-American President) that the costs for tooling up for a modern car were in those ranges, he would say stuff like 'Well, we might as well stop the program right now.'"

But like a freight train with no engineer at the controls, the project moved forward into the unknown, even picking up speed as it went. Bryant was in an engineer's nightmare dealing with marketing types who refused to look what it cost in the real world to engineer a car from scratch. Another example, he points out, "is that Olds told us the Aurora engine was certified for smog on the basis of being mated to an automatic. We got Olds to re-certify it for a manual shift, which we specified, but that alone got them a bill from Delphi for $330,000."

Eventually it got to be too much for Bryant. The last straw was when Ron Zarella took over marketing at GM and, when told the Series 1 was being readied to be the pace car at Indy, snapped: "No, it won't, it will be the Aurora."

In May of 1997 the Series One Concept car was driven onto the stage at the MGM Grand hotel in Las Vegas for a party for Oldsmobile Management to celebrate the Division's 100th birthday, Bryant left Shelby's employ shortly thereafter and went on to help develop a safety device and start a company that makes SUVs safer. He still lives in Las Vegas and is still working as an engineering consultant. He said that the final blow dealt by Rager was when he refused to pay Bryant the $7,500 bonus promised to Bryant for completing the concept cars both on time and under budget. Bryant had designed and built two concept cars for less than $1.4 million dollars. (In 1996 Oldsmobile paid Troy Design $1.5 million to build a concept show car without any chassis or interior.) But the project moved forward.

Rock selected early retirement at the beginning of 1997. His successor, Darwin Clark, was, to be fair, knowledgeable about sports cars, having worked in Europe and he even owned a Lotus, but, by all accounts, he was a man less inclined to stick his neck out. He didn't have the fast shoot-from-the-hip operating style of Rock. And no doubt found himself wondering more than once "Who the hell is this Shelby guy with all these demands?"

And for a conservative guy seated at a desk in East Lansing Michigan, it was pretty obvious what Shelby was trying to do. Call it "the fast hustle." Shelby was driving the Series 1 program foot to the floor toward GM with the hopes that Oldsmobile would adopt this wayward child, and put their badge on the nose. If Shelby succeeded, he could walk away clean, a million or so in his overall pockets, and leave the production and marketing of the car up to Olds.

But even though Shelby had come to Oldsmobile at the right time to make some money, he had come at the wrong time as far as GM Corporate was concerned. The GM Corporation had fallen in love with the concept of "brand marketing," marketing cars like toothpaste or breakfast cereal. A sports car coming into the picture out of left field didn't fit into the grand scheme of things. As Eric Davison wrote: "after Rock left, the Series 1 became a hot potato. No one wanted to touch it." Clark even resigned later on and, after him, Davison says, "nobody wanted to stick their neck out and champion the car that had come from outside the system."

The irony was that a little of Shelby's magic elixer was, in fact, just what Olds needed. The market for Oldsmobiles was piss-poor with their average buyer approaching 60. Only Buick and Cadillac in the GM offerings had older buyers. While these were buyers who, age-wise, might remember the name "Shelby," the car wouldn't have been aimed at them but at a younger age group in an effort to rapidly move down the average age of Oldsmobile buyers. The concept had worked for Dodge with each Viper proving to be a veritable people magnet. Once the curious walked into a Dodge dealership to see a Viper, they were caught in the salesmen's clutches and could be sold Neons, Dodge Rams, whatever—the key, as always, was to get a prospect into the showroom.

It could have been wonderful. Oldsmobile with their own Corvette, in effect. Better, their own Viper. That's if it all worked out. But there was a lot about the modern car business that Shelby didn't know even after being in on the Viper program. Problems? He didn't want to hear about them. As they say in in Texas, "You can always tell a Texan, but you can't tell him much."

Shelby pressed on regardless. You could say, when talking of the Series 1's descent toward hell that this particular train actually came off the track right from the beginning but those driving the locomotive paid no mind. Instead of pumping in money or sending some MBAs from Harvard to shape them up, Oldsmobile turned its back on the Series 1 as soon as the project became troublesome and the Shelby company became mired in controversy. Olds itself died a slow and painful death, ironically the nameplate being tabled only a year past their 100th anniversary.

Just one example of how unsympathetic Oldsmobile was to the success of the Series 1 was when Shelby was handed a bill for 530 engines at $4,000 each. This was a huge price for the engines. Shelby had been assured at the outset of the program that they would get a sweetheart deal on engines, ie. something close to GM's cost (it probably didn't cost GM much more than that to make the whole Aurora car with the engine). This was almost a retail price, and just one factor in the constant repricing of the Series 1. A car that he had talked about costing $75,000 before the first one was built eventually ballooned in price to $140,000, and even at that price was losing money.

Most of these price changes occurred after Shelby had sold out his interest in the car to one of the suppliers—Venture—and walked away from it. Each time the supplier ran into a problem, the solution was to raise the price. Shelby had followed the old Texas rule: "If you find yourself in a hole the first thing to do is stop digging."

Venture Industries was a reportedly 2.3 billion dollar enterprise based in Fraser, Michigan, run by a hard driving man named Larry Winget. At first they were only a supplier to Shelby but at some point they became the owners of his business. It is said that Winget poured more than $50 million into the money-losing car, surprising for a company that was 100% in the auto business and should, Eric Davison implies, have been able with all their experience, to spot a money loser from a distance.

Good publicity can make a car, as one sees in the original Cobra marketing. And, conversely, bad publicity can sink it. Shelby discovered to his chagrin that, as far as the Series 1, he no longer could automatically count on having the press on his side. Things were far different from the good ol' days back in the Sixties when reporters like John Christy of *Sports Car Graphic* would willingly "omit" mentioning that things were falling off the Cobras in exchange for the privilege of being the first reporter to drive one. (Today you call this type of journalist an "imbedded" journalist). Many reporters of the 1990s could be bought off as well with a nice press lunch and a chance to thrash a car on a racetrack, but there had been a subtle change in the way the automotive press worked—there was a new breed of whistle-blower reporter who fit the description of a Doberman— "sleek and clean and liable to turn on you any moment." These new consumer-conscious reporters could be counted on to leap on any reported flaw in a new car so they could bask in the glory of being the first to spot a flaw in a car being heavily promoted.

The Series 1, alas, was not ready for prime time and exposed to the press in less than perfect form. It was vulnerable. The automotive press, which had been so favorably disposed toward the car before they drove one, grew impatient and began to make hay out of each flaw that appeared, and each delay in production. Such as the fact that the cars were years late in being ready for market and once they were ready and shipped, it was discovered by the recipients that certain things hadn't been designed, like convertible tops. One story said tops would be shipped later and a man would come from the factory and install them.

The most serious problem the Series 1 cars had was price. Announced before production at one projected price—$75,000—once they began building them, there were periodically announced price increases, each one attempting to make the car profitable. At one point it was $134,975, at another point $165,000 and at still another point $175,000.

A second problem the car had was power, or lack of it. The performance, after all that was promised, was not even close to a 427 Cobra. Not a real 427 Cobra, but even your average big block replica with a mild 428. Even a well-tuned 289 Cobra could make mincemeat of it. Part of the problem was the Olds engine wasn't that big, 4.0 liters not being anywhere near the size of the 8.0 liter V-10 in the much lower cost Viper, and even smaller than a 1962 4.2-liter 260 Cobra. The irony was that Cadillac had a 4.6-liter version of the same engine which the Series 1 should have had. But do you think they would share that with Olds? No way. Their attitude was "Let Olds fry in their own oil." That's the spirit!

The power might have been adequate if they had kept to the originally projected weight target. The car, originally supposed to be 2600 lbs., had fattened up to nearly 2900 lbs. as a result of having to use gallons of body filler to smooth out the rippled body panels.

A last ditch effort to improve the horsepower was to supercharge it. But though that pumped up the power, the supercharged version was not run through the EPA tests so the supercharged version couldn't be sold as a new car. You had to first buy a normally-aspirated car, then take it back and have a supercharger installed on an aftermarket basis. The car magazines again bent over backward to promote the supercharged version in road tests, never mentioning that they were, at that point, all aftermarket conversions.

The third problem the Series 1 had was quality control, or lack of it. It was abysmal, so much so that the founder of the Series 1 Owners Club, a Newport Beach sports doctor, turned from a fawning fan to an enemy, launching lawsuits to recover his expenses in trying to get his car sorted out. Shelby sold his interest in the company so he would have some business entities left but the new buyers of the Series 1 were not able to keep the car going once word got out about the quality problems.

And the new buyers thought they could get along without Shelby. They failed to realize that part of the magic of buying a Shelby product was going to the factory and having your picture taken with its creator as he hands you the keys. He had done it with the Cobras and the Shelbys, creating lifelong fans for those cars, fans that remain loyal four decades later.

Without the ol' Snakemeister on scene, the car suddenly had less appeal than it had before. If was like the car was being disowned by its father more or less. De-ranked from the status of crown prince to the status of being a mere pretender to the throne.

And all the while, Shelby had to worry about the car magazines. *Motor Trend*, long a friend to Shelby, gave a five page glowing report about the car. But then Petersen Publishing was always pro-Shelby. *Road & Track*, the more patrician of American car magazines, to their credit, returned the first test car they had been loaned, saying something like: "It's not developed enough for us to test yet" i.e. "If we do write about it, you won't like it."

They did test one later on, damning it with faint praise. At first the test seemed complimentary, but the more you read between the lines, the more you realized they were advising their readers to step carefully around this car.

Shelby had always had a running battle with *Car and Driver*, but personally got along good with Brock Yates, who was for decades their long time senior editor. Shelby perked up when he found out that, after first sending a test car back untested saying it was not ready, *Car and Driver* agreed to test the supercharged version. And Shelby was buoyed up by the news his old pal Brock Yates would be writing the story. But Shelby found out too late why Brock Yates is called "the assassin." Yates was invited to Las Vegas to drive the supercharged car but the two examples provided both failed in the 100-degree plus Nevada heat. Brock condemned them in print and, without the power of a major automaker who could imply they might be reviewing their ad schedule, the marketers could do nothing to kill the story. But each issue of *Car and Driver* sold with the damning report was like another little nail being pounded into the coffin of the Series 1.

Shelby still won some points from his friends in the press. Just one example of how his PR minions were able to lean on them was when several magazines, including the *Robb Report*, ran Shelby Series 1 driving impressions in the early 2000s, without ever mentioning that if you bought one, it would have to be titled as a 1999 since that was the only model year Shelby had received government approval to produce it as a production car.

With any other automaker such an important omission would be a cardinal sin!

But his friends in the press couldn't save him. The car was flawed; it had no soul. The plug was pulled at 250 cars, half of what they had said they were going to make.

One suspects that there was one group at GM who were secretly cheering at the funeral for the Series 1. That was the Corvette group at GM—proud that they had once again deterred an interloper from burrowing into GM's money vaults. Shelby had, after all, tried to get into GM's coffers back in '58 with his end run involving the Italian-bodied Corvettes. Once again, they had prevented Shelby from setting up an operation inside the walls of Fortress GM. (Would he come back? Best deploy the concertina around the perimeter...)

To an objective analyst, their worries were for naught—because the Series 1 wasn't in the same price range—being basically at the outset priced more than double the Corvette's price (and later three times the price of a Corvette) and less of a highway cruiser, being more along 1st generation Viper lines, something you own just to take to the track and time trial on weekends; a car decidedly more track-biased and hard-edged.

Why didn't GM lift a finger to save the car? Well, it wouldn't have taken much digging to find that the phrase "rock solid" didn't apply to the company Shelby had set up to produce the car. From the beginning, the GM philosophy had been—if Shelby was an asset, they would maintain ties. If he turned into a liability, well, they could always cut him loose. So, in the end, they cut him loose.

And GM had troubles of their own, Olds' market share plummeting. The Division at the time Landy approached them was like the Titanic five minutes after hitting the iceberg. They were still afloat but word hadn't yet filtered up to the bridge that they were taking on water faster than the bilge pumps could bail them out.

In the end the Shelby Series 1 faded into automotive history.

Oldsmobile followed it to that same auto graveyard in the sky. And, because the Series 1's engine had been tied to the Aurora, no more development was done on it. Any chance of that engine achieving cult status (such as the L88 of the Sixties) disappeared.

There was conceivably one man in all of Detroit's auto industry who could have saved the car. That man was Bob Lutz, a former powerhouse at Chrysler, and one who truly qualifies as a "Renaissance man" despite the fact that he was still active in the auto industry at an age when most high execs over 60 had cashed in their millions in stock bonuses and retired to the comfort of a Lazy Boy overlooking the beach in West Palm. Lutz even owned a Cobra, more or less, if you want to count his aluminum-bodied A.C.-built Mk. IV as a real Cobra. Reportedly Lutz had been the friendly Ford official who backed Ford supplying engines for that retro car.

And it was Lutz who earlier had talked the Chrysler board into backing the Viper show car as a production model.

GM, recognizing his acumen in choosing future car models was an asset too good to lie fallow, hired him in 2001. Hopes were buoyed in the minds of enthusiasts. Lutz at GM! He will save the Series 1.

Why didn't he? Davison in his book *Snake Bit* says Shelby was still mad at Lutz for making the Viper too heavy when they had worked on the car at Chrysler. Shelby supposedly had been in favor of a small block V8 aided by a supercharger or twin turbo arrangement. Instead they had gone with the truck-derived V-10, although with a lightweight alloy block. Shelby and Lutz likely wouldn't have gotten along on what to do with the Series 1. Shelby didn't see Lutz as a savior for the Series 1, though he wanted someone to save it because he was sick and couldn't deal with all the problems in production and clashing personalities, not to mention the angry customers who had waited as long as two years for their car.

But Lutz was perhaps too much the politician to stick his neck out for a lost cause. He began tinkering with GM's upcoming cars, cutting some projected plans and revising others, such as helping Pontiac get the GTO revived, and talking Cadillac into redoing the XLR sports car after the first body (designed before he got there) had a two-year run to at least reap some benefit out of all the money spent on tooling. He had too much work to do at GM to worry about Shelby.

According to Paul A. Eisenstein writing on a website called The Car Connection, back in January 2001 (before coming to GM), Lutz was hot on his own sports car project, as co-owner of the new Cunningham Motor Co., teaming up with Cunningham's son, Briggs II. The car they developed was aimed fairly high, Lutz, a noted watch afficionado, joking it was for those "who consider a Rolex watch commonplace." The plan was for all-wheel-drive 2-plus-2 with an aluminum space frame, and presumably an aluminum block 48-valve V-12 turning out somewhere around 500 horsepower. The svelte prototype—looking vaguely Aston Martin-ish, weighed in at 3,550 pounds. The goal was to market about 500-600 a year at around $200,000-$250,000 apiece. Ironically, once Lutz was hired on at GM, he dropped the Cunningham like a hot potato. GM wanted him working on real cars for the masses, not rich men's toys.

The irony was that, when Rock had been in charge, Olds had succeeded in gaining a toehold with enthusiasts. But nobody after Rock retired had a clue to what they would lose if they didn't support those programs. Rock's successor cut loose Olds' performance fans—a carefully nurtured audience—to let them twist, twist slowly in the wind.

And they did the same with Shelby. Shelby's enemies were no doubt enjoying seeing him in difficulty. They were waiting for his creditors to close in for the kill. He might not go broke but they wanted to see him lift his paws and say please and play dead.

Not that Shelby was worrying. With his usual flare for separating the wheat from the chaff, Shelby managed to separate the making of his continuation Cobras from the doomed Shelby Series 1 venture (no pun intended), a wise move as it later turned out. Shelby announced: "I've spent the past 40 years of my life building some of the world's fastest cars," said Shelby. "Now I'm shifting gears. I'm taking my companies public. This will allow us to continue to grow the business now, and long after I'm gone." He did this through a brilliantly arranged shuffle of stock, buying a firm called Ginseng Forest, an already existant corporate shell that didn't really do anything but was listed on NASDAQ. No revenues—and no real expenses. But it was a public company. Once you have spent the money to make a company public, it means that you have some liquidity which is a lot easier than when you own a private company. The typical approach is for the private company to be "bought" by the corporate shell. The private company then gets to "go public" on the cheap and then ends up with the stock. Shelby became the largest shareholder in Ginseng Forest, Inc. Whoever owned it originally no doubt got some nominal dollars for giving up their corporate shell. In a press release Shelby appeared to grant the Shelby name, rights, etc. to the new company. Shelby was claiming that Shelby-American International were in default and that he can do whatever he wants with them. If SAI objected, Shelby wanted a corporate shell to use in the fight. The shell meant that SAI would potentially have to sue Ginseng Forest instead of Shelby himself. If they won, Shelby would still get to keep his ranch and SAI just ends up with the seeds or whatever is on the shelves at Ginseng Forest. If it turned out that Shelby actually had a case, he could go out and raise investment dollars on the stock market (since this is technically a public company) and that would allow him to go after SAI's parent company who had very deep pockets. In the end Shelby ended up buying back Shelby-American International for a tiny fraction of what he had sold it for. It's amazing that Shelby had the fortitude to fight this battle!

While the Series 1 saga was going on, Shelby's health had been in more than the usual jeopardy. He needed a kidney, and couldn't find a good match. His old employees, who he ran into at reunions, would joke "Hell, Shelby's gonna keep going. He's already made of ol' junk parts."

At last a donor came forward—his own son, Michael, and reportedly the transplant went well, though Shelby had to take drugs to make up for his lost immunity, drugs that swelled up his features.

Shelby also had a disaster happen in his personal life. His fifth wife, the Swedish-born Lena Dahl, to whom he had been married for ten years, was killed in a single car accident while driving on his Texas ranch. She had hit a ditch, been thrown out of her Jeep, whereupon it rolled on her.

Shelby remarried less than a year or so later to Cleo, a vivacious British woman several decades his junior who he had known from his racing days, but these changes in his personal life made him want to be free of the Series 1 and all its difficulties. He had a life other than cars: three grown children, a passel of grandchildren, a ranch or two, a car collection, airplanes, livestock, and other priorities in life.

Shelby decamped to his cloneworks to produce basically replicas of big block and small block Cobras. By the time the last Series 1 had been built, that car, in his mind, seemed to be but a distant memory. He was merely practicing that Texas saying, "If you're ridin' ahead of the herd, take a look back every now and then to make sure it's still there."

But the operative phrase in the Shelby world is "Never say never." As we go to press, Shelby has rolled out a redesigned Shelby Series 2, a Series 1 slightly warmed over in details by Tom Tjaarda, an American who has been working in Italy for four decades, famous for designing the Pantera for DeTomaso back in 1969. The Series 2 is now supercharged. The pricetag now soars above $220,000. Will it succeed? Will anyone care there is no Oldsmobile any more? Is it too early to sell replicas of a car that was never a success in the first place? Stay tuned....Shelby could still pull this iron out of the fire yet....

Chapter 18- Shelby with Ford (Again)

Scottsdale, Arizona, sometime in the early 2000s.

The Ford official looked at his watch. Golf frankly bored the hell out of him. He had managed to slip out of the foursome he had been committed to on the links and was seeking something else to do before having to go back and face the Detroit winter. He saw in the Phoenix paper that there was some sort of old car auction over at a place called Horseworld.

An hour later he was there. A Shelby Mustang was rolling across the stage. The crowd was stumbling over each other to bid on it.

"One hundred thousand," the auctioneer crooned, but the bidding kept going at a rapid pace. The Ford executive fought his way outside the tent and called Dearborn on his cellphone.

"Hello—product planning? This is Ted, with the Product Clinic in Scottsdale. You wouldn't believe what 40-year old Shelby Mustangs are going for out here. Tell me—is there any way in hell we can get Shelby back on board?"

Ford Motor Company was on a mission in the early part of the new century. They wanted to recapture the Ford fans that worshipped the cars they had built in the Sixties but who weren't buying Fords now.

Some Ford executives actually laid down their *Wall Street Journals* at times and read the enthusiast press and therein observed with much churning of their stomach, how cars like your run of the mill street model 1965 Shelby GT-350, a model which had sold for less than $6,000 new, were now going for over 100 big ones time and time again at auctions like the Barrett-Jackson in Scottsdale, Arizona.

While this was good for Ford's reputation—that fans liked to pay heavy bread for their old stuff—this blind worship on the alter of Ford's past wasn't making Ford a dime in the present, in the new century.

The only way Ford had found to horn in on the burgeoning popularity of cars they had made 30-40 years before was to provide crate engines through its racing parts group—off-the-shelf engines that produced more horsepower than the ones they could legally sell in production cars. The new trend called "retro-rodding" had come at the right time because, besides the purists, many hot rodders were restoring old cars but putting in new state of the art high performance engines (which they didn't have to have smog checked because, after all, their cars were built prior to the first year smog laws began to apply).

But that was small potatoes. In the new century, Ford wanted to create brand new cars that would sell for the same big bucks that the blue oval enthusiasts were paying for 30 and 40-year old Fords.

But Ford's marketers knew that, in order to crack that market, they had to build a car of legendary performance and design—something truly worthy of their dollars. Something that would—like the original Shelbys and Cobras— appreciate in value. Their first attempt to break into this market was the Ford GT, first shown as a concept car around the year 2002.

Back then the show car was called the GT40, and was very much like the original GT40 Mk. I, as long as you didn't park it too closely to an original, whereupon it made the original—a legendary car that had dominated sports car racing for four solid years—look the size of a kiddie car.

The new Ford GT would have a robust 5.4 liter supercharged engine, basically a truck engine lifted intact out of their Lightning concept F-150 show car. It used Navigator tooling but an aluminum block was ordered from a Michigan casting firm. Ford rated the production version, introduced in 2005, at 550 hp. And proved it will do 205 mph (actually it'll go faster but, with tires in mind, they thought it safer to electronically limit the top speed).

From the very inception of the road version, Ford's public relations releases made it clear that the ol' Snakemeister, Carroll Shelby, was the seminal influence. The Godfather. The *capo di tutti capi,* as it were. He never lifted a wrench on the car, but the implication was that not a step was taken without his learned opinion being solicited first.

Shelby's return to the Ford fold was a long time coming. Shelby had been on the outs with Ford for years, ever since young Edsel, son of Henry Ford II, while stationed down in Australia for the company, had copied the paint scheme of the 1965 GT-350 for a car sold down there as the "Cobra." That aggravated Shelby, but he didn't go ballistic until decades later when Ford also tried to liven up the Mustang II (a model based on the lowly Pinto chassis) by reviving the GT-350 name again. Actually Ford had been perfectly within their rights when they used the name "Cobra" but no one at Ford had thought to check if they owned the name "GT-350" before re-using it.

Mistake. Shelby nailed them. The lawsuit dragged on for years but was finally resolved after a meeting between Shelby and Edsel Ford II, a major stockholder and great grandson of the original Henry Ford. Both parties saw that they had much to profit from burying the hatchet.

Edsel, who had been a young lad in the company of his proud papa (Henry Ford II) at Le Mans when Ford first won that event in '66, and remembered how at one time he'd been Shelby's biggest fan (he had even restored a Cobra and a Ford GT40 for his personal car collection). He realized that Ford had almost lost the youth market, and that there was no living icon anywhere in the American auto industry that could rev up hero worship quite like Shelby. If Ford could once again have Shelby hawking their cars it would be as if Zora Arkus-Duntov— "the father of the Corvette" (though in truth he had been hired by GM after the Corvette was already in the showrooms)—were still alive and able to make public appearances on the introduction of each new model Corvette. Well, Duntov was dead and Chevrolet had no comparable personality to tout their wares. Neither did Chrysler.

That gave Ford the advantage. Shelby was not only alive, but available. In 2003, after a ride in the Ford GT40 concept at Pebble Beach, he signed on, and was back on board with Ford with a handsome retainer.

Not everybody in the press was deliriously happy to see Shelby back on board. Christopher A. Sawyer, the outspoken editor of an industry website called Autofield Guide wrote in 2003, "What was the big news coming out of the Pebble Beach concours this year? It was the resurrection of Sixties legend Carroll Shelby. Let me hasten to point out that I mean 1960s legend. Shelby is 80....However I don't understand what good an 80-year old man who had a stint at Chrysler putting his name on hot Omnis and Horizons, and who has spent the recent past years suing various Cobra kit car copycats and trying to produce the Shelby Series 1 sports car brings to the party. Hell, his Texas chili mix has a best-buy date, shouldn't he?...Is there no one either inside or outside the company with the talent, drive, ideas and ability to do for Ford what Shelby and others did in the 1960s?..."

In a word, Mr. Sawyer: no.

In publicity pictures released by Ford, Shelby was subsequently pictured deep in conversation with Neil Hannemann, the Ford GT chief engineer, when the production car was still in its rude and crude "mule" stage. How much advice did he actually give to Ford? No one has said, but it was certainly encouraging to the Ford GT team that Shelby—in effect their Yoda—was on scene, checking things out.

They might not have been aware that Shelby was, back in the day, entrusted to sell some street GT40s that had been sent over from England. Only a few were sold and the car was much too low to be drivable on modern streets with curbs, speed bumps and the like. Shelby probably didn't mention to his new friends at Ford what a turkey the first version had been in its debut as a road car.

Ford also reeled in some of Shelby's premier old drivers, such as Dan Gurney who Ford pictured inspecting the prototypes and invited to the long lead preview to schlep car magazine editors around Laguna Seca in the new Ford GT as well as some restored originals. The implication was that these historic drivers were willing to field questions on whether the new crew building the new Ford GT were doing it right. It was a winning PR concept. How can you not respect the advice of someone who drove the original Ford GTs over 200 mph hour after hour at Le Mans in a pouring rain? (Especially after Ford's re-test of old GT40s in the wind tunnel revealed that the front tires were often off the ground as they neared 200 mph.)

Ford's move in retaining Shelby once again might have been less for his inspiration than purely a defensive move. They had no doubt considered the alternative—if they didn't have Shelby on board, there was always a chance he could criticize the new car saying "That weren't nuthin' like the car we raced."

Best to have him aboard. And, fortunately for Ford, it all worked out, with Shelby appearing in publicity pictures not only by the side of the new Ford GT but with later Ford concept cars connected with his name.

The new GT was one of the few successes for Ford in the 2005-2006 period when the firm's market share was falling south of 25% of the market share it had commanded in the year 2000 down to 17% by 2006. Their only successes were the Ford F-150 pickup truck, the new Mustang (itself a retro car reprising some styling cues of the '66 and '67 Shelby Mustang models) and the Ford GT, which managed to sell for as much as $20,000 above list price for a solid year.

Once Shelby was on board, Ford was eager to see what configurations of their present cars could be best "Shelbyized." One that was run up the flagpole right quick—only to be pulled down just as fast when no one clamored for it—was a Shelby Expedition, a gussied-up SUV. As shown at the SEMA show (Specialty Equipment Manufacturer's Assn.) it had a 500-hp supercharged V8, navigation equipment, full leather, the whole nine yards, but a Shelby official calculated that for a production model so equipped, it would have to have listed for $110,000, which at that time was thought excessive for an SUV (though times have changed and there are SUVs that cost that and more).

Ford subsequently came up with two Cobra concept cars, both of which Shelby dutifully posed with. Both were powered by an all-aluminum V-10 which could achieve a heady power output of 650 hp while naturally aspirated.

Ford looked around for a chassis they could base a new Cobra on. There was absolutely no thought whatsoever given to resurrecting the original 427 twin tube chassis—how could they be a modern company and try to hawk a 40-year old chassis? They would get laughed out of the car business.

Then they began looking at the Ford GT chassis, which weighed under 500 lbs. and was made with the new technique of extruded aluminum square section tubes plugged into aluminum modules at each corner. Ford was also using the same concept on the new Aston Martin DB9, made by the prestige English firm they had bought years earlier.

"We were already planning to use the Ford GT suspension systems, and we asked ourselves how much more of the GT we could borrow," a Ford official said. Turns out they concluded, "Why just use the suspension—why not use the whole chassis?"

Even though the GT is a mid-engine car, and the proposed roadster was front-engined, a decision to mount the transmission at the rear made the connection. The new Cobra would really be a front mid-engined car. The engine would still be in front, but moved far back, almost amidships.

In keeping with J Mays penchant, it was "retro."

Mays, a graduate of Art Center College, had been first hired by Audi, for whom he had directed the final design of the Porsche 356-inspied Audi TT, then achieved fame at the VW studio when he came up with the design for the New Beetle.

Before the Ford GT40 concept car, he had designed a concept called the "Forty-Nine" which looked for all the world like a '49 Ford "Shoebox" chopped and channeled by George and Sam Barris around 1953. Ford decided to go with the Ford GT40 as a production car instead.

"Retro" is a term that came to the American auto industry in the late '90s when Chrysler rolled out the Prowler, a hot rod-like car that looked more like a chopped '32 Ford than anything from Chrysler history. They followed that with the PT Cruiser, a little wagon that looked similar to a '40s Ford. BMW matched them with a remake of the Mini, even offering a hotter Cooper model. Ford came up with the Ford GT, a faithful re-do of their Le Mans winning car of the Sixties. Then Chevrolet followed with a two seater pickup truck with a retractible hardtop, the SSR, a vehicle that looked like a custom '53 Chevy pickup truck and pretty soon each Detroit automaker had a retro product.

But when it came to the new Cobra, Mays wanted something different than merely aping what Shelby had done 40 odd years before. He wanted the flavor of an original Cobra, the bunched-up ready-to-pounce look of a jungle cat ready to spring, but a more modern interpretation of the front.

It turned out that the front of the concept car was what most enthusiasts took issue with. Mays failed to adopt the traditional oval grille shell shape of the Cobra. He later announced that they had done it different "so everybody wouldn't think we were rolling out a kit car."

A small error perhaps but unlike the GT, with that one mistake Mays had irreversibly offended the hardcore Shelby fans and created a car that had no soul.

The interior almost made up for it, though. Knowing enthusiasts love parts carved out of solid aluminum, Mays called for the entire dash to be hewn out of one solid billet of aluminum with switchgear holes carved out of it. It is perhaps the most beautiful "homage to the machine" interior ever done because there is no plastic visible, just metal.

Ford Public Relations worked the "Shelby-proud papa" angle for all it was worth. When the first running car was built, Shelby was pictured on the cover of *Autoweek* driving it, and saying inside the magazine that it was what he imagined a new Cobra would be like.

At the Detroit Auto Show, Shelby was there, dressed in black like Johnny Cash, with only the beaded hatband missing from his Sixties wardrobe (the striped overalls featured in the early Shelby ads seem to have been long forgotten).

Ford succeeded in the Cobra concept roadster as far as finding out how far they could push the envelope. What they were doing, if you looked at the 1966 Shelby roofline on the 2005 Mustang, was marching through Shelby-American history year by year. Once they had the Ford GT in production, and a Shelby-like Mustang and a Cobra roadster design, the next retro step would of course be a Cobra coupe.

Accordingly, Ford rolled out their own version of a Cobra coupe at Monterey in 2004, displaying it initially before a select group of concours fans at a party held on the lawn of Pebble Beach. This was a wise place for a rollout, as the attendees at the Pebble Beach concours represent the *creme de la creme* of car enthusiasts in America, many of whom are to buy a luxury sports car with their pocket money.

If Ford could get favorable word started at Pebble, the ripples would spread far and wide.

The coupe concept was called the GR-1 and wasn't nearly as "retro" as the Shelby concept roadster was. Instead it was an all-new shape, though eerily reminiscent of a one-off coupe A.C. Cars had built for Le Mans in '64, a car that is blamed for bringing a maximum speed law to England's motorways after A.C.'s test driver had been caught doing 181 mph motoring down the new M1 excpressway.

This time, the grille cavity is was more reminiscent of a Cobra but divided into various compartments, as it would be on a racecar, each intake feeding air to a different cooler.

There is a hood hump, an indication of the bulging V-10 wedged under it.

Phil Martens, the British born group vice president, Product Creation, said at the car's announcement, "Our goal this time around was not to create the ultimate top-speed, high-performance sports car. Really, we intended to strike a better balance of design, capability and usability that might appeal to someone considering a Ferrari 575M Maranello."

This was the first indication that Ford planned to continue in the exotic market after the Ford GT. Some had thought the Ford GT—aimed at the Ferrari 360 Modena—would be their one and only shot at grabbing some of the supercar money away from Europe but by mentioning the Ferrari Maranello, Martens revealed that some at Ford did not consider it inconceivable that Ford could permanently offer cars that will dent Ferrari's sales.

GM had reason to worry if Ford was serious. They themselves had cold feet about the domestic exotic earlier and cancelled the mid-engined Cadillac Cien they had been showing around. Chrysler, owned by Daimler-Benz in Germany, was no doubt peeved as well, as they had cancelled the equally exotic mid-engined ME Four Twelve. If Ford were able to move ahead with yet another supercar, Ford could effectively "own" the domestically produced "exotic" market. (Though of course the Viper still exists, and as we go to press, Chrysler has shown an alternative body for the Viper, which would allow them to market the chassis under another name; in effect to create a sort of half-price Aston Martin clone).

In some of the PR photos released at the time, Shelby was pictured happy as a clam, looking as proud as if he had created it himself.

Alas, after all had been said and done, Ford was forced by their declining market share to table production plans for both the roadster and the coupe. The board of directors had in effect practiced "tough love" and ruled "no dessert until you eat your dinner, boys."

The fact was that the corporation had failed to come up with a winner in a bread and butter car for the masses, a replacement for the old Taurus which had withered away while its rivals—the Honda Accord and Toyota Camry—were still selling in the millions. But hopes spring eternal among enthusiasts that, once Ford again has a hit in a car for the masses, that will release some funds for new developments in the toy department. One phrase that ought to be tattoed on the biceps of Cobra fans after all the water that's gone under the bridge is "Never say never."

One Ford Division that probably breathed easy when the two seaters were tabled was Aston Martin, a purchase that has taken more than five years to earn its first dime for Ford but who had two new models in the pipeline in '06. All they needed was something from the lower class blue oval brand to upstage them. A Cobra coupe could do that, appealing to a wider audience than the Aston.

Exactly how Ford would co-ordinate the production of a two seater Cobra with the still existent Shelby replica Cobras being built in Las Vegas remains to be seen. Shelby may sell those companies before Ford rolls out any new two seater Cobra production car.

The big news for Shelby fans in '06 though, was the forthcoming Shelby GT500, marketed as an '07 model. At the '06 Detroit auto show, on January 8, Ford announced that they were bringing back the Shelby muscle car, based on the current Mustang, with a 475-horsepower supercharged V8, 6-speed manual transmission, race-tuned suspension, and four-piston Brembo brakes.

Ford called it called "the most powerful, most capable Mustang ever."

Shelby was quoted saying: "It's one thing to put 450 horsepower in an exotic supercar," says Shelby. "It's another to put that much power in something as affordable as a Mustang. The fact that they not only met their goal but pushed on to 475 horsepower is a remarkable achievement." (That was before, we might add, they found another 25 horses.)

The heart of the '07 Ford Shelby GT500 is the supercharged 5.4-liter, 32-valve V8 which is force-fed an air-and-fuel mixture via a 'Roots-type' super-charger providing 8.5 pounds per square inch of boost.

While the Ford GT, at about four times the price, had an aluminum block, the GT500 uses a cast-iron engine block, but borrowed from the Ford GT the aluminum, four-valve cylinder heads, piston rings and bearings.

Ford saw the market for the GT500 as "baby boomer boy racer," though they would never admit it, so a 6-speed manual gearbox was the only gearbox going in. The Special Vehicle Team of engineers developed the car from the standard Mustang, retuning and upgrading key chassis components such as the shocks, springs and stabilizer bars.

Shelby himself, if we are to believe the PR photos, was in on the testing at one point or another, scaring the beejeesuz out of Ford test track personnel as he flung the prototypes around corners and took hills at four times the recommended speed limit of the ancient test track, which dates back to Ford's Model T days. He was also there at the press preview in California, taking reporters for rides. He admitted to several reporters that he didn't have much to do with the car but was damn proud to have his name on it.

The '07 GT500 features a MacPherson strut independent front suspension with Reverse L lower control arms, and a solid-axle, three-link rear suspension with coil springs and a Panhard rod for precise control of the rear axle.

This rear suspension design, Ford claimed, was validated on the track by Ford Racing in the Ford Racing Mustang FR500C race car which won its first race in the season opener at Daytona International Speedway in February 2005 and went on to dominate the season and clinch the championship.

Italian-designed four-piston Brembo calipers are fitted to 14-inch Brembo vented rotors up front, and 11.8-inch vented discs in the rear so at least the GT500 has the same brand brakes as the Ford GT supercar. The tires are Goodyear Eagles, sized 255/45ZR in front and 285/40ZR in back. Wheels are 18 inches by 9.5 inches.

Motor Trend, in a story run before the car was in production, dared to ask that "when-did-you-stop-beating-your-wife" question that comes with any discussion of an independent rear suspension, such as Ford offered in the 1999-2004 Cobra. Like where was it? Hal Tai-Tang, the engineer in charge of the car's development, gave them a straight answer: "Sure, we could've done it. We looked at the marginal handling improvement attainable by going to an IRS, and we didn't feel the gain justified the cost. The incremental benefit of an IRS is refinement, but not much more in terms of all-out performance. We've got good geometry and good shock-motion ratios, and we're happy with the suspension we have. We won't hesitate to have you do a driving comparison against IRS-suspended competitors."

What Ford didn't want to admit was that the Corporation was hurting financially, and that any dollar they could cut out of any new product was a help, so cutting something the public couldn't see from the showroom window was done. And besides, the decision proved right. When the GT500 was announced, Ford dealers were swamped with orders and nobody was seen picketing their local Ford dealer carrying a sign reading: "I'm not gonna buy one until they offer IRS."

Ford was in a hurry to make money by getting the car in production fast, which translates to minimal body changes. The nose was changed to accommodate wider upper and lower fascia openings with a functional air splitter.

The hood has heat extractors protruding near the leading edge, combining to provide improved airflow and aerodynamics. Shelby was actually pictured inspecting these in the clay model phase, silencing somewhat critics who felt he didn't influence the cars. Maybe his only suggestion was "raise the lip a hair here, boys" but you had to recognize that this advice was coming from a guy who had been there (here, there and everywhere in fact).

The GT500 nomenclature is prominent in the lower bodyside racing stripe, another cue from the classic Shelby Mustangs. (Oddly Ford decided no stripes would be available on the GT500 Convertible, but they are making up for that by offering a premium cloth top in the convertibles.)

Car and Driver's Tony Swan, in a 2006 driving impression of the convertible published in Sept. 2006, said that stripe decision might be a mistake. "We have mixed reactions here to the absence of the Shelby stripes on this convertible —they're a dealer option. We judged the stripes as a 'low' in our July test, but we are not unanimous on that score, and it's fair to say the Shelby doesn't really have much curbside charisma without them. Along these lines, we also think the SVT people could have taken more pains with this car's interior. Aside from a couple of badges, there's not much that sets the Shelby apart from its Mustang GT counterparts, and it's pretty plain considering the car's price. And speaking of price, we're already hearing tales of dealers asking $15,000 to $20,000 over the MSRP. Ford has no real control over this, and the sad part is these gougers will probably get their markups."

Inside the GT500, Ford swapped the locations of the speedometer and the tachometer because they said, "It provides performance-oriented drivers with a better view of shift points while changing gears."

Front seats received additional lateral support to help keep the driver in place during cornering. The '07 interior is offered in a choice of two colors, Charcoal Black or Charcoal Black and Crimson Red. The charcoal/red offering features Crimson Red seating surfaces and door panel inserts. For those not around in the Fifties, two-tone was very big back then.

Seating surfaces are leather with both interior treatments. The interior is also chock-a-block with Shelbymania: Snake logos in the seat backs, Shelby GT500 script and the Cobra image on the steering wheel cap.

To their credit, Ford did a quality upgrade over the Mustang, the gauges in the GT500 wearing light-colored faces in keeping with SVT tradition. The normally-chromed bits on the dash are now satin aluminum finished, including the aluminum shift lever knob that is nicely positioned for quick, positive shifts.

Ford originally announced they would make about 8,000 and then revised that estimate upward to 10,000 when they saw the demand building. Shelby was claiming they were sold out before the first one hit the showrooms.

Ironically, the new Shelby was the only one of three Shelby-connected Mustang models for '07 that is *not* built in Shelby's Las Vegas, Nevada plant. The Ford Shelby GT500 is built at the Ford-Mazda joint venture, AutoAlliance International, in Flat Rock, Michigan.

The press, starved for real performance at a more affordable level than the previous Ford GT, praised the car but it was still possible to find some criticism, such as *Car & Driver's* Tony Swan saying the convertible had a "rubbery chassis." Still in the end of his convertible driving impression Swan wrote; "There's no question that these cars will be instant collectibles. That alone makes this Shelby another winner, whatever expectations we may entertain."

Ford was hoping the general public would think "Ford GT" when they thought of the GT500 engine because it too has supercharged 5.4-liter DOHC 32-valve V8. But *Car and Driver*, in a preliminary preview of the car set their readers straight: "there are important distinctions. The GT V8 is all aluminum with a dry-sump lubrication system, whereas the GT500 has an iron block and a wet sump. The GT engine is force-fed by a Lysholm screw-type supercharger; the GT500 will use an Eaton R122 Roots-type blower and an air-to-liquid intercooler, adding 10 psi to the intake system at peak boost."

"The Lysholm unit is a little more expensive," *Car & Driver* quoted a Ford official, "but the big problem was supply. They can't make as many as we're going to need. There are performance differences, too. The Lysholm type gives you a little more top end, and the Roots type is a little fatter in the midrange. We think owners will be satisfied with this setup."

Car and Driver also pointed out that the car has a pronounced forward weight bias—about 57/43, "due to increased mass. The supercharged iron-block 5.4 weighs about 175 more pounds than the naturally aspirated 4.6 SOHC 24-valve aluminum V8 in the Mustang GT. That factor, plus a bigger front-brake package, bigger wheels and tires, and other GT500 package elements, add up to a curb weight projected in the 3850-pound range versus 3575 pounds for the last Mustang GT we tested."

In the braking department the Shelby GT500 scores well over the regular Mustang GT, its 18-inch wheels covering 14.0-inch vented front rotors with four-piston calipers with 11.8-inch vented rear rotors at the rear (by contrast the Mustang GT has 12.4-inch front rotors and 11.8-inch rears, all vented.)

Ford and Shelby believe in anti roll bars so the GT500 has tubular 1.4-inch diameter bar up front and a solid 0.9-inch bar in back with spring rates and damping profiles customized for this model.

Automobile Magazine's Don Sherman (a veteran who goes back to the days of musclecars at *Car & Driver* in the Sixties) had a little fun making fun of all the Shelby regalia in his road test: "To prevent onlookers from confusing this with an ordinary 'Stang, there's a liberal sprinkling from Ford's jewelry box. We counted seven snake emblems, seven SVT logos, four GT500 badges, three Shelby escutcheons, and two Ford ovals adorning interior and exterior surfaces. In lieu of a Mustang badge, there's a silk-screened horsey galloping across the windshield. Le Mans-style skunk stripes are exclusive to the coupe. If that's too over-the-top for your tastes, you can delete them. Choosing the delete option is a smart move, because the white-striped red coupe we drove on back roads in Northern California popped up on law enforcement radar more vividly than three cherries in a Vegas slot machine. Those serious about speeding should select the evil black or super stealthy alloy (charcoal bordering on black) monotone exterior hues."

He also describes the sound: "Unless you've got the Shaker cranked up with Bob Seger hammering out 'Old Time Rock & Roll,' there's no escaping the sound track revolution. Thanks to the government's pass-by noise standards, heavy exhaust rumble is a thing of the past. Instead of the horny honk of the Cobra Jet's Holley four-barrel sucking holes in the ozone layer, you get a blower serenade with the level of whine directly proportional to the engine's rpm. Chief engineer Jay O'Connell acknowledges that resonance chambers capable of quieting the yowl were considered but rejected because of the void they left in the Shelby GT500's character."

Sherman, being an engineer, can't help but knock the choice of a live rear axle. "The Shelby GT500 behaves while attacking smooth road courses, and it's a model of deportment on the drag strip, but one circumstance does hitch its stride: Steer smoothly into a fast bend, and all systems feel nicely poised until you encounter a significant heave in the road. When hundreds of pounds of unsprung mass are so excited, the rear axle momentarily loses track of what it was doing. There's a wonky feeling that must be addressed with steering corrections. Because of its Achilles' heel, the musclebound Mustang is unlikely to pose any serious threat to BMW's eminence."

But then he goes on to say that the true Shelby fans don't care about BMWs, or fancy phrases like "unsprung weight" they just view this car as the "muscle car's second coming."

Shelby, seeking to repeat the success of his 40th Anniversary Cobra replicas, also announced a 40th Anniversary package for the GT500 at the SEMA show in Vegas in Nov. '06.

Among the ingredients would be:

—Shelby/Eibach coil-over suspension (lowers the car by as much as 1.6 inches).

—Larger stabilizer bars for flatter cornering.

—Twenty-inch American Racing Shelby Razor wheels (optional).

—Shelby Signature Borla cat-back exhaust system.

—Shelby billet-aluminum caps and covers for power steering, radiator, brake master cylinder, windshield washer fluid bottle and oil dipstick.

—Consecutive number plate of authentication.

—Carbon-fiber lower front fascia splitter and mirror covers.

—Aluminum hood grille inserts, sequential taillamps and front/rear brake duct kits.

—Anniversary badging.

—Convertible models get an anniversary stripe package.

—Shelby door-sill plates with consecutive numbers.

—Center dash-mounted gauge cluster with three Carroll Shelby/Autometer carbon-fiber gauges (boost, oil and fuel pressure).

—Shelby snake door handles.

—40th Anniversary armrest cover.

—Light bar with solenoid-activated light system for convertibles.

Since the GT500s are made in Detroit, the installation of the packages will be done in Shelby's Las Vegas HQ or at his appointed dealers.

And then was the Hertz re-connection. Harkening back 40 years—in July 2006 Shelby and Ford announced that Shelby would be converting 500 black Mustangs into souped-up versions for Hertz. The black and gold cars were destined only for Hertz. Though rental rates vary by city, they rented for $129 a day in San Francisco for a midweek September booking, a 25% premium.

Hertz planned to distribute the 500 units through the Hertz Fun Collection at select airport locations Arizona, California, Colorado, Florida, Hawaii, Massachusetts, Nevada, Oregon and Washington.

"Like the original Hertz cars, the Ford Shelby GT-H will be fun to drive," said Carroll Shelby. "We started with a terrific Mustang and modified it with some Ford go-fast parts and gave it a distinct look for Shelby-style driving. Whoever gets the opportunity to rent one of these unique cars will get an experience of a lifetime."

But will they, as rumored in the Sixties, take them to the racetrack? The new Hertz, unlike the '66 models, won't have the same size engine as the GT500. Instead, Ford Racing Performance Group is supplying its popular Power Pack (FR1) to add a genuine 25-horsepower Ford performance kick to the 300-horse Mustang GT 4.6L V8/five-speed automatic transmission powertrain and an increase of 10 lb.-ft. of torque.

The package includes Ford Racing's 90mm Cold Air kit, the Muffler Kit, a new X-pipe similar to the one used on the new Ford Shelby GT500 Mustang, and a performance calibration. Most important, though, in order to feed that boy racer in all of us, is that guttural throaty growl created by what is called a "cat-back performance exhaust" that will make this car unmistakably sound like a Shelby.

In order to put that extra horsepower to the ground, the Ford Shelby GT-H also comes with the Ford Racing Handling Pack (FR3) installed, including specially-tuned dampers inspired from the FR500C, lowering springs, sway bars and a strut tower brace—plus a Ford Racing 3.55:1 ratio rear axle assembly more off-the-dig.

Ironically, there was such an immediate clamor among those who wanted the Hertz version (which they could presumably only buy as a used car from

Hertz and 500 cars wouldn't be near enough to meet the demand) that Ford hastily pressed Button A and offered a civilian version which they called the "Shelby GT."

The ace reporter from Edmunds.com, a popular website on cars, attended the press preview of the Shelby GT and reported:

"If there's one thing Ford has learned in recent months, it's the magic that comes with combining the words 'Mustang' and 'Shelby.' Throw in the harsh reality that Ford needs all the magic it can conjure these days, and you have the makings of yet another Shelby Mustang. Following closely (some might say too closely) on the heels of the Shelby GT500 and Shelby GT-H, this latest hot-rod pony is simply dubbed 'Shelby GT' and is, for the most part, a retail version of the GT-H rental car offered through select Hertz agencies....

"Shelby Automobiles, based in Las Vegas, begins with a stock Mustang GT and adds a Ford Racing Power Pack and Handling Pack to each car. The Power Pack consists of a 90-millimeter cold-air intake, reworked engine calibration, upgraded exhaust flow (via a new X-pipe) and a shorter rear axle ratio (3.55 versus the GT's 3.31). And while the rental GT-H comes in automatic form only, the Shelby GT can be had with a slushbox or a five-speed manual transmission featuring a Hurst short-throw shifter.

"The Handling Pack consists of shorter springs, stiffer dampers and an upgraded front antiroll bar. The shorter springs drop the car 1.5 inches, which is unfortunate in the sense that it makes seeing these upgraded parts—all of them painted a shimmering shade of Ford Blue—even harder to see unless you have access to a vehicle lift. A front strut-tower brace and P235/55ZR18 tires complete the Shelby GT's handling upgrades.

"Cosmetically, the Shelby GT gets a modest re-do—a pair of silver Le Mans racing stripes over your choice of only two colors—white or black. And there is no convertible. On the side there are 'Shelby GT' side stripes.

"In front there is a lower front fascia with a brushed-aluminum grille—but no foglights—and, Lord deliver us, a non-functional hood scoop. The obligatory 'SHELBY' lettering is there, spelled out across the trunk lid in separately placed classic-font letters, reminescent of the days of Sixties Shelbys.

"Inside the Shelby GT there are plenty of Shelby cues, including 'Shelby GT' floor mats, Shelby doorsill plates and an authentication plate above the center stack featuring a CSX number (a matching CSX numbered tag is located in the engine compartment), and that is the most important part of all as there will no doubt be fake Shelbys being made as we speak."

One of the really classic re-visits to Sixtiesland is the use of a Hurst shifter, which Brauer praises "both for its classic chrome-and-cue-ball look as well as its powerful, purposeful feel. It's this sort of shifter action, along with the Shelby GT's baritone exhaust warble and immediate throttle response, that truly evokes the muscle car era from which the Shelby legend springs."

But Brauer, who owns a $160,000 205-mph Ford GT and knows from whence he speaks, isn't fooled by just badges and throaty exhausts. "The real difference," he says, "comes with 40 years of progress, meaning you now can enjoy those traits plus inspired steering feel and predictable at-the-limit handling.

On the proving grounds we repeatedly tossed this newest pony car into sharp corners for the sheer joy of throwing the tail out and reeling it back in." (Hey, we hope the Hertz guys don't read this.)

Brauer in his report on the Shelby GT on his website addresses the same subject as the writer from *Autofield Guide*, who three years earlier had roasted Ford's decision to bring Shelby back on board. Brauer, with the advantage that comes with hindsight and seeing the first '07 Shelbys sell like hotcakes, says: "Of course, some might argue that building a new car inspired by a 40-year-old car doesn't seem like 'forward' thinking. But Ford's desire to offer 'a steed for every need' means the company is recognizing the increased fragmentation of the marketplace while simultaneously answering it with highly specialized, limited-production vehicles. If Toyota can sell dealer-customized Scions to the youth of America, why shouldn't Ford provide a series of Mustangs that range in price from $19,995 (V6 Coupe) to $45,755 (Shelby GT500 convertible)?

"This Shelby GT version of the Mustang will cost approximately $35,000 and go on sale at the beginning of 2007. If you still believe in that 'Mustang' and 'Shelby' magic, but you don't want to spend Porsche Boxster-like money, Ford's got a new steed to meet your need."

What Brauer didn't say, but needs saying, is that while it would be nice to have found a young man (we'll be generous and say 50 is "young") who could imbue a product with legendary status, the problem is that you have to first go out and do a lot of stuff first in order to *become* a legend. Shelby did all that. So when he comes to a product and helps the maker ready it for production, he brings a lot to the table—is that not so?

Only time will tell whether Ford over-did it with the use of the Shelby name brand in the '07 model year. Let's see, 10,000 GT500s, 500 GT-H and an unlimited number of Shelby GTs—they might be taking a chance on over-proliferating more Shelbys in one year than the original Shelby-American firm cranked out in five years. On the other hand, they want to get them out now, when Ford needs the money, and for nostalgia's sake, while Shelby is still alive to personally bless them as they come off the line.

Just to leave no stone unturned Ford also announced a CS/GT package which is in the spirit of that special '68 model—a raft of small goodies that you can order installed on a Mustang which sort of give you a Shelby-like image—sort of.

Autoweb.com describes it as "a modern interpretation of the classic 1968 Mustang 'California Special,' a $1,895 option package available in five colors. Highlights of this special 'feature car' include restyled front and rear fascias, side scoops, a unique bodyside racing stripe, and chrome rolled-tip exhaust outlets. Ford fits polished 18-inch wheels to the 2007 Ford Mustang GT/CS, and if you order the optional GT Appearance Package, you'll get a hood scoop, too. Inside, there's plenty of aluminum and chrome accent trim, black leather seats with Dove or Parchment GT/CS inserts, and embroidered floor mats. And finally, under the hood, there's a special engine cover that Ford says gives the car a custom appearance.

The 2007 Ford Mustang GT/CS doesn't get any engine or suspension modifications, but Ford reminds buyers that Ford Racing Performance offers a variety of aftermarket equipment designed to improve the Mustang's power and handling. The GT/CS will be available as a coupe or convertible in Redfire Metallic, Performance White, Vista Blue Metallic, and Black. A Valencia Yellow will be added to the product mix after the car arrives."

In short J Mays, the Ford VP in charge of design, has beat the retro bushes for all they're worth to re-create the ambiance of Shelby-American, mid-to-late Sixties. Now he's already off in another direction, reviving the Bullitt Mustang again (linked to a Mustang driven by Steve McQueen in a movie of the same name) and talking about a Boss 302 revival.

As Ford was readying a new Shelby Mustang, old Shelby cars were going through the roof. Colin Comer, an authority on Shelby values, commented in *Sports Car Market* magazine after Reggie Jackson's '65 Shelby Mustang reached a cool $324,000 at Russo and Steele's Monterey, California, auction. This was not even an R-model Shelby but an early street car. Comer explains the appeal of the early Shelby: "The earlier the car is, the better, where values are concerned. 'Two digit' cars, as they have become known, are the most valuable. These were Shelby's first allotment from Ford, and as such, occupy a unique place in Shelby Mustang history. Early cars have the battery in the trunk, 16-inch Moto-Lita steering wheels (just like the Cobra) and other unique features. As production increased, many running changes occurred. Soon the GT350 went to a 15-inch steering wheel, the quality of the fiberglass hoods improved and the battery (was) moved up front around car 325. So if you're shopping for a '65 Shelby, you want to buy a car with the battery in the trunk, a shoddy hood and as low a serial number as you can find."

What a topsy-turvy world we live in, where the crudest of a given series is considered the most valuable!

Another factor in the popularity of the original Shelby Mustangs and Cobras, and a factor which would be difficult to document unless you did interviews, is the fact that many of the people who built the cars, crewed them at races and piloted them remained "on the scene" at various vintage race events during the last 40 years, many times appearing as speakers at various Shelby club gatherings. It is one thing to own an old Italian race car made by obscure Italians who a guy from Kansas will never meet but it is quite another to be able to go to a vintage race and hobnob with Billy Krause, who drove the first Cobra in competition or with Phil Remington, who was Shelby's main development engineer during the entire Cobra era. Many of these men are now the age of WWII veterans and fading from the picture fast, but their "presence" at various events in the last four decades has greatly enriched the owning experience for many an owner of a genuine Shelby product, sort of akin to owning a World War II-era warbird and being able to run into someone at an air show who helped build it or who maybe even flew it in combat. It's sort of like meeting a distant uncle who is not just interested in what you are interested in, but can tell you what jets work best in the Weber carburetors at 6,500 ft. altitude!

Shelby, meanwhile, continues to expand his replica connections. After years of making Cobra replicas, in recent years, he has expanded the franchise by tying in with firms that make replicas of Shelby Mustangs. At a recent Shelby-

American Automobile Club convention, there were no less than three such firms with large displays, two of them offering customized Shelby-like Mustangs in the modern retro-rod style, and the third making replicas of '67-'70 models which use newly tooled bodywork.

Will they be recognized decades from now as Shelby Mustangs? No one knows. But one thing's sure—no matter what Shelby has done lately with replicas, it hasn't hurt the price of the original Cobras and Shelbys one bit, because the replicas continue to expand the market by educating newcomers about the lore of the marque. The newbies may be wet behind the ears, but that's not to say that some of them don't have a sizable amount of change jingling in their pockets. Even if only a few will be able to afford real Shelbys, or real A.C. Cobras, a great many more will be able to write out a check that won't bounce for the clones. But, that's only a handful. Ford has bet millions that these same fans will embrace the modern Shelbys coming out of Dearborn. If the Ford engineers, in their huddles with Shelby, correctly devined the elements that make for that indefinable thing called soul, we may have yet another winner....

Advance orders for the '07 Shelby Mustang are strong; demonstrating that Ford is on the right path, and getting to where they want to be vis-à-vis the rock solid true blue core of Ford fans, the ones paying those inflated prices for old Shelby Mustangs at Scottsdale.

What Ford said with the Ford GT and is saying all over again with the new Shelby Mustang is: "Hey, Ford fans, what we made way back when is nice, but it's what we make now that's important."

Amen, brother.

While at this writing, the new Shelby Mustang is just reaching the showrooms, Shelby's eagerness to get out of the gate must have bowled over some Ford execs, for back in '05 he was already displaying a supercharged '05 Mustang, one which looked awfully close to what Ford was planning to sell as a Shelby in '07. But since Shelby's car was based on a V-6, and Ford is desperate to have enthusiasts recognize that a V-6 in a Mustang is not a bad thing. Ford resisted publically reprimanded him for jumping the gun with his own new model introduced before they could get their own Shelbys rolling out of Michigan. Hey get used to it—it's just Shelby being Shelby.

Shelby combined forces with a company called West Coast Customs, famous for being the shop that is featured on the cable show "Pimp My Ride." With them doing the designing, Shelby's Mustang upgrade package looked almost better than what Ford was planning to do with the GT500. It had a blue paint job and a silver diagonal stripe as well as Silver Le Mans stripes. As originally announced it had two stages:

Stage 1 was mostly cosmetic, with 20-inch American Racing wheels, a custom hood, stripes, custom interior, upper and lower grilles, side scoops, a Shelby front fascia, hood pins and all those things that identify it as a Shelby related car, including the rear logo, dash plaque, door kick panel inlay set, interior upgrade it and aforementioned stripes.

For those insistant on adding performance (and what's a Shelby for?) Stage 2 delivered an intercooled Paxton Supercharger that jumped the stock 210 hp to 350hp! Other hot-rod type improvements in this package included different rear gears, a Borla dual exhaust system, and Baer Signature Series brakes with custom calipers carrying the Shelby logo.

Whether Mustangs retrofitted with this package will be accorded the status of bring true Shelbys depends on what some historical association decides down the road. The next logical step is for Shelby to publish his own Registry, whereupon whatever he calls a Shelby is a Shelby....

And, of course, Shelby still has a life of his own—that of a family man. The public doesn't see much of it beyond an occasional glimpse. In a 2005 interview done by *Autoweek's* Pete Lyons, Lyons said he asked Shelby that, considering the races he won, the cars he built, the businesses he founded what did he consider his most important achievement? "Without hesitation," Lyons wrote, "Shelby replied 'Three kids who have never been dopes, who have the work ethic, who are three wonderful human beings. The world is better off because they are in the world: Sharon, Pat and Mike, that's No. 1.'"

Despite all his afflictions, which make it near impossible to pin down whether he will make this or that appearance, Shelby loves making public appearances.

Leo Levine in an article in *Classic Automobile Register* described a Shelby appearance in the '90s: "He looks worn out, drained—until he gets out of the car. Then the old Shelby takes over, and sagging pants, slumping shoulders, silver grey hair and all, his eyes are bright under the battered cowboy hat. It's showtime. He loves it."

His usual activity at such appearances is for him to sit down at a table and sign autographs or even parts of cars he built like Shelby glove compartment doors. Since he began his charities, there is usually a donation required and the price for each signature has steadily risen until it presently is at $100. Shelby at one time signed things for free but with the advent of eBay, it didn't take him long to realize that the picture he signed at 10 a.m. was often being offered as a genuine autographed Shelby picture by 10:10 am on ebay.

As Leo Levine summed it up, in his *Classic Automobile Register* story "He is a legend, this laughing, raggedy assed high-mileage ancient.... living on borrowed time with a borrowed heart and still pursuing his private Moby Dick."

Somewhere in Texas, the early 2000s.

The old man walked out into the Texas sunshine. Birds were chirping and somewhere on the farm he heard some steers making noise. He walked into the barn.

He walked down the row of cars, debating which one would be right for this fine morning.

He chose a long-time favorite—a 427 Cobra S/C in raw aluminum, the one wearing his favorite racing number: 98.

He got in and started it up. Something caught his eye and he saw his dog come a-runnin'. That fool hound loved ridin' in an open car and you had only to start the engine to call him. The dog leapt over the door and landed in the passenger seat, breathing hard and bright-eyed and bushy-tailed.

The old man checked his valise—yup, it was still there, the check made out from his heart fund for the hospital—twenty five thousand smackers. Hell, even with the high cost of medicine, that ought to buy sumpthin'!

He started it up and backed her out of the stall. He rumbled down toward the open highway and stopped, checking the traffic.

It was clear. He let out the clutch and floored it.

A minute later, he was clocking 4500, passing everything in sight at 120 mph.

He saw a trooper go by the other way and gave him a lazy wave. They knew it was him, Ol' Shel. No use in giving chase, there wasn't anything in East Texas that could catch him.

And that sound… the old man reveled in that sound. It was the same sound he had heard at Sebring, at Daytona, and at LeMan so long ago, back in those golden years of the Sixties.

Bibliography

A Guide to American Sports Car Racing, William S. Stone, Doubleday 1967 3rd Edition A

A.C. Martyn Watkins, Haynes Publishing Group 1976

A.C. Cobra The Complete Story, Brian Laban, Crowood, 1991 HC

A.C. Cobra: The Truth Behind the Anglo-American Legend, Rinsey Mills, Haynes 2002

A.C. (Shelby) Cobra 1962-67; Marks I, II, III; 260,289,427, F. Wilson McComb, Osprey 1984

The American Sports Car, Jerold Kelman Editor, Consumer Guide 1979

American Sports Car Racing in the 1950s, by Michael Lynch, MBI 1998

American Car Design Now, C. Edson Armi, Rizzoli International Publications 2004

Automobile Quarterly Vol 44 No 4, Gary Witzenberg

Boss and Cobra Jet Mustangs: 302, 351, 428 and 429, Dr. John Craft, Motorobooks 1996

The Carroll Shelby Story, Carroll Shelby & John Bentley, Pocket Books 1967

The Certain Sound, Thirty Years of Motor Racing, John Wyer, Haynes Publications 1986

Classic A.C.'s: Auto-Carrier to Cobra, John McLellan, Sutton 2000

The Cobra–Ferrari Wars 1963 – 1965, Michael L. Shoen, CFW 1988 & 1990

The Cobra Ferrari Wars (DVD), Jonny Lieberman

Cooper Cars, D. Nye, 1st ed. 1983

Essential A.C. Cobra: The Cars and Their Story 1962-67, Rinsey Mills, Motorbooks International 1997

Ford Cobra Guide, Bill Carroll, Sports Car Press 1964

Ford: The Dust and The Glory - A Racing History, Leo Levine, MacMillan 1968

Ford: The Men and the Machine, Robert Lacey, Random House Value Publishing 1988

Ford Total Performance: The Road to World Racing Domination, Alex Gabbard, HPBooks 2000

Ford vs. Ferrari: The Battle for Le Mans, Anthony Pritchard, Zuma Marketing 1984

Glory Days: When Horsepower and Passion Ruled Detroit, Jim Wangers, Bentley Publishers 1998

Holman Moody, The Legendary Race Team, Tom Cotter, Motorbooks 2003

Illustrated Shelby Buyers Guide, Lamm & Nicaise, Motorbooks 1992

The Inside Story of the Fastest Fords, Karl E. Ludvigsen, Style Auto Editrice 1970 & 1971

Just Call Me Carroll, Phil Henny, Editions Cotty 2004

Motor Racing Mechanic Emil Cuoghi with Jeremy Walton, Cooper cars, Doug Nye 1983

Mustang Race Cars, Dr John Craft, Motorbooks 2002

Mustang! The Complete History of America's Pioneer Ponycar, Gary L Witzenburg, Automobile Quarterly, Inc. 1979

New VW Beetle, Matt DeLorenzo, Motorbooks 1998

PROTOTYPE 1968-70, Mike Twite, Pelham Books Ltd. 1969

Shelby-American Guide: Revised 2nd Edition 1992, Richard J. Kopec, Motorbooks and SAAC, 1982

Vintage American Road Racing Cars 1950-1969, Harold Pace & Mark Brin, Motorobooks 2004

Viper, Matt Stone, MBI 2004

Viper: Pure Performance by Dodge, Giametta, Consumer Guide

BOOK PROPOSALS

Iconografix is a publishing company specializing in books for transportation enthusiasts. We publish in a number of different areas, including Automobiles, Auto Racing, Buses, Construction Equipment, Emergency Equipment, Farming Equipment, Railroads & Trucks. The Iconografix imprint is constantly growing and expanding into new subject areas.

Authors, editors, and knowledgeable enthusiasts in the field of transportation history are invited to contact the Editorial Department at Iconografix, Inc., PO Box 446, Hudson, WI 54016.

www.iconografixinc.com

More great books from
Iconografix

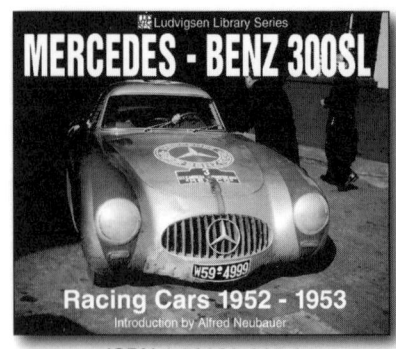

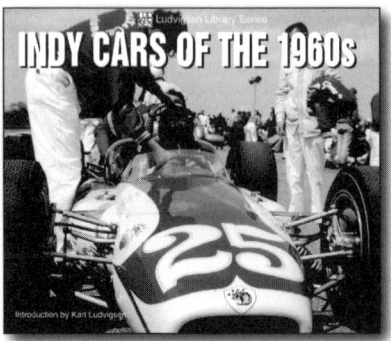
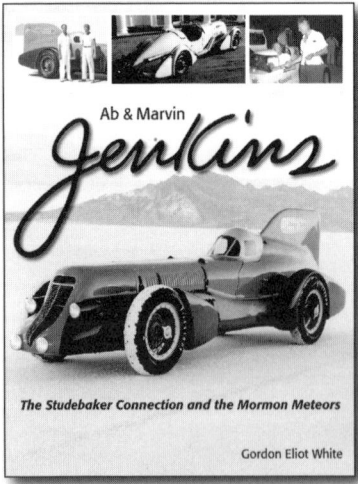
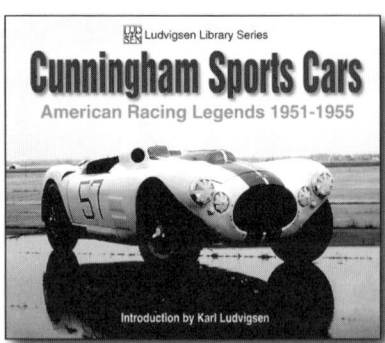

Iconografix, Inc.
P.O. Box 446, Dept BK,
Hudson, WI 54016
For a free catalog call:
1-800-289-3504
info@iconografixinc.com
www.iconografixinc.com